T0277355

IN THE HEAT OF THE
MIDDAY SUN

IN THE HEAT OF THE MIDDAY SUN

The Indelible Story of the 1986 World Cup

STEVEN SCRAGG

First published by Pitch Publishing, 2022

Pitch Publishing
9 Donnington Park,
85 Birdham Road,
Chichester,
West Sussex,
PO20 7AJ
www.pitchpublishing.co.uk
info@pitchpublishing.co.uk

© 2022, Steven Scragg

Every effort has been made to trace the copyright.
Any oversight will be rectified in future editions at the
earliest opportunity by the publisher.

All rights reserved. No part of this book may be reproduced,
sold or utilised in any form or transmitted in any form or by
any means, electronic or mechanical, including photocopying,
recording or by any information storage and retrieval system,
without prior permission in writing from the Publisher.

A CIP catalogue record is available for this book
from the British Library.

ISBN 978 1 80150 097 5

Typesetting and origination by Pitch Publishing
Printed and bound in Great Britain by TJ Books, Padstow

Contents

For Sam, the biggest little man in the world, who suffers with a semi-uncomfortable sense of pride when his teachers buy my books.

Acknowledgements

THIS BOOK wouldn't have been possible without the support of my wife, Beverley, and our wondrous children, Sam, Elsie and Florence, who have all knowingly or unknowingly saved an increasingly frazzled mind, body and soul at one point or another. I would also like to thank Jane at Pitch Publishing for their continued support and trust in what I produce, with a big nod to the excellent Duncan Olner for producing the book cover, which totally smacks of the 1986 World Cup.

Added to this, I can't express how much gratitude I have for my *These Football Times* brethren, Stuart Horsfield, Gary Thacker, Aidan Williams, Paul McParlan, Will Sharp and Chris Weir, who tend to be the ones goading me into these projects, but more than all others to Omar Saleem, whose support always goes above and beyond. You're a gentleman, and a true friend.

Honourable mentions must also go out to the people who took time out to chat about all things Mexico '86. Ric George, Ian Stewart, Hamish Tindall, Clive Toye, Barry Davies, Martí Perarnau. I also need to thank the beautiful soul who is Hayley Coleman. She always has my back and a handy bumper bar of chocolate dropping through my letterbox. Plus my brother and sister, David and Alison, who think this is all surreal/cool, as do their fabulous children.

Finally, I would like to thank everyone who took the plunge to purchase this book, and any of the three that preceded it. Whether you're a new customer or one of the regulars who have been along for the ride from the start, your support is never taken for granted.

Introduction

I'M A great believer in how the finest of lines can often make a monumental difference. I'm convinced that the merest of deflections in certain circumstances can change the complexion of how events pan out, to the most dramatic of effects.

Half an inch here, a few extra seconds there, a glance in the opposite direction at a pivotal moment. They can all make a landscape-altering difference. For instance, how would the 1960s have evolved culturally had Paul McCartney and John Lennon not crossed paths at a garden fete in Woolton, Liverpool on Saturday, 6 July 1957?

Some things are meant to be and some things aren't. Football works by the same rule of thumb. Take the 1974 World Cup finals as a case in point. So often it's lamented that the *totaalvoetbal* of the Netherlands, Rinus Michels and Johan Cruyff fell agonisingly short of fulfilling their widely expected destiny. The Netherlands the 1974 World Cup winners in all but actual outcome? You can argue that it's a whimsical thought. You can argue that it insults just how good the 1974 West Germany were. After all, Franz Beckenbauer, Gerd Müller, Paul Breitner, Sepp Maier and Uli Hoeneß, on home soil, as the reigning European champions, were always going to have something to say about the final outcome at the Olympiastadion in Munich against the *Oranje*.

A sliding doors effect is in operation. Somewhere, in a parallel universe, the Netherlands won the 1974 World Cup Final. Conversely, in a further parallel universe, the Netherlands failed to qualify for the 1974 World Cup at all. Famously, England failed to qualify for those finals by the narrowest of margins. Goal-line clearances and the outrageously brilliant goalkeeping of Jan Tomaszewski kept Sir Alf Ramsey's team at bay on a legendary night of football at Wembley Stadium in October 1973, when Poland qualified instead.

Largely forgotten, one month later Belgium's Jan Verheyen scored what appeared to be a perfectly good winning goal at the Olympic Stadium in Amsterdam against the Netherlands. Played onside by three orange-shirted individuals, Verheyen's goal would have been enough to take Belgium to the World Cup finals, and in the process broken the hearts of their near neighbours and great rivals. Verheyen's goal was erroneously disallowed, however. The goalless scoreline instead sent the Netherlands through, while Belgium, who hadn't conceded a goal throughout the entire qualification campaign, became one of the biggest hard-luck stories the World Cup has ever known.

Just think about that for a moment. The Netherlands and Poland, second and third-placed nations at the 1974 World Cup, were only in attendance at all by the skin of their teeth.

The Cruyff turn. The tectonic de facto semi-final between the Netherlands and Brazil in Dortmund. Johan Neeskens's first-minute penalty in the final, before anyone in a West German shirt could touch the ball. Poland sending Italy home early. The goals of the tournament's top scorer, Grzegorz Lato. None of those images might have been there at all had it been for half an inch here, a few seconds there, or a glance in the right direction at a pivotal moment.

Imagine a 1974 World Cup shorn of the Netherlands and Poland, and instead inhabited by Belgium and England. It almost came to pass. It could have looked so very differently in West Germany.

Every World Cup qualification campaign has its hard-luck stories, the closest of near-misses. Twelve years on from Verheyen's moment of infamy, in November 1985, the Netherlands and Belgium were fighting it out over World Cup qualification once again. This time the match took place in Rotterdam, and De Kuip was the venue. Once more there was another late goal for Belgium, this time a goal that was given. The Netherlands had come to within five minutes of qualifying for Mexico '86. Instead, it was Belgium who won the day this time, and it was Belgium who would go on to reach the semi-finals of the 1986 World Cup. Belgium, a nation who were only there by the skin of their teeth.

It's the concept of how a landscape that sits evocatively within your mind's eye could so easily have been markedly altered, had it not been for the finest of lines.

Which is your favourite World Cup? Mine is 1982. Which of course means it was an obtuse decision to write a book about 1986 instead.

But 1982 was my first fully conscious World Cup. The sights, the sounds, the hazy shimmer seeping from the television, the commentaries of John Motson, Barry Davies, Martin Tyler and Gerald Sinstadt, which felt as if broadcast from the surface of the moon, or at the very least through a yoghurt pot and a length of string. 'That' Brazilian team, which boasted the sensory overload of Sócrates, Zico, Éder, Falcão and Cerezo. My version of the Netherlands being denied in 1974 was the denial of Brazil in 1982.

It wasn't only Brazil either. There was also the wonderful French team of Michel Platini, Alain Giresse, Dominique Rocheteau, Bernard Genghini and Jean Tigana, with their heartbreaking penalty shoot-out defeat to West Germany in the semi-final in Seville, after the near maiming of Patrick Battiston by Toni Schumacher. Machiavellian deeds at their worst; a campaign made more intriguing thanks to the brooding resentment between Platini and his one-time friend – and Saint-Étienne team-mate – Jean-François Larios, after the latter was rumoured to have had an affair with the wife of the former.

Added to Brazil and France, we had the slow start yet sudden blossoming of Enzo Bearzot's Italy. Paolo Rossi's burst of goals and Marco Tardelli's exuberant, legendary celebration of his goal in the final itself; great beauty that was protected by the glorious brutality of Claudio Gentile and the commanding goalkeeping of Dino Zoff.

Good and bad, everything about 1982 hit the spot for me. Cameroon going home unbeaten, the cruelty of Algeria's exit, the joy and pain of Honduras, El Salvador conceding ten against Hungary, Northern Ireland in Valencia against the hosts. Zbigniew Boniek, the fallibility and the genius of Diego Maradona, Scotland going home in what was an equally hypnotic and shambolic style, and then you had Kevin Keegan and Trevor Brooking belatedly arriving to the party for England, against Spain, only for their World Cup to end almost as soon as it had begun for them.

I have a theory that you're chemically hardwired to your first World Cups. The first couple set the tone for what you demand from all other subsequent tournaments. Once that happens, then you're primed only for disappointment. The football doesn't seem quite so magical, the social setting within which you watch them isn't as carefree.

The thrill of watching Brazil vs Italy in 1982 as an impressionable eight-year-old, then heading out with a ball to recreate it with your friends, can't be improved upon by watching the abject negativity of the West Germany vs

Argentina final in 1990, while a moody teenager. From there onward, you're simply chasing something elusive that you'll never again attain.

The 1990 World Cup is international football's greatest sleight of hand. It simply wasn't as good as many people would have you believe. Take the peak of his powers Des Lynam, and Luciano Pavarotti out of the equation, and what are you really left with?

That World Cup is all about the surrounding aesthetics. Lynam, Pavarotti, those dots down the sides of the television screen courtesy of the host broadcaster RAI. Balmy evenings and the afterglow of the second summer of love. 'World in Motion', some fantastic football kits on display and a sense of expectancy that wasn't fulfilled. A much put-upon Diego Maradona, the blossoming of the man-child that was Paul Gascoigne, and after an initial Italian reluctance to unleash him, the belated arrival of Roberto Baggio aside, where was the artistry at World Cup '90? Where was the flair of World Cups past?

Reigning champions Argentina were a pale shadow of their former self. Arguably the worst side to ever reach a World Cup Final. Erroneously accused of being a one-man team four years earlier, it was much fairer to suggest such a concept in 1990. Brazil were far too Europeanised in their approach; where was the romance of the Telê Santana era? Colombia strode forth as the most authentic South American team, yet they self-destructed against Cameroon in the last 16.

Cameroon brought the romance, but it was laced with an iron fist. The first African nation to reach the quarter-finals. When Benjamin Massing hit Claudio Caniggia with enough velocity to remove his own right boot in the opening match, it set a high benchmark that just couldn't be sustained throughout the remainder of the tournament.

England reaching the semi-finals and coming so close to the final itself simply propagates the myth surrounding the 1990 World Cup. Held to a draw by Ireland in a dour, very British sort of match, functional against Egypt, outplayed, even fortunate against Belgium, and progressing by the seat of their pants against Cameroon. England's best performances were saved for two matches they failed to win. The Netherlands during the group stages and West Germany in the semi-final.

Ireland were a ball of momentum, and like England they held their own in their highest-profile matches, against England, the Netherlands and Italy. Like England, they didn't win any of their high-profile matches, despite the commitment and endeavour shown. Uninspiring against Egypt and locked in a 'defend what we start with' stalemate with Romania, Ireland exited 1990 in the quarter-finals, without having won a match in regulation play.

Scotland were, of course, unremittingly Scotland. Stoic and accepting in defeat to Costa Rica, ebullient against Sweden and wonderful in a cruel loss to Brazil. Organised, yet self-destructive.

Italy, as hosts, played while shrouded within a fear of failure. Reluctant to field Baggio and equally reluctant to drop a misfiring Gianluca Vialli, it was only when Azeglio Vicini finally yielded to popular opinion that *Gli Azzurri* clicked into a higher gear. The genius of Baggio, coupled with the eye of the storm goalscoring of Salvatore Schillaci, brought them a momentum that was eventually halted, but only when they moved from Rome to Naples for their antagonistic semi-final against Argentina and Maradona.

Yugoslavia, the hipster's team of choice, weren't the visage of Eastern European promise the mind conjures them up to be either. Dismantled by West Germany, half of the goals they scored at the 1990 World Cup were plundered against the United Arab Emirates. Lucky to navigate their way past Spain, had Yugoslavia really been the team so many felt they were, then they would have breezed past Argentina in the quarter-finals. As for Spain. Well, Spain were just the Spain of old. Potential to win the tournament, offset by a propensity to shoot themselves in the foot.

West Germany. It always came down to West Germany, however. Clinical and efficient. Fluid movement and no shortage of percentage-playing skill. On the footballing dancefloor, they were all robotics and body-popping. They don't get enough credit for winning that World Cup because it was expected. Four goals against Yugoslavia, as part of a ten-goal haul during the group stages, they then picked their way past the Netherlands, Czechoslovakia, England and Argentina on their way to collecting a third World Cup. It was a success that even the West German population seemed to roll their eyes at.

The anticipation of the 1990 tournament had propelled me to quit my first job, in the name of spending a month in front of the television, to be able to watch every second of the action. Hydraulic retail never got over the loss, I'm sure. However, 1990 only delivered a vague sense of unfulfillment. It gave with one hand and took with the other. It was all a footballing illusion.

Things would never be the same again. I don't remember the 1994 World Cup. I suffered a head injury in September 1994, an injury that wiped out two years' worth of my memory; memory that I've never recovered. During the following two years, as my scattered brainwaves tried to recalibrate, my memory banks failed to record most days. I lost up to four years in total. I came to just in time for 1996 European Championship.

From 1998 onward, each passing World Cup has lost a little bit more of its shine. The hosts shouldn't have won in 1998. They had no striker of purpose, and had the Netherlands beaten Brazil in the semi-finals, then I think it would have been a very different outcome.

The 2002 World Cup was an awkward and generally disappointing one, hindered by too many shock results. Germany in 2006 promised much but didn't deliver any iconic images, apart from Zinedine Zidane headbutting Marco Materazzi in the solar plexus during the final itself.

South Africa in 2010 was of course evocative due to its location, but again didn't offer the on-pitch enjoyment.

Brazil in 2014 was mostly noticeable due to the way the host nation self-destructed, not just in footballing terms but also in societal circumstances too.

The 2018 World Cup was stained long before it began. While I'm not sure that FIFA will ever fully recover its composure from the 2022 World Cup in Qatar.

So, 1986 and Mexico essentially stands in my mind as the last great World Cup. I was by then a more sensory-attuned 12 years old. Liverpool had just won the league and FA Cup double, and semi-regular live First Division football had started to be broadcast at the beginning of the 1983/84 season. The European Cup had been won in 1984 by Joe Fagan's team, heading to Rome to face AS Roma in their own backyard, the greatest achievement by any British football club. Tottenham Hotspur had lifted the UEFA Cup too. Twelve-year-old eyes, yes, but increasingly football centric ones they were. By 1986 I was a seasoned veteran.

Twelve-year-old eyes tend to operate with a filter system, however. Hooliganism blighted the game in the mid-1980s, and in the early months of 1985 talks between the Football League, the Football Association and the cartel of the BBC and ITV had broken down over a new deal for televised football for the forthcoming 1985/86 season. World Cup season.

A combined BBC/ITV bid of almost £20m was turned down by the powers that be. While football felt it was worth much more, the aura that surrounded the game at that point was a damaging one. It wasn't the time to play hardball. The elite clubs, the 'Big Five', which comprised Liverpool, Everton, Tottenham Hotspur, Arsenal and Manchester United, were making regular noises about the launch of a potential Super League, but attendances had been receding year on year and hooliganism was a stain on the game.

The biggest clubs were worried, and busy trying to safeguard their positions. From their perspective, they were English football's biggest selling point, but the rest of the league, and particularly the lower divisions, were riding on their coat tails, holding them back from achieving their true potential. The Big Five wanted a larger slice of the cake, and if they weren't going to be handed it by the existing structure, then they would just bake a new cake of their own and sell it to the highest bidder.

By May 1985 the domestic game had reached its nadir. In March, visiting Millwall fans had dismantled a section of Kenilworth Road and occupied the much-lamented artificial pitch, in the name of an FA Cup quarter-final defeat to Luton Town. Before the end of May there had been the horrors of the Bradford City stadium disaster, and on the very same day there was also the tragic death of Ian Hambridge, a teenage Leeds United fan, at St Andrew's, amid riots between Birmingham City and Leeds supporters, when he was trapped under a collapsed wall. Then came Heysel, and the grim finale of a dark month.

The 1985/86 season began without an agreement between the rulers of the game and the television companies. Domestic club football was under a blanket television blackout. The only way you could see a football match was by clicking through the turnstiles. The sport and those who followed it, be that peacefully or aggressively, found themselves to be persona non grata. An agreement on a new television deal wouldn't be reached until December.

Still, football was everything. As children we watched it and we played it. We consumed it. Football wasn't yet a squad game, and you knew every player from every team. My team, Liverpool, won trophies on an annual basis. It was expected.

Football was an occasion. Football in person wasn't always the feral environment it was portrayed as. Despite Heysel, Anfield was one of the safest places to watch football. Heysel was inexcusable, but it was also massively out of character.

Football on television was savoured, more so beyond the blackout. Highlights were becoming increasingly rare, instead it was live matches that the BBC and ITV wanted more of. In the Granada region we were blessed to be in a geographical hotspot for football teams, so we were luckier than other parts of the country, but the times they were a changing.

In May 1986 Liverpool won the double in England, while Heart of Midlothian blew the double in Scotland. Terry Venables took Barcelona to the European Cup Final, one of the very worst European Cup finals of all time. Steaua Bucharest won it on penalties, ending the first season of the European ban on English clubs meekly. An earlier than usual start to the season meant that the World Cup would be kicking off before the month was out.

A year on from Heysel, and seen as undesirables, there had been talk and in-depth conjecture over whether the FA should back out of the tournament altogether. Under Bobby Robson, England had qualified comfortably for Mexico, but the appetite for the World Cup wasn't high. Off the pitch, the problems were clear and obvious, while on the pitch the football was largely uninspiring.

Just two years earlier and despite the English domination at club level on the Continent, there had been no British involvement at a glorious 1984 European Championship finals. It had been a tournament that was criminally ignored in the UK. With England having been edged aside in qualifying by the surprise emergence of Sepp Piontek's 'Danish Dynamite' team, and Scotland failing to mount a serious challenge on reaching the finals in France, both were left in the dust of their lesser-considered neighbours, Northern Ireland and Wales.

Northern Ireland became the only nation to beat West Germany, and subsequently the unified Germany, both home and away during a qualifying group for a major international tournament, yet still contrived to miss out on reaching the finals of the 1984 European Championship after dropping crucial points in Albania and Turkey. They came to within ten minutes of qualifying when Albania frustrated *Die Mannschaft* on their final evening of qualification, only to see Jupp Derwall's team eventually snatch the winning goal they required late on. Wales's heartbreak was even more pronounced. They came to within seconds of qualifying, until Yugoslavia procured an injury-time winner against Bulgaria in Split.

While participation in the 1984 European Championship from the UK still looked a distinct possibility, the BBC and ITV had come to an agreement to each broadcast one of the two group stages live, with a semi-final apiece, and both covering the final. Late on, ITV backed out of the agreement, and they largely blanked the tournament, apart from goal round-ups on *World of Sport*. Left with a clear run, the BBC then diluted its coverage rather than extending it. They covered only one match live prior to the final itself, the dramatic end-of-group match between Spain and West Germany, when Antonio Maceda's last-minute winner at the Parc des Princes propelled the underachieving Iberians through to the semi-finals and sent the West Germans home.

Despite this, the iconic semi-final between France and Portugal only made it on to television screens in the UK in late-night highlights form. Subsequently, what was arguably the greatest European Championship finals took place without many people even realising it was being played out. On the evening that France and Portugal were trading beautiful and artistic on-pitch blows, in the UK we were watching *The Val Doonican Music Show* on BBC 1, *The Gentle Touch* on ITV, *Saturday Review* on BBC 2 and *Cervantes* on Channel 4.

Due to this, many of the greatest elements that came to the fore in Mexico in 1986 were previously little known, or even completely unknown. There was a blasé attitude going into the tournament. The television companies were operating with football under an air of suspicion and near mistrust. Both parties were trying to play the role of the one who was needed most by the other.

Given the time difference, both the BBC and ITV were making noises that the early kick-offs, which would coincide with early evening in the UK, might not be broadcast in full. While the 1984 European Championship was being shunned, England undertook a tour of South America and, in an act of foretelling, ITV showed an unwillingness to move the ratings puller, *Surprise Surprise*, one Sunday in early June, meaning that England's match at the Maracanã against Brazil was only broadcast live for the second half. Thus, that incredible goal John Barnes scored, which came shortly before half-time, was missed by a frustrated nation of football fans.

So, it was under these strained circumstances that the 1986 World Cup finals approached the horizon. Culturally troubled as the era was, on my timeline it came at a period where my eyes were still set to wide when it came to football. Four years beyond the unbridled wonderment of the 1982 finals, and four years away from the first pangs of how football can let you down, during the 1990 edition, Mexico in 1986 was something of an oasis or a mirage. Appearing through waves of heat for a month and then vanishing once again, the 1986 World Cup finals was the perfect time to be 12 years old.

Chapter One

Colombia '86

MARCO TARDELLI'S unbridled joy at scoring Italy's second goal in the 1982 World Cup Final was for a long time the indisputable benchmark of all daydreaming football fans. Somewhere along the way, however, it became an overplayed image. There's much beauty in Tardelli's goal, much to please the eye in the build-up to that iconic goal, but that wonderful outpouring of a celebration became so familiar a sight that it lost some of its power to thrill in the way it once did.

Anything to do with future World Cups would tag on the visuals of Tardelli, running free and unfettered at the Santiago Bernabéu on 11 July 1982. Behold, this is what it means to win the World Cup. It was like switching on the radio and feeling a pang of frustration because when they play the Stone Roses they've opted for 'Ten Storey Love Song', rather than 'Daybreak'. 'Ten Storey Love Song' is a great song though, which should never be taken for granted.

Way up in the stands of the Bernabéu there was a prominent advertising hoarding. Emblazoned upon this hoarding was the slogan of Colombia '86. There was no Mexico '86 to speak of at that point in time, but there were some sizeable question marks over whether Colombia could host the next World Cup or not.

Despite a deployment of Colombian dignitaries, happily handing out Colombia '86 embossed freebies at the 1982 World Cup Final, when FIFA's movers and shakers pressed them on just how feasible the next tournament was, they were blithely met with the intonation that it would certainly be under the condition that the World Cup reverted to a 16-team tournament, regressing from the newly extended 24-nation event it had become for España '82.

While Colombia can be afforded a degree of sympathy that they launched a bid for a future World Cup at a time when it was a smaller tournament than the version that they would be expected to deliver, it was always entirely unlikely that they could have floated a 16-nation tournament, let alone one with places for 24.

As peculiar a choice as Colombia seemed, there simply was no rival bid. In June 1974, within the looming shadow of the finals in West Germany, and amid the upheaval of Sir Stanley Rous being overthrown as FIFA president, to be replaced by João Havelange, Colombia being awarded the hosting rights of the 1986 finals slipped under the radar somewhat.

It shouldn't have been that way. This was the first time since 1966 that a future World Cup host had been decided. Colombia was afforded the luxury of not just a clear run to collect the prize, but also 12 years in which to deliver on their promises.

The overthrow of Rous ensured that Colombia's prospects of hosting the 1986 World Cup were strangled at birth.

Havelange swept to power preaching the need to increase the number of participants of football's biggest event, opening the door wider to those not living under the umbrella of UEFA and CONMEBOL. Upon his coronation as the new president of FIFA, immediate and serious efforts were made to increase the number of competitors at the 1978 World Cup finals to 20 nations.

Eventually accepted to be a logistical accomplishment too soon, the 1978 finals proceeded without expansion, but 1982 and beyond would bear Havelange's hallmark for change. None of this would have come as a surprise to Colombia in June 1974, let alone at the Bernabéu in July 1982.

Within the closed-off era, when the location of the World Cup finals was still alternated between Europe and the Americas, by virtue of the swinging FIFA pendulum the 1986 tournament was roundly expected to be a Latin one. With Argentina set to host the 1978 finals, Spain having been allotted the 1982 tournament for Europe, and Uruguay, Brazil and Chile all having previously carried a World Cup, there was a paucity of obvious Latin American nations who could claim the 1986 prize of host nation.

Previous calendar aesthetics meant there was no big-hitting CONMEBOL nations either able or willing to step into the 1986 breach. Peru would have been a sensory fit, having contested the 1970 finals so admirably, but in June 1974 theirs was a country that was just four years beyond a devastating earthquake in the Ancash region, just off the coast of Chimbote. The largest natural disaster to hit Peru, bringing with it a human cost of up to 70,000 souls, the tremors were felt as far away as the central areas of Brazil, while damage and casualties were reported in Ecuador.

These terrible events were inclusive of what was the deadliest avalanche ever known, when the north face of Mount Huascarán was affected to such an extent that 80 million cubic metres of water, rock and mud travelled at speeds in excess of 200mph for 11 miles, consuming the towns of Yungay and Ranrahirca within its destructive path.

The Ancash earthquake took place on the opening day of the 1970 World Cup finals, at a time when an expectant nation was eagerly looking forward to their footballing heroes playing their first match of the tournament just two days later. It was Peru's first World Cup since the inaugural tournament in 1930. The monetary cost of the disaster was estimated at around $1bn, which would equate to over $7bn in the late summer of 2021.

With Peru out of the picture, Argentina's World Cup just four years away, and Uruguay, Brazil and Chile having had their turn already, CONMEBOL was running low on realistic options. Weighing up the logistics and then taking Bolivia, Ecuador, Paraguay and Venezuela out of the equation, with only Bolivia and Paraguay from that quartet having competed at a World Cup, it left only one possibility. Colombia.

Whereas common sense prevailed in Asunción, Caracas, Sucre and Quito, when it came to the potential for grandiose notions of over extension of their means in bidding for a World Cup, in Bogotá there was a very different sentiment. Inspired by the fervour of his country during the 1970 National Games of Colombia, the first time the multi-sport event had been contested for a decade, the sporting visionary, Alfredo Senior Quevedo, began to formulate his plan to bring the World Cup to Colombia. Winning the approval of Colombia's President, Carlos Lleras Restrepo, as part of what the Liberal Party leader billed as an era of national transformation, Quevedo, by now a newly installed member of the FIFA Executive Committee, immediately put the wheels in motion for his ambitious project.

Despite a change in president in August 1970, seeing the Conservative leader and cautious progressive Misael Pastrana Borrero sweep to power, Quevedo's plans continued largely unchallenged to his date with FIFA destiny in June 1974. With a clear field and a complicit government, FIFA awarded the 1986 finals to the only bidder. Colombia '86 was conceived.

Within two months of being awarded the 1986 World Cup, the sands hadn't only shifted unfavourably at FIFA, as far as Quevedo was concerned, but also at home. In August 1974 the Liberal Party once again reclaimed power, but the former president, and the man who gave Quevedo the initial encouragement to pursue the World Cup, Restrepo, had been beaten in his party primaries in his bid to once again stand for the presidency. It was another hammer blow to Quevedo's plans, when Alfonso López Michelsen instead took power for the Liberals. It was here that Colombia's silent efforts of gradually unpicking themselves from hosting the 1986 World Cup began.

Over the course of the next four years little progress was made on the construction of stadiums and the required improvements to general national infrastructure. FIFA had implored the need for a new international airport with regional links, hotels for visiting spectators, improved communications, and a motorway system that would ensure fluid movement between host cities. None of FIFA's demands were in danger of being met between 1974 and 1978. The distant nature of 1986 enabled the concept that the World Cup would be another president's problem.

When widespread riots broke out on the streets of Bogotá in September 1977 over food shortages and high unemployment, unrest that led to 80 people losing their lives and the injury of more than 2,000 others, Quevedo's dreams of Colombia being the centre of the sporting world were massively at odds with the brutal reality of his nation's volatile backdrop.

Michelsen's successor, Julio César Turbay Ayala, who came to power in 1978 and was Colombia's head of state during España '82, found his presidency consumed by a constant battle to contain the growing influence of left-wing guerrilla groups, inclusive of the potent 19th of April Movement. Growing dissent over the lack of improvements in the levels of social decay, which had prompted the September 1977 riots, and Turbay's increasing use of corporal control through military force in trying to subdue 'undesirables' all meant that Quevedo's attempts to advance the preparations for the World Cup were either met with empty platitudes or a wall of silence. The closer the 1986 World Cup loomed, the louder the silence became. Turbay was safe in the knowledge that he would soon be out of office.

Eventually it was left to the new incoming president, Belisario Betancur, to deliver the last rites on Colombia '86, stating in a radio and television address, towards the tail end of October 1982, that his nation lacked the economic capacity to meet FIFA's criteria for hosting the 1986 World Cup. He went on to class much of FIFA's criteria as extravagance, declaring that Colombia had more important priorities than a football tournament.

FIFA had in fact been forced to call Colombia's bluff. Having set a deadline for action of early November, there was no longer any time to lose. The next World Cup was little more than three and a half years away and FIFA knew that Colombia couldn't deliver on their promises. A new host would need to be identified as soon as possible. Commercial partners were beginning to get nervous.

Viewed in black-and-white terms, Quevedo's legacy is one of failure. He led a successful bid to procure a World Cup from FIFA, and for the only time in history it was a hosting right that was handed back. Colombia '86 remains a mirage, a trick of the mind's eye. Quevedo, however, was a visionary. His dream of a World Cup was born before a pronounced fault line opened in the global development of the sport. Mexico would haunt him in many ways. Mexico

'86 could have been his World Cup, the fruition of his dream for his nation, but in many ways Mexico '70 went a long way to destroying his dream.

Mexico '70 marked a meeting of the new world and the old world. While a Colombian World Cup might have been more feasible in the old Rous-led world order, it was totally infeasible in the new royal court of Havelange. The globalised nature of Mexico '86 sat 16 years beyond its iconic sibling, and with its shimmering if somewhat fragile satellite-fed colour images being beamed around the world it makes it hard to mentally visualise a Colombian version of the event.

Conversely, 16 years prior to Mexico '70, when the World Cup was that little bit quainter, Colombia wouldn't have seemed out of place sat amid the likes of Switzerland, Sweden and Chile in hosting the tournament. Quevedo's dream of a Colombian World Cup was born prior to the tectonic plates of football shifting between 1970 and 1974. The look, the feel, the very aura of not just football but the world at large altered dramatically beyond that clashing of eras at Mexico '70. Asking Colombia to host the World Cup in 1986 was akin to asking Alain Prost to win the Formula 1 title in a Citroën 2CV.

Quevedo was far from the failed PT Barnum character he was painted as. He was ambitious, he was creative, and no other man could have brought Colombia so close to hosting a World Cup as he did. He was the driving force behind the inexorable rise of the Bogotá outfit Millonarios Fútbol Club. The original *Galácticos*. Elected as president of the club in June 1946, he set out to create what became known as 'The Ballet Azul'. Taking advantage of a major players' strike in Argentina, Quevedo swooped for the services of stars such as Alfredo Di Stéfano, Adolfo Pedernera, Néstor Rossi and Julio Cozzi, much to the ire of the giants of the Argentinian game. Quevedo even dipped into British football for Everton's Billy Higgins, and Bobby Flavell of Heart of Midlothian.

Questions were raised over the legitimacy of these signings, and FIFA stepped in, ultimately banning Colombia from the organisation, and giving birth to the El Dorado era, when Colombia's league operated outside the jurisdiction of FIFA. The ban also affected the national team, causing their non-participation in the qualifiers for the 1954 World Cup.

Quevedo's Millonarios swept all before them, dominating as they collected four league titles in five years. The heady days of the renegade league finally ended in 1954, and it was from there, ever the opportunist, that perhaps the World Cup began to play on Quevedo's mind. Big ideas for a relatively small country, Quevedo's vision was essentially doomed from the outset. As Belisario Bentancur finally pronounced the worst-kept secret in world football, the vultures began to circle.

Brazil, Canada, the USA and Mexico all declared an immediate interest in stepping into the breach. Yet, with the Havelange factor, Brazil soon dropped out of the running, fearing potential accusations of sleight of hand. However, a persistent aura of sleight of hand hung in the air regardless of Brazil's withdrawal. Stories surfaced that Havelange had flown out to Mexico within days of Colombia handing their hosting rights back to FIFA. Havelange was among friends in Mexico, powerful friends who had stood with him in 1974 when he'd dethroned Rous for the presidency of FIFA. A facilitation to guide the 1986 World Cup to Mexico had begun.

The media mogul Emilio Azcarraga, and his Televisa empire, was set to benefit from the World Cup returning to Mexico, while Guillermo Canedo, Havelange's most vocal advocate within the FIFA executive committee, was another powerful influence on the direction of the reallocation of the 1986 World Cup.

With the continued interest of both the USA and Canada, a barely subtle charade was played out. A FIFA commission was formed to assess the viability of the potential host nations. Mexico received a visit, yet the USA and Canada didn't. This broke FIFA's own rule book, which states that every potential host nation must be inspected. Canedo was the man who guided the FIFA commission on a tour of Mexican stadiums and facilities. Everything was ultimately kept in-house.

The combined visitation snub towards North America was handily excused through omissions on the applications of both the USA and Canada, omissions that would likely have been forgiven had Mexico made similar ones. The FIFA commission returned to Europe instead, where they unanimously recommended the choice of Mexico as host of the 13th World Cup finals.

Despite this, there was no immediate disqualification of the USA and Canada. The public projection of a competitive bidding process was all too valuable to FIFA. In Stockholm on 20 May 1983, all candidates convened to present their cases to Havelange and his collection of executives, inclusive of the newly promoted general secretary, Sepp Blatter.

Canada, the rank outsiders, and in with very little chance of prevailing, put forward a still-impressive 30-minute presentation. The fact that Canada would still have a role to play at the 1986 World Cup finals is one of those wonderful yet inexplicable turn of events. Until 1986, never had Canada contested a World Cup finals tournament, and nor have they done so since.

The USA were meticulous in their planning and presentation. The hierarchy of the United States Soccer Federation (USSF) were primed with every possible answer to every imaginable scenario. Led by no less a megalith than Henry Kissinger, the former secretary of state under the presidencies of Richard Nixon and Gerald Ford, and more recently the conduit for the potential dream of peace between Israel and Palestine, the USSF had pulled out every stop to try to convince FIFA to go against the expected Mexican grain.

There was more, however. Kissinger was joined in his mission by his successor as secretary of state, Cyrus Vance, who served under the administration of Jimmy Carter. Then they also had the far from insignificant figures of Pelé and Franz Beckenbauer to assist. It was a powerful US delegation that swept into Stockholm with the hope that even if they couldn't win the vote, they could at least be granted a one-month deferral to allow a visit by the same FIFA commission that had been to inspect Mexico's facilities.

What followed was a compelling 60-minute presentation of a vastly superior bid to the one that Mexico would win the process with. Stadiums, transport, general infrastructure, communications, accommodation – the Mexican bid wasn't even second best in some categories when compared to the USA and Canada. Almost four decades later it seems incredulous that these three nations will pull together in hosting the 2026 World Cup finals.

Delivered by Rafael del Castillo, the president of the Mexican Football Federation, Mexico's presentation lasted just eight minutes, with the fine detail reputedly printed upon six pages of foolscap paper, in comparison to the glossy 90-page brochures that the USA and Canada produced. Later, when Del Castillo was asked about the swift nature of his presentation, he was heard to boast that he'd only needed 60 seconds to win the bid.

In the lobby bar of the Sheraton Hotel in Stockholm, tequila cocktails were being prepared for a public show of

Mexican jubilation before FIFA had even made an official announcement. Although the USSF would eventually win the right to host the 1994 World Cup, there remains a sense of a powerful enemy having been created by FIFA in the shape of the USA in Stockholm.

It's impossible to speculate just where the game of football would be now in the USA had they won their bid for the 1986 World Cup. Was it an opportunity lost perhaps, to make a labouring North American Soccer League (NASL) the centre of the footballing universe? Conversely, Clive Toye, the former general manager of the New York Cosmos and later the interim president of the NASL itself, offered me the opinion that not even being awarded the 1986 World Cup could have helped save his rapidly deteriorating league.

Either way, there almost feels like there was something preordained that the USA would be so instrumental in bringing down the old empire at FIFA three decades later.

Before the end of the 1980s, Del Castillo and the Mexican Football Federation would fall from FIFA grace when caught out fielding overage players during the qualifiers for the 1989 Under-20 World Championship. Known as the Cachirules scandal, the repercussions would eventually lead to a two-year suspension of all senior- and junior-age Mexican national teams from international competitions. Not only did this mean that the under-20 variant found themselves denied entry to the 1989 World Championship in Saudi Arabia, but also the increasingly talented senior team were banned from taking part in the 1990 World Cup qualifiers.

For the USA, the loss of the 1986 World Cup was a massive setback. There were understandable reservations harboured by the powers that be at FIFA towards the USSF and the potential Americanisation of the World Cup. The

NASL had been a thorn in FIFA's side, and Havelange was never going to water that dying plant.

In Ian Plenderleith's wonderful book, *Rock 'n' Roll Soccer: The Short Life and Fast Times of the North American Soccer League*, Phil Woosnam, the commissionaire of the NASL in its heyday, was moved to comment, in respect to the USSF's bid and the influence the NASL was trying to levy upon it, stating that you can't kick at FIFA's door for well over a decade and then expect them to invite you in.

Swimming upstream from the word go, there was even rumour of some self-sabotage from within the USSF, with stories of a phone call being made to FIFA insisting that the USA wasn't yet ready for a World Cup. If there's any truth to the rumour, at best it could perhaps be classed as an underhand way in which to make a valid point, while at worst it could be seen as a deliberate act to assist in the demise of the NASL, of which the USSF was no more than an uncomfortable bedfellow within the bidding process. In 1983 the USA was technically and logistically ready for the 1986 World Cup, yet maybe not culturally ready as a nation.

The NASL would grind to a halt in 1984, and the hypothetical awarding of the 1986 World Cup to the USA in 1983 either would likely have kept the league in operation for longer or given life to a replacement league. Instead, it would be over a decade later until the first ball in anger was kicked in the MLS (Major League Soccer).

In Stockholm, not everyone at FIFA was happy with the way the 1986 World Cup was guided into Mexico's possession. Harry Cavin, the FIFA vice-president at the time, had plenty of sympathy for the USA bid team, stating that much of the blame for the situation lay with FIFA. It was his contention that the commission should have visited the USA, just as it had Mexico. Cavin even indicated that he would favour a postponement of the vote. But, of course, that never came, and Cavin voted for Mexico regardless.

Ironically, within a year of the USA having been denied the chance to host the 1986 World Cup, FIFA's head had been turned by the packed-out stadiums for the football tournament at the 1984 Los Angeles Olympics. The seeds that would bloom at the 1994 World Cup had been sown.

Clearly, none of this was known by me at the time. All I saw ahead was a month of football and a Panini sticker album that I was never going to complete. The filter system of a 12-year-old boy kicking in as required once again.

Chapter Two

Paco's Panini Album

'I WAS talking to Paco at work, and he was asking about your book. He was saying he's still got a 1986 World Cup sticker album.'

It was a simple throwaway remark or two that my wife blithely made.

'I had one of those,' I replied. 'I don't know anybody that completed one though,' I continued.

'I think Paco did,' she responded, as if it were something and nothing.

'He ... did ... what? went the riposte.

So, a couple of weeks later I came into possession of Paco's prized Mexico '86 Panini sticker album. Albeit on a regrettably temporary basis.

It was with passing thoughts that I really should be donning white cotton gloves and using a set of page-turning prongs that I took Paco's sticker album from its plastic protective sleeve. The 35 years since I had last held my own partly completed one just fell away.

Paco is a workplace nickname for a man called Stephen Taylor. I've pondered its origin and I could probably make an educated guess, but I've never questioned why they call him that. I've never even met Stephen. He was, however, the first person to give feedback on the early content of this book and he liked it, so I was a long-term but distant fan of his, way before he produced his wondrous sticker-brimmed Panini album. Suddenly I had a new chapter two, Stephen pushing no less than Diego Maradona into chapter three.

Emblazoned with the classic Mexico '86 double-lined typeset at the top of the front cover, with a self-explanatory 'STICKER ALBUM' crammed in above, beneath this rests the tournament logo. Three spheres that make a vague nod towards the rings of the Olympiad, but also to the 1980s *BBC News* backdrop.

These three spheres comprise the two sides of planet Earth in a lined format either side of a red-and-white visual representation of the Adidas Telstar, the ball of choice for the 1970 and 1974 World Cups. Odd, given that it had been the Adidas Tango that had been in use for the previous two tournaments in Argentina and Spain. Imitated relentlessly to this very day, the Telstar remains the globally accepted image of a stereotypical football, to the point that it has its own emoji.

On the lower third of the front cover is the tournament mascot, Pique, the humanised chilli with upturned moustache, sombrero brim, red Mexico shirt, oversized feet and a Telstar that's at shoulder height to him. He's framed by the flags of all 24 competing nations, a goalmouth directly behind him. To his right it simply states, 'WORLD CUP', and to his left is the Panini logo, that evocative jousting knight of the realm.

Market competitors, Merlin, might have been created by the people who were the driving force behind the glory days of Panini, but they simply don't hold the same thrall as a jousting knight does. It would be like Nike taking over as the tournament's ball supplier, if Merlin were ever to usurp Panini as the World Cup's official sticker album of choice. Some things are sacrosanct; some things are sacred.

Turning over to the back cover, you're implored to purchase a 'Fabulous Souvenir' stamp collector's dream, that included 24 large and unique colour stamps, a free wallchart and, intriguingly, a 'Fantastic World Cup Hologram' that 'has to be seen to be believed', all at the extortionately priced £3.95 from The Stamp Centre in Southampton.

At the foot of the back cover is the array of global distributors. What an Aladdin's cave 116–120 Goswell Road, London must have been in 1986. No longer the centre of the sticker collector's universe, I wonder whether the workers who now occupy the building have any idea of the historical significance of their surroundings?

Carefully turning the first page, it seems familiar, yet also unfamiliar. The first sticker is of a ball – yet another representation of the Telstar – which is orbited to its northern hemisphere by the words 'WORLD CUP', and to its southern hemisphere by the word 'MUNDIAL'. It's presumably an unfamiliar sticker because I never obtained it. The accompanying stickers of the World Cup logo and Pique are more familiar, however, either because I managed to get those ones, or due to them being images that are instantly recognisable.

To the left, the list of national abbreviations and translations are both evocative and comforting. There's an entire generation who don't know of the simple joys of seeing scoreline captions part way through games, where the teams are referred to in the host nation's language. Among the European teams to set sail for Mexico '86 there were Alemania, Bélgica, Escocia, Francia, Inglaterra, España, Dinamarca, Italia, Irlanda del Norte, Polonia and the URSS.

In the list of contents, however, and as each nation's page-to-page banner identification, the teams are referred to in their native tongue. While England, Scotland and Northern Ireland are simply – and boringly – England,

Scotland and Northern Ireland, we instead have Belgium, Hungary, West Germany and Morocco billed as Belgique-Belgie, Magyarorszag, Deutschland-BRD and Maroc.

It all worked towards adding that layer of mystique to a Latin World Cup, when combined with those crackly commentaries and hazy, vulnerable broadcast images.

Beneath those first three stickers there's a picture of the World Cup itself, flanked by another reminder of what the tournament is called and a list of previous World Cup winners. The teams are named in their native vernacular. Up to 1970 it's referred to as the Rimet Cup and from 1974 it's branded the FIFA World Cup.

At the top of the page 'MEXICO 86' is proclaimed once more. Sport Billy's presence is also evident in copyright form. Sport Billy being the annoyingly gifted animated sports star from the planet Olympus, who seemed to be everywhere in the early to mid-1980s, with his equally annoying sidekicks, Lilly and Willy.

Inside the back cover is the teaser page, where you're told what to do if you come to within 50 stickers of completing your album. As if anybody other than Stephen Taylor came close to such a feat of endurance.

Exploring further within, we have a glorious page where there's a sticker of each official World Cup poster from 1930 to 1982. While some of these posters were quite simplistic and others tried a bit too hard to get it right, they're all beautiful in their own way. Some stand out as pieces of art that transcend eras, yet others are entirely of their time. For instance, there's the art deco feel to the 1930 offering, an almost foreboding aura to the 1938 image, a vague nod to the space race in 1962 and a shadowiness to the 1978 version.

Next, we have a wallchart that isn't quite a wallchart. Stephen strikingly stopped filling in the scores after Argentina beat England. This is followed by stickers of each stadium and an image from each hosting city. Most of these are of a landmark of civic pride, although Monterrey opts for a panoramic view of itself instead. Intriguingly, the stadium shots are all artistic impressions rather than photographs. A primitive form of airbrushing that suggests the stadiums and surrounding areas weren't as pristine as they had hoped for, at least when the stickers went to print.

Turning the next page, this is where the teams kick in, beginning with Group A and the holders, Italy. A foil badge, of course, a pre-match team picture and 16 individual player stickers. It was always unsettling that you didn't get a full squad of 22, and given that the stickers went to print not long after the draw for the finals was made, a degree of guesswork had to take place when it came to the selection of each 'squad'.

Perceptively, whoever it was that predicted the *Azzurri* squad got it correct, as all 16 players did indeed make Enzo Bearzot's 22 for Mexico. The retrospectively interesting part, however, is that Gianluca Vialli didn't get a sticker and nor did Walter Zenga. Both junior members of Italy's travelling party, they would become cornerstones of the post-Bearzot Italy, under Azeglio Vicini.

From page to page there's also a list of each team's results since the previous World Cup, up to early February 1986.

Throughout the rest of Group A, the standout images are of how beautiful Bulgaria's kit was, the erroneous presence of Argentina's 1978 World Cup-winning goalkeeper, Ubaldo Fillol, who didn't travel to Mexico, and the insult to South Korea in their players being reduced to two players per sticker, just as was the case with Scottish Premier Division stickers in Panini's domestic club version.

In Group B, Iraq befalls the same shrunken fate as South Korea, while Mexico, Belgium and Paraguay are given the full works.

José Touré is part of the France page, in Group C, although a serious knee injury eventually ruled him out of the tournament. It was the loss of Touré that opened the door in Henri Michel's squad for Jean-Pierre Papin. Beyond this, Group C is cemented by the no-nonsense camera poses of the Soviet Union players, inclusive of the very precise moustache of Aleksandr Chivadze, the impressive beards of the Hungary squad and Canada having the same temerity as the Soviet Union in printing their team name across the front of their shirts.

Group D's pages are illuminated by Algeria's marvellous kit and their unenviable fixture list. It's also the place where we find Brazil, where Stephen clearly had a bit of a nightmare in putting Júnior in his space, as he's at a pronounced jaunty angle and without question the most creased sticker throughout the entire album. In fact, Júnior is so cockeyed that he even manages to marginally overlap Falcão to his left.

Brazil and Algeria are complemented by Spain, upon whose page Hipólito Rincón is the only player sporting an Adidas-embossed Spain shirt, while the rest are wearing Le Coq Sportif. A portentous harbinger of sartorial doom perhaps, Rincón travelled to Mexico without playing one single minute of the World Cup.

And then we have Northern Ireland, providing Spain with cold sweats in memory of Valencia four years earlier. A combination of youthful mullets, hairstyles stuck in the 1970s, a smattering of receding hairlines and yet another iconic Adidas kit. Led symbolically by Pat Jennings, who was officially an Everton player at this World Cup, having spent most of the season back on the books at Tottenham Hotspur for registration purposes and as extra cover for Ray Clemence, before answering the call from Howard Kendall to be the back-up to Bobby Mimms, who in turn was covering for the injured Neville Southall. Despite the presence of Jennings, the captain's armband was the property of Sammy McIlroy.

In Group E, West Germany are clean-cut, with not a hair out of place. Even Stephen's work in putting their stickers in place is admirably efficient, with only Michael Frontzeck creeping outside the lines, and he didn't even go to Mexico. This neatness continues into Uruguay's page, another team bearing the Le Coq Sportif logo.

On the next page, Scottish faces are predominantly set to pensive, although Roy Aitken, David Speedie and Kenny Dalglish look genuinely happy. Dalglish would be a late withdrawal, while Speedie would miss the cut. Graeme Souness has opted for a menacing pose and Steve Archibald looks quite satisfied with himself, which is probably due to him being a resident of Barcelona. Scotland's team photo is unsettling, as it's of them lining up at Ninian Park on the evening Jock Stein died. There's also a wistfulness at the sight of the tragic Davie Cooper.

Denmark's page is magical. The carefulness of the sticker placement from West Germany, through Uruguay and Scotland, has now worn off, as the more freestyle nature begins to kick in again. This is eminently in keeping with Denmark as a footballing ethos. Wild, unkempt, yet skilfully hypnotic. The Hummel chevrons are as eye-catching as the players. The Mexico '86 kit isn't yet in evidence, but the equally as attractive Arsenal-esqe version is. I could stare at this page forever.

Finally, we have Group F. Poland with yet more beautiful kits and the brilliant Zbigniew Boniek, plus Portugal and the curious case of António André, who has a massive double plaster over his left eye. How did he receive this injury? We have Morocco too, the last of the nations to be restricted, insulted even, by having their team condensed to smaller stickers. They're almost an afterthought, crammed in next to the instructions on how to send off for your last 50 stickers. It's no way to treat what would be Group F's winners.

This leaves England. The penultimate team in the album, Mark Wright and Paul Bracewell are in attendance, yet neither would go to Mexico. A broken leg in the FA Cup semi-final sidelined Wright, while Bracewell was unlucky not to make Bobby Robson's squad, left on the outside looking in by the multi-positional adaptability of Steve Hodge, who could play both centrally and wide, whereas the Everton man was a central midfielder in an already competitive field.

As an oddity, of the 13 England players to take to the pitch for the World Cup quarter-final against Argentina, four of them were omitted from England's Panini page. Along with Hodge, Peter Beardsley, Peter Reid and John Barnes were also missing.

A vision of wonderment, a fully realised version of something I could only dream of having completed, Stephen Taylor's Panini album represents the end of an era for me. At 16, I was too moody to own an Italia '90 sticker album, but at 12, this one was perfectly timed, and it added to the sense of awe the tournament provided. I'm blessed to have been able to look at it.

Chapter Three

The Hand of God

CONTENTIOUS, OF course, it's the defining image of the 1986 World Cup finals, and it's perhaps even the most distinguishing aspect of the entire history of the tournament, stretching back to its very inception in 1930.

To be able to properly assess Argentina as World Cup winners in 1986, I believe that you need to initially remove their first goal in the quarter-final from the equation. You need to detach it and view it for what it was, to desensitise it before reattaching it to the match from which it came. Only then can you look at their wider World Cup campaign more expansively and with greater clarity. Confront the pantomime before considering wider, ultimately glorious kitchen-sink drama.

I mean, with immediate recall, does anyone, off the top of their head, automatically know who Argentina played in the four matches that led them to the 1986 World Cup quarter-final? This is a strange phenomenon that's arguably unique to the Argentina vintage of 1986, when it comes to World Cups played out within the colour television era.

Many people could pick out most of the matches Brazil played during the process of winning within a blizzard of beauty in 1970. A lot could probably point to West Germany facing East Germany in 1974, or Argentina sitting within

1978's group of death against France, Italy and Hungary. And if you don't know about Italy facing Argentina and Brazil in 1982, then this really isn't the book you're looking for.

Argentina at the 1986 World Cup, prior to facing England, remain a mystery to many, however. So, the need to separate the 'Hand of God' and later return to the wider cause and effect of Argentina's success is quite imperative, as is the need to isolate a fleeting moment that many people can't see beyond, at least in the hope that the two can be reconciled and reunited with a degree of balance and perspective later in the book.

If the 'Hand of God' isn't the World Cup's most defining image, then it must be its most identifiable, in a similar manner to how thoughts of the Olympic Games, despite all the glorious moments you can linger on, will swiftly drift to Tommie Smith and John Carlos, as they defiantly display the Black Power salute in 1968. An event that ironically also took place in Mexico City, just eight miles from the Estadio Azteca, at the Estadio Olímpico Universitario, a stadium in which Argentina played two of those four matches that took them into their 1986 World Cup quarter-final encounter with England.

Politically charged at the time, due to the relative proximity of the Falklands War just four years earlier, in a more contemporary frame the 'Hand of God' remains politically divisive. This is something that largely boils down to the two men who decisively duelled for the ball in mid-air when that fateful opening goal was scored.

On one side of this divide sits Diego Maradona, a man celebrated and demonised in the most pronounced of measures, but somebody who, willingly or not, represented those who see themselves as oppressed, wronged and marginalised, to whom he remains a hero and anti-hero all rolled into one, even within death. Maradona is a beacon, even to those who fall into the category of the footballing romantic, those of an artistic soul, or simply those of us who have an anti-authoritarian nature.

Opposing the street urchin's street urchin of choice is Peter Shilton, a goalkeeper who has gone on to become something of a social media standard-bearer for the right wing of the political spectrum of the UK, an unofficial tub-thumper for Nigel Farage and an admirer of the works of Boris Johnson. This has been a turn of events that's left him open to ridicule and invective responses from some who think differently. In his new role, Shilton has become the very personification of John Bull.

Within this, the 'Hand of God' has become a stick with which to beat the former England goalkeeper. Shilton is regularly goaded for not getting off the ground in his dealings with Maradona on that blisteringly hot day in Mexico City. Ironically, on a smaller scale, Shilton has almost become as polarising as Maradona. His critics sift through YouTube for evidence of his mistakes as a player, of which there are quite a few glaring ones. It's led to an increasing revisionism of his talents as a goalkeeper, which is seemingly gaining more and more traction.

As World Cup footballing incidents go, it's become the moment where the elephant runs amok on *Blue Peter*, leaving wee, poo and a struggling zookeeper in its wake, much to the amusement of that category of child that never coveted being handed a badge by Valerie Singleton or John Noakes.

'My amigos' was how Maradona used to describe them, yet for over three and a half decades, Ali Bin Nasser and Bogdan Dochev weren't on cordial terms with one another. For over 35 years, they mutedly blamed each other for the events that surrounded the opening goal of the 1986 World Cup quarter-final between Argentina and England. A subdued and long-distance feud of sorts was at play, one that was arguably unrequited by Bin Nasser, towards the man who ran the right-hand-side touchline on that fateful day.

There was beauty, there was sleight of hand and there was controversy; there was confusion, there was anger and there was jubilation. Time stood still as the ball rolled over Shilton's goal line; two men dressed in all black looked at each other, and neither of them knew the answer to the question that was asked of them. A goal was given.

Bin Nasser was the referee who was unsure of what he'd just seen, and Dochev was the linesman with his flag down. They had stared at one another in a prolonged manner, each in hope that the other had spotted a vaguely sensed infringement. Instead, they both ran back to the halfway line, referee with no option but to give the goal and linesman having made no signal either way.

Even though eight World Cups have passed since the 'Hand of God', it's a goal that's still one of the most widely discussed in the history of the game. Wide open to debate, it's maybe even the most famous goal in football history. There are numerous still photographs of the fateful moment when Maradona's clenched left hand meets the ball. It was more the clenched fist of God, perhaps.

In Mexico City, at the Estadio Azteca, a match was played out between Argentina and England on 22 June 1986, the midday sun blazing high in the sky, that spidery shadow lurking ominously in the centre circle, just inside the Argentina half and to the right of the centre spot. Not one of the myriads of still photographs in circulation successfully captures the moment of contact of ball with Argentine hand. Each one of them is either a split second too late or too soon. The ball is on the way down or on the way up. Maradona's arm is more outstretched than it was when contact was made. The camera does lie from time to time.

There's a common misconception about just how obvious Maradona's handling of the ball was for the opening goal of the match, an incident that came six minutes beyond the restart for the second half. Time has distorted the occurrence to a large extent. Many people are of the mind that it was impossible to miss the infringement; many people are of the mind that beyond Bin Nasser and Dochev, of those present within the stadium only the BBC's Barry Davies missed it too, so flagrantly obvious it was.

'They're appealing for offside,' proclaimed Davies, during his initial reaction to what was unfolding. There was confusion both on and off the pitch, and it took over 30 seconds for the first inkling of what had occurred to filter through and even then very few people were entirely certain of what they had just seen.

Many of those in the stands of the Azteca failed to notice it too. Ric George, not much more than a couple of weeks after securing journalistic employment with the *Liverpool Echo*, was there as part of a wonderful odyssey around Mexico to take in the World Cup on a holidaying basis. He only discovered the method of conversion of Argentina's first goal when boarding a bus after the match.

It was a similar story for Hamish Tindall, a member of Scotland's massed ranks of support in Mexico, who continued to take in matches beyond his nation's exit from the tournament. He too spoke of having no inkling of foul play, not even of vague rumblings of discontent around him in the stadium.

On the pitch, only Maradona himself, Peter Shilton and Terry Fenwick had any real certainty over what had happened. Fenwick raced to the halfway line in pursuit of Bin Nasser, protesting animatedly as he did. Glenn Hoddle belatedly joined him in protest, but with no more conviction than that of a man who had been told a first-hand account of the footballing crime he was now trying to report, as opposed to having witnessed it himself. It wasn't the first time during the match that Hoddle had turned up belatedly.

It all happened so quickly, and it was almost out of sync with a match that was predominantly slow-paced due to the baking climate.

The two goals Maradona scored that day are sold as classic examples of the double-sided coin of his personality. If the second goal was a beauty, then the first one was the beast? Yin and yang in footballing form. Yet there was beauty within that first goal too. The beauty was in the build-up, and from some perspectives there's also beauty to be found within the finish.

He who robs a thief has a hundred years of pardon. It was a saying and a sentiment that hung heavy in the celebratory air in Buenos Aires in the aftermath of the final whistle of this match. Thousands of people took themselves to the streets and chanted anti-Margaret Thatcher slogans long into the night, actions that would have won the nod of approval of a great many voters in the UK at that very time. The enemies of Margaret Thatcher resided both overseas and on home shores. The two nations at play in the Estadio Azteca had of course been at war just four years earlier.

Tensions were higher off the pitch than on. In fact, apart from a small number of isolated and short-lived outbursts of pre-match aggression, tensions seemed to be higher in the press box and back home than they were in the stands.

Argentina's players had handed each opponent in the England team a personalised pennant before kick-off, in a gesture of friendship, or at least in a disarming manoeuvre that had the intention of killing the opposition with kindness. In many respects, the sting was taken out of the occasion before it had begun, only to be injected back into the game in the 51st minute.

In the stands the atmosphere took on a more laid-back aura to the tinderbox one that had been feared and, unlike in the UK, cold beer was available for the spectators to imbibe in clear view of the pitch. With the midday sun at its most fierce, it could almost have been a relaxing, if scorching day at the beach. Argentines and Englishmen go out in the midday sun – 114,580 spectators were in attendance.

Even after the match, in some instances there was sympathy, or at least sportsmanship from Argentina supporters to England fans upon their exit from the tournament. Clive Toye, the former New York Cosmos general manager, was heading back to his rental car when he feared the worst from a cluster of Argentina followers, only to be embraced by them, having mistaken him for an isolated England supporter.

Back on the pitch, Argentina moved the ball around with ease, probing for gaps. England, almost like a fear-infused challenger in a boxing ring, ducking and bobbing with the heavyweight champion of the world elect. The longer the punch took to land the more England began to sleepwalk, hypnotised by the seemingly sedentary nature of the movement of both the opposing players and the ball.

Just 90 seconds before the first goal rolled over his goal line, Shilton was busy winding an imaginary spinning wheel with his right hand, attempting to wake his slumbering defence. He recognised the signals and England were sending out regular invitations to Argentina to go for goal. The 'Hand of God' conceals more than it illuminates.

Six minutes after the restart for the second half, another unforced long ball out of defence from Terry Butcher was subsequently returned to the England half of the pitch with measured Argentinian passing, via Sergio Batista and Héctor Enrique, and into the possession of Julio Olarticoechea. A square ball from the left-hand side of the pitch to Maradona

The Hand of God

in line with the edge of the centre circle was played sedately, as if the match was being played within an unspoken truce of walking pace.

A burst of speed and the ball was in the England net just ten seconds later.

For every Shilton with his arm raised there was an oblivious Trevor Steven ambling back into place for the restart. While Fenwick argued with Ali Bin Nasser, Peter Beardsley stood there with arms outstretched, as much in confusion over what the argument was about than joining the protest. For every Hoddle racing in to back up Fenwick there was a Steve Hodge sheepishly blending into the background.

Maradona picked up the ball in line with the edge of the centre circle. He turned inwards and carried it to England at medium pace before he then dipped to his right to evade the advancing Hoddle. It's here that the accelerator hit the floor. The converging Peter Reid and Steven saw him go past in a blur. Fenwick advanced, only to see Maradona repeat what he'd just done to Hoddle. Butcher and Kenny Sansom then closed the door to the edge of the England penalty area, yet as Maradona prodded the ball diagonally to his right towards Jorge Valdano, he continued his run, breaking past a mesmerised England defence, who had now fragmented and were busy ball-watching.

Valdano flicked the ball up with his left foot, taking himself by surprise at how high it spun upwards, looping over his shoulder, and as it dropped down it was marginally out of the Real Madrid striker's reach, but not that of Hodge. Right foot planted, leaning back, left foot stretched out and far too raised, possibly put off from heading the ball by Valdano spinning towards it with his elbow jutting forward, it wasn't the first time in this match that Hodge had sent the ball backwards over his head inside his own

51

penalty area. He also did it during the first half, to less damaging effect.

The next time the ball would make any kind of contact, it was to be with Maradona's hand, as it looped far into the air and landed to him around seven or eight yards from the goal line. Having run at speed for around 35 to 40 yards, the first 20 yards of those with the ball at his feet, he met it at a forceful velocity, launching himself from around ten yards short of the goal line.

From the opposite direction, Shilton was slow out of the blocks and there's no discernible lift-off in his jump to meet the oncoming player and ball. In those still photos that don't quite capture the moment perfectly, the England goalkeeper strikes the image of somebody who has all the leaden-footed intent of a man stretching to open a window. While Maradona had speed of momentum, Shilton had a height advantage. Use of hand or not, at eight inches taller, the grey-attired England No. 1 should never be second best in that duel for the ball.

Before the ball rolls over the goal line, both Shilton and Fenwick have arms aloft in protest. Within four seconds, Maradona has exited the England penalty area, stage right, taking a quick glance over his shoulder to see whether the referee has called play back or not. Beckoning over his team-mates to celebrate, his tracks have been covered and the illusion of a legitimate goal is complete. Genius is at play, and the British sense of fair play was, of course, insulted.

The concept of the British sense of fair play is a selective commodity, however. For the same nation that embraces the getting away with it ideals of the Great Train Robbery and *The Italian Job*, to be so aghast at the actions of Maradona doesn't sit right.

One person's cheat is another's opportunist. Sir Bobby Robson, Chris Waddle, Shilton and Butcher lamented long and loudly about the injustice of the event. They're complaints that are regularly aired to this day. When Maradona was still with us, Shilton often spoke of the lack of an official apology, yet how could he apologise for something he had no remorse for?

From Maradona's perspective, he cunningly outwitted his opponents – thundering Anglo-Saxon opponents. He defeated brawn with brain, and many of the broader-thinking newspaper reports in the days directly after the match made little of the manner of the first goal. While the tabloids made greater sensationalist purchase of it, the broadsheets were more considered. They instead focused on England's limitations in comparison to Argentina, and the physical nature of their approach to *La Albiceleste*'s ultimate maestro.

David Miller in *The Times* wrote of how England had tried to stifle their opponents rather than play to win. He contended that England's players had been somewhat agricultural in their dealings with Maradona, concluding that 'they closed around him like a gang of farmhands gingerly trying to grapple with a bull which had slipped his pen'.

Jeff Powell of the *Daily Mail* has since offered the opinion that the 'Hand of God' was possibly accidental, perhaps more in hope than genuine belief.

While it's hard to sell as an accidental incident, neither was it premeditated. Maradona didn't set off for goal in the 51st minute with the idea in his head that he would strike forth and punch the ball into the England net. It was a spur-of-the-moment opportunistic incident that even he has admitted to having happened in other matches before 22 June 1986. Maradona was a man with that inbuilt drive to win at all costs, something that many British sports stars have had too.

In 2015, Diego Maradona was in Tunisia to film a television advert, and while he was there, he met up with Ali Bin Nasser. Maradona gave him a signed shirt with the personalised message: 'To my eternal friend'. Bin Nasser in return gave him the framed picture from his wall. It was an enlarged image taken in the centre circle of the Estadio Azteca just before kick-off, at the World Cup quarter-final between Argentina and England. Maradona and Shilton are shaking hands, and Bin Nasser is in the background. They were gifts exchanged by unlikely friends who had managed to generate a distant, yet enduring friendship born of infamy.

As for Bogdan Dochev, the man who was harshly classed by many in Bulgaria as a national traitor for his part in the 'Hand of God', well he sat and he awaited his own home visit from Maradona, a visit that never came. Dochev sadly died in May 2017, three and a half years prior to the death of the man who was born with a hand that was reputedly guided by God himself.

Chapter Four

A, B, C, as Easy as 1, 2, 3

WHEN JOÃO Havelange finally pushed through his proposal to increase the number of World Cup competitors for the 1982 finals to 24 nations in a bid to retain symmetrical integrity, a format was conjured up that consisted of six, four-team first-round groups, from which only two teams per group would progress to the next stage, for a total of 12 continuing competitors.

It meant that despite the introduction of two extra groups and eight further qualifiers to the tournament, there was still a sink or swim nature to progression, and that the tournament would continue to shed half of the teams that began the race by the time that initial group stage had come to an end.

Nice and neat in terms of structure. The curveball was that the numbers being crunched didn't fit in with the pattern of most previous World Cups, where the latter stages would be contested by a collection of teams that added up in multiples of the base number of teams in the final. Two teams in the final, four teams in the semi-finals, and eight teams in the quarter-finals, or in the case of 1974 and 1978, two further groups of four teams.

Just what could be done with 12 teams was a conundrum that was solved by a second round of group matches, the continuing nations being split into four groups of three teams, from which only the winners would move on to a pair of traditional semi-finals, a concept reintroduced in Spain after what had been a 12-year hiatus.

This was a format that looked sound on paper, but on green, rectangular patches of grass with goalposts at each end there proved to be a cluster of flaws. There ended up being two very clear instances where winning the initial group stages did the victors no favours when it came to the tasks they were handed for the second round of group matches.

When England topped Group 4, and Brazil led the way in Group 6, both teams winning all three matches in the process, their dubious rewards were to be thrown into second-round battle with West Germany and Spain, and Argentina and Italy, respectively. Meanwhile, the teams they marginalised into the runners-up spots of their first-round groups both landed kinder-looking landscapes, pitted alongside the likes of Austria, Northern Ireland, Belgium and Poland.

Obviously, karma was very much preoccupied in the summer of 1982, as in the instance of Brazil it all facilitated to ensure that one of the best teams to ever grace a World Cup failed to even make it to the last four, while in the case of England, they exited the tournament at the same stage, despite being unbeaten and only having conceded one goal in their five matches played.

Added to these phenomena, there had been a bad taste left behind by the idea that both African qualifiers had been bundled out of the tournament, one by unfair means and the other via a lack of fortune. This was when Algeria were denied their projected place in the second round of group matches by a shameful collusion between West Germany and Austria in Group 2, which earned itself the moniker of 'The

Disgrace of Gijón', an outrage further irked by Cameroon's own unbeaten exit, after they had matched Italy's trio of draws in Group 1, only to go out due to having scored one goal fewer than the eventual world champions.

When West Germany's role of the pantomime villain was completed later, due to Harald Schumacher ruthlessly mowing down the onrushing Patrick Battiston, in their iconic semi-final with France in Seville, it amazingly propagated a situation where a once-maligned Italy were cast in the unlikely role of the saviours of the tournament when overpowering Jupp Derwall's team in the final.

While not entirely of the making of its organisers, the 1982 World Cup found itself the recipient of a high degree of negativity, something that was an enormous shame, given that it had been a tournament with a massive amount going for it, be it the often-wonderful football or the sights and sounds of a hugely atmospheric month of vivid aesthetics.

Whether it was the unsatisfactory outcome of the format or the perceived lack of footballing justice on display in 1982, changes were demanded for the 1986 World Cup finals. Having been dispensed with after the 1970 World Cup, also in Mexico, the exclusively knockout format for the second stage of the World Cup returned.

It was in the name of modernisation that knockout football had vanished from the 1974 and 1978 World Cups. A peculiar move, given that both of 1970's semi-finals had been classics, with Italy's victory over West Germany even being declared the match of the century. On top of this, the quarter-finals had provided rich entertainment too, inclusive of a six-goal thriller between Brazil and Peru, plus West Germany's stunning comeback win against Sir Alf Ramsey's England. Over the course of the seven matches that had made up the quarter-finals, semi-finals and final of the 1970

World Cup, an incredible 33 goals had been scored, with a third of them belonging to Brazil.

Only one of these seven matches ended with fewer than four goals being scored. Apart from the potential increase in revenue from the six extra matches played in 1974 and 1978, compared to 1970 and the three preceding World Cups, it's bewildering that FIFA felt change was necessary. It certainly wasn't initiated in the name of producing more entertainment and goals.

Escalation being the name of the game, the increase to 24 teams for the 1982 World Cup finals upped the fixture count to 52, and not wanting a decrease in that amount for 1986, the permutations were pondered and the rejigged format gave back with one hand and took away with the other.

While a return to a knockout system beyond the group stages was presented, the problem lay within the task of condensing 24 teams into that knockout format without taking a step back in the high threshold of 52 matches. It meant that there was no way that FIFA's new knockout stage would completely mirror the old one in running from an eight-team quarter-final. It would have to contain an extra round of 16.

A simple decision and an incredibly opportunistic and convenient way of maintaining 52 matches, yet it would mean that four of the six third-placed teams in the initial group stage would need to advance, alongside the 12 teams to occupy the top two positions across the six groups. This meant there would be potential reward for underachievement and that 36 group matches would be played out across a span of two weeks, in the name of eliminating just eight teams.

Group stages diluted; although this was the tournament that's classed as being the one that gave birth to the phrase 'the group of death', it's also the tournament that took a giant step towards killing off that very concept. A format of

A, B, C, as Easy as 1, 2, 3

anomalies, both Hungary and Portugal would make their exit at the group stages, despite picking up a win each, while Bulgaria and Uruguay managed to progress to the knockout stage without a victory, and in the case of Uruguay a 6-0 drubbing at the hands of Denmark.

It's impossible to deny that some teams that reached the last 16 should have instead been homeward bound. This was a very different World Cup to the ones that had preceded it. While 1982 may not have been perfect, it offered a much more exacting challenge to the first-round group stages, where, for instance, Scotland found that a win and a draw wasn't enough to see them through. Eight years earlier at the 1974 World Cup it was an even more unforgiving system, when a win and two draws hadn't been enough.

In a satisfyingly symmetrical manner, half of the eight nations to depart the 1986 World Cup at the group stages waved goodbye to the tournament from groups A, B and C, as South Korea, Iraq, Hungary and Canada fell by the wayside. Of this quartet, Hungary were the most illustrious, at least in historical terms. Beaten finalists in 1938 and 1954, it had, however, been 20 years since they had navigated their way beyond the group stages of a World Cup. They had failed to qualify in both 1970 and 1974, two absences that bookended a now seemingly out-of-character run to the semi-finals of the 1972 European Championship.

Led by György Mezey, a man who went against the grain of the usual identikit for the stereotypical gnarled and grizzled footballing elder that you might expect to be found in charge of an Eastern European national team, Hungary's head coach had been in football management since the age of 29 and was still only in his mid-40s when he took the Mighty Magyars, as was, to Mexico. A coaching odyssey that had begun in his mid-20s while still a player, Mezey had ascended to the Hungarian national job after spending the

59

1970s at the forefront of Budapest club football, inclusive of three years at the helm of MTK, before gaining employment with the Magyar Labdarúgó Szövetség (MLSZ), the Hungarian football governing body.

At the MLSZ, Mezey filled an array of positions between 1980 and 1983, from assistant to Kálmán Mészöly, whom he served under at the 1982 World Cup, to taking charge of Hungary's youth levels, duties that were added to with leading their Olympic team. By 1983, Mészöly had stepped aside after an ineffectual qualifying campaign for the 1984 European Championship, upon which Mezey was handed the top job and the unenviable task of plotting a path to the 1986 World Cup past not only the Netherlands but Austria too.

Undaunted, that's exactly what Mezey did. While his Hungary team comfortably had the measure of Austria both home and away and managed to pick off a stunning victory in Rotterdam against the Netherlands at De Kuip early in the qualifying campaign, the *Oranje* conspired against themselves when picking up just one point from their two matches against Austria. It meant that by the time they were obtaining themselves a narrow final night victory at the Népstadion, it was by then a result that could only gain the Dutch a play-off spot. Having won their first five qualifiers, Hungary had already booked their ticket for Mexico, scoring more goals than any of their opponents, and conceding fewer.

It was a hugely impressive turnaround in fortunes for Hungary. Mezey had taken over during a time of disarray in the Hungarian game, within the wake of wider investigations into match-fixing. Inheriting the job from his mentor, on his 42nd birthday, the new head coach instilled a heightened sense of discipline and focus to work alongside their undoubted skill.

With much to be positive about during qualification, Hungary even had time to pick off a victory in Hamburg over West Germany in January 1985, while they wrapped up their official warm-up matches for the World Cup surprisingly prematurely, two and a half months prior to the tournament, albeit with an incredulous 3-0 demolition of Brazil in front of 70,000 enthralled spectators in Budapest.

Between the conclusion of their qualification campaign and the first ball they kicked in anger at the World Cup, Hungary suffered only one reversal, and that came in December 1985 in Toluca against Mexico, during a four-team acclimatisation tournament. Arguably a team in a rich vein of form, in one respect Hungary can't be blamed for curtailing their more expansive World Cup preparations after their stunning defeat of Brazil, yet two and a half months without a serious test prior to taking to the pitch for their opening match was an undeniable error.

An era might have unwittingly been coming to an end for Hungary, with the 1986 World Cup proving to be their last major international tournament for three decades, but the team that qualified for Mexico were one of underappreciated substance, one that married experience with a cluster of younger players. Half of Hungary's squad were under the age of 27, and with a strong nod towards an Eastern Bloc that was still a few politically fraught years away from dissolution, only three of the 22 players that Mezey took to Mexico were playing their club football away from the Nemzeti Bajnokság, each of whom had only gained their footballing freedom later in their careers.

They relied heavily on the skills and eye for goal of Lajos Détári and Márton Esterházy. The former had scored goals aplenty in a 1985/86 title-winning campaign for Budapest Honvéd, while the latter had been allowed to move to AEK Athens two years earlier, at the age of 28, markedly ahead of the usual narrative of freedom only being permitted once a player had reached his 30s. For Esterházy, this concession owed a lot to the unusual fact that he was the descendant of a family of great Hungarian nobility.

Of the rest of Détári and Esterházy's fellow squad members, only the defender and twice Hungarian player of the year Antal Róth and the talented striker József Kiprich went on to embrace careers with substantial Western European clubs while still within their expected peak years, swiftly taking advantage of a loosening of Hungarian borders after the 1986 World Cup. Both players were soon in the employment of Feyenoord, although Róth was to struggle with a succession of injuries that would eventually end his career prematurely. Détári would go on to play in both the Bundesliga and Serie A, sandwiched by a productive couple of seasons with Olympiacos in Greece. Others would also venture beyond their once-restrictive borders, but to more modest destinations.

Key to the problems Hungary encountered in Mexico was the absence of the prodigiously talented Tibor Nyilasi. Veteran of the 1978 and 1982 World Cups, the latter as captain, he'd been the pivot upon which the team revolved. Metronomic playmaker, with an outrageous goals tally from midfield, he was the archetypal all-action hero, with added playmaker status. He was both indispensable and irreplaceable. Without Nyilasi, Mezey's team struggled against opponents of quality, swept aside as they were by the Soviet Union and France, to the tune of an aggregate of nine goals conceded without reply.

Hungary were victims of the Soviet Union's finest performance of the World Cup, trailing 2-0 with only five minutes elapsed in Irapuato. They could even have been on the end of the tournament's widest margin of defeat in a match in which they could comfortably have trailed 5-0 after just half an hour, hindered as they were by the early loss to injury of Róth. But Hungary still showed occasional flashes of their true potential, especially during the second half. However, the Soviet Union prevailed 6-0.

After being comprehensively undone by the magnificence of Valeriy Lobanovskyi's team, Hungary started their second match with a mean streak of ultimately unfulfilled intent against Canada, Esterházy giving them the lead after just 110 seconds. Sticking to the formation with which they ended the Soviet Union match, rather than the one they started it with, along with dropping his first-choice goalkeeper Péter Disztl in favour of József Szendrei, Mezey's team failed to build on their dream start, and it wasn't until 15 minutes from time that Détári doubled Hungary's lead.

Hungary were essentially guilty of being too tentative against what were extremely inexperienced opponents, a team who were struggling for rhythm, to live up to the stubborn endeavour they had shown in their opening match against France, and eventually discipline, when ending the match with ten men. Mezey's players had spurned the opportunity to remedy their abject goal difference and left themselves with the unenviable task of procuring a positive result when shifting to León to face Michel Platini and his merry band of outrageously gifted team-mates.

With Disztl being fortunate to reclaim the goalkeeping duties from Szendrei, the beleaguered Videoton shot-stopper then conceded another three goals to add to the six that the Soviet Union had drilled past him.

As the introduction of three points for a win was still two World Cups away, Hungary's victory over Canada, added to their losses to the Soviet Union and France, was classified as no more valuable than two draws and a defeat. In finishing third in Group C, their hopes of progression rested in them having either more points or a better goal difference than two other nations to finish third across the span of the other five groups.

With a goal difference of minus seven, despite having a group-stage win under their belts, Hungary were left clinging on to a hope and a prayer that was never answered. In terms of World Cups past, Mezey's team were more than deserving of their early exit, but regarding the new format, they were massively unlucky to go home, with a combination of results that would have been enough to take them into the last 16 at the expense of Uruguay had three points for a win been in operation.

Of course, also exiting the 1986 World Cup from Group C, were Tony Waiters' Canada. First time qualifiers in Mexico, and up to their qualification for the upcoming 2022 World Cup, in Qatar, the only occasion they have reached the finals of the tournament.

It's something which provides a lingering ambiguity that means 1986 remains at the forefront of the Canadian footballing consciousness. A singular oasis, across fast approaching a century of World Cup history, *The Canucks* finally gate-crashed the global football party for its 13th edition.

With Mexico competing as substitute hosts in 1986, they left behind a qualification bun fight for the second CONCACAF (Confederation of North, Central America and Caribbean Association Football) berth, which Honduras were the favourites to obtain, having reached their first World Cup in 1982. While they were unable to progress beyond the group stage in Spain, Honduras had been impressively durable, and having taken a point off both the hosts and Northern Ireland, it was only in the closing minutes of their clash with Yugoslavia that their very active hopes of reaching the second round were ended.

Alongside Honduras, El Salvador had also been present at the 1982 World Cup, the second time they had qualified in 12 years, upon which they left an indelible, historical imprint for the part they played in being on the receiving end of the World Cup's biggest margin of defeat, when beaten 10-1, by Hungary in Elche.

For the fourth successive time, the CONCACAF Championship doubled up as World Cup qualifiers, with a finals section that consisted of three groups of three teams, from which the three winners progressed to one last, decisive, three-team group, the winner of which would be off to Mexico.

With Honduras and El Salvador drawn together in Group 1, alongside Suriname, it meant that one of the two CONCACAF representatives from the 1982 World Cup wouldn't even reach the final round of matches. This dramatically opened the field, and Canada found themselves placed in Group 2 with Guatemala and the 1974 qualifiers, Haiti, for company, while in Group 3, Costa Rica, the United States, and Trinidad and Tobago went up against one another.

Of the competitors for the 1985 CONCACAF Championship, apart from Suriname, Canada were the team with the least-impressive back catalogue. Four of the nine nations involved had previously taken part in a World Cup. The United States had even reached the 1930 semi-finals and defeated England in 1950, while of those who had still to reach a World Cup, Costa Rica and Guatemala had dominated Central American international football throughout the 1960s, and both had won the CONCACAF Championship that decade, Costa Rica twice. Even Trinidad and Tobago had been runners-up as recently as 1973, whereas Canada had never finished any higher than fourth.

Honduras advanced from Group 1, getting the better of El Salvador in San Salvador, thanks to a magnificent winning goal from Eduardo Laing, a goal ruthlessly struck from distance, but one in which he displayed a wonderfully deft piece of technique and control to set himself up for the shot. A goalless draw four days later in Tegucigalpa clinched Honduras their progression, two results that overhauled El Salvador's advantage, which had previously been gained via their better handling of Suriname.

It was a similar story in Group 3, where the decisive matches between Costa Rica and the United States were finely poised, after both had faced Trinidad and Tobago. While Costa Rica were held to a careless 1-1 draw in one of their two matches against the 'Soca Warriors', the United States had narrowly won both fixtures, the first thanks to an 89th-minute strike from Mark Peterson.

Due to Trinidad and Tobago's lack of an adequate venue in Port of Spain, Costa Rica and the United States had been gifted home advantage for both of their matches against them, the southern Caribbean islands having not kicked a ball in anger during the first qualification round, thanks to obtaining a walkover when Grenada withdrew.

When it came to the face-offs between Costa Rica and the United States, a valuable 1-1 draw in Alajuela left the United States needing only to avoid defeat at the Murdock Stadium in Torrance to reach the final round. Yet, in California, with a big and vociferous backing, it was the visitors who edged through, thanks to a goal procured via a set piece on a day when they employed a classic counter-attack system.

Meanwhile, Canada's progression in Group 2 had been relatively sedate. By the time Guatemala were overpowering Haiti in the final match of the group, Canada were already through, thanks to three wins and a draw from their four matches. Two victories within a week in Victoria over their two rivals had set Canada up nicely, with Igor Vrablic, Michael Sweeney and Dale Mitchell the goalscoring heroes. A valuable point gained in Guatemala and a comfortable win in Port-au-Prince against a Haiti team that was no longer liberally funded by Jean-Claude 'Baby Doc' Duvalier, as was very much the case when they reached the 1974 World Cup finals, and Canada were through to the final stages of qualification.

Still, Canada very much remained the underdog. Led by a former Blackpool and England goalkeeper and propelled on the pitch by a collective of players that included an Italian-born goalkeeper, a Trinidadian-born defender, a Welshman and a couple of Scots in midfield, plus a Mancunian striker, who was backed up by Czech- and Yugoslav-born partners, they all sat among an array of eclectically travelled team-mates, and the odds were very much stacked against them.

Another aspect working against Canada was that, given that the NASL had folded in 1984, half of their squad were restricted to playing their regular club football in the Major Indoor Soccer League (MISL), on downsized hard-court pitches in front of often sparsely populated crowds. These were events that struck the prototype image of the 1980s six-a-side tournaments that would annually pop up on *Sportsnight* shortly before Christmas, usually sponsored by Guinness, or the Masters Football series of tournaments throughout the noughties, for ex-players who still fancied a kickaround.

Nobody could have suggested with a straight face that the MISL was the ideal preparation for international footballers who had designs on qualifying for a World Cup. To compound matters further, only five of Canada's squad were employed by European clubs, and the majority of those five weren't getting first-team appearances under their belts.

While Waiters's players' club careers were widely dysfunctional, the plus side was that whenever they were together as a unit for Canada, they were eager to make use of a full-sized football pitch and a competitive match. It was inspiration, via adversity, and even subjugation, so shackled by their club careers were some players.

Three months separated Canada's victory away to Haiti and the beginning of their final qualification group campaign. Six days after Costa Rica and Honduras had got proceedings underway, sharing a 2-2 draw in San José, Waiters and his team welcomed Costa Rica to Toronto, where the hosts came from behind to claim a second-half equaliser from Paul James, going on to see out a 1-1 draw.

A useful point, and nothing too damaging, given the stalemate between Costa Rica and Honduras, it was the next two matches where Canada's hopes would either sink or swim, as they set off for the away double-header in Tegucigalpa and San José.

Totally against all expectations, Canada simply stunned Honduras. George Pakos made himself a national hero as he guided in a spectacular volley after a smart piece of opportunism, combined with a complete lack of Honduran concentration. Just shy of the hour mark, it was to be the only goal of the match, and a week later they consolidated their position at the top of the group with a priceless goalless draw against Costa Rica, during which their goalkeeper, Tino Lettieri, pulled off a string of magnificent saves to defy their hosts the win they would have arguably counted on.

Seven days later, Costa Rica were out of the running when throwing away an early lead to go down to Honduras, 3-1. It was a result that left Canada one point ahead of Honduras, with the two teams set to face each other the following week at King George V Park in St John's, Newfoundland. The equation was easy enough. Avoid defeat and Canada would be going to the 1986 World Cup finals.

Strategically chosen with an understandable and perfectly acceptable Machiavellian streak, St John's in mid-September was an inhospitable landscape for the visiting Honduras team, a set of players who had left behind Tegucigalpa temperatures that were skirting 30°C. Geographically, St John's is closer to the British Isles than it is to Vancouver, and Honduras walked into something of a clinical and climatical ambush. Arriving to torrential rain and freezing winds, their players and staff didn't venture outside the hotel for the first 48 hours of their stay, and when they did finally begin training preparations, they opted for an indoor arena.

The chosen venue for the match had taken virtually everyone by surprise. Offered generous financial increments, the Canadian Soccer Association was quick to sign the deal with St John's. Monetary gain aside, there was also a degree of subsidiary and tactical method in the madness to the decision to play the match at what was no more than a makeshift stadium, which sat centrally within a public park and where temporary bleachers were brought in to enclose the pitch from surrounding car parks.

When the Bratislava-born Igor Vrablic bundled the ball over the Honduras goal line for Canada just beyond the hour mark to reclaim his side a lead that they had surrendered shortly after the restart, on that cold Saturday afternoon he stepped into Canadian footballing immortality. It was a goal that eased Canadian shoulders as, had the next goal fallen the way of Honduras, then it would have been into their hands that a place in the 1986 World Cup would have been provisionally placed.

Twice holding their nerve, having taken 15 first-half minutes to obtain an initial lead, with Pakos once again the hero, the most impressive thing about Canada's performance in this decisive match was their composure and the lack of panic in their display when up against opponents that were infinitely more experienced, and the prize on offer was of the most precious value imaginable. The weight of the situation could so easily have made Canada buckle, yet they were almost formulaic in closing out on qualification for their first World Cup on an afternoon when they were always in pole position.

Cohesive, focused and stubborn, they were fully deserving of their place at the 1986 World Cup finals, with Waiters almost having fostered a club mentality. This was something that was inclusive of the Manchester-born Carl Valentine, playing despite struggling badly with influenza, rising above how ill he felt to play a pivotal role in both of Canada's goals on that incredible day.

There was something marvellously symbolic about the two players who clinched Canada's victory over Honduras. Scorer of the first goal had been the 33-year-old Pakos, who had returned from the periphery of the squad, a player who had faded entirely from Waiters's thinking until being called upon once more after the damaging loss of the excellent Dale Mitchell to a ruptured anterior cruciate ligament.

As for Vrablic, a player at the other end of the age spectrum, he hadn't long waved goodbye to his teenage years and had just spent the season as an impact sub for FC Sérésien, as they successfully, if narrowly, fended off relegation from the Belgian First Division. It was a club he'd joined via the Toronto Blizzard and Golden Bay Earthquakes, having emigrated to Ontario with his parents as a young child. Prodigiously talented, Vrablic, just like 13 other members of Canada's 1986 World Cup squad, was part of the pool of players that represented the nation at the 1984 Olympic football tournament, when they had progressed beyond the group stages at the expense of a Roger

Milla-inspired Cameroon, before coming stunningly close to beating Brazil in the quarter-finals.

One of the few players in the Canada squad to be playing his club football at a perceptively higher level than the MISL, an own goal aside, Vrablic, along with Pakos again, were the only players to score for Canada throughout their seven competitive World Cup warm-up fixtures.

Towards the end of January 1986, Canada headed to Florida for the Miami Cup, where they played three matches in eight days. In many respects, it was the perfect dry run for the demands of the upcoming World Cup, undertaking a trio of fixtures in not much more than a week, in high temperatures, albeit in a location that's only nominally above sea level, thus was clearly in no position to be able to replicate the altitude Waiters's side would experience in León, and Irapuato.

Canada rounded their three matches out with a goalless draw against the USA in an exceptionally sparsely populated Orange Bowl, on a day when roughly 70,000 seats went unused. Prior to that, they had taken on two fellow World Cup qualifying nations in the shapes of Paraguay and Uruguay, playing out another goalless draw with the former, and finding the latter too powerful when going down to a 3-1 defeat, in which Pakos scored Canada's only goal.

Far from disgracing themselves in Miami, Waiters was able to fine-tune his squad, and four more formal friendlies carried him and his team towards the World Cup, as firstly they headed off to Mexico City to experience playing at altitude, against the expectant hosts.

A losing scoreline of 3-0 was deceptive to the naked eye, as Mexico, without the services of Hugo Sánchez, laboured against a stubborn Canadian defence and midfield. It took a goal shortly before the interval and two late strikes in the last five minutes to enhance the outcome for Bora Milutinović's team. For Waiters, the biggest plus point to go alongside the dogged determination of his team was the return to action of Mitchell.

A match played out just over a month before the start of the World Cup, the loss to Mexico was then followed by a three-match tour of their homeland, which for Canada acted as a protracted send-off to their first-ever World Cup, with dates penned in for Toronto, Vancouver and Burnaby.

Wales were invited to play the first two matches, the opening one landing on the same day as the 1986 FA Cup Final, thus meaning that Mike England's team were without the considerable talents of Pat Van Den Hauwe, Kevin Ratcliffe and Ian Rush. None of them would join up with the Welsh party for the second match, despite the nine-day gap between the two.

Shorn of nine regulars, inclusive of the injured Neville Southall, whether it was down to pronounced squad depletion, their players having been preoccupied by events at Wembley, fatigue of travel, or just completely underestimating the capabilities of Canada, Wales were comfortably beaten in Toronto on a day when the Cardiff-born Paul James was one of the heroes for The Canucks. Vrablic opened the scoring, before a Joey Jones own goal on the brink of half-time gave Canada their first victory since overcoming Honduras eight months earlier.

Once bitten, when the two teams reconvened in Vancouver, with only two changes made to the Wales line-up, it was a very different result, with the 21-year-old Brighton and Hove Albion striker Dean Saunders scoring twice, as part of an efficient 3-0 win, in which a teenage Malcolm Allen netted the final goal.

More of a concern for Waiters than the result was the continued absence of his first-choice goalkeeper, Lettieri, with Paul Dolan again covering, while Mitchell, deployed again from the start, was showing signs of understandable rustiness.

Five days later, Canada went up against Bobby Robson's England in Burnaby. With big decisions to be made, Waiters opted to drop Mitchell down to the bench, pairing Vrablic with Valentine. Armed with a disciplined shape and no shortage of determination, England were repelled for almost an hour, until Mark Hateley grabbed what was to prove the only goal of the match.

They might have ridden their luck at times, but this was a significant performance from Canada, as they had proved to themselves that they could be awkward opponents for even the most vaunted of teams, despite being without two of their best players. Nine of the England starting line-up would take to the pitch for their opening match of the World Cup, so this had by no means been a mix-and-match team that Robson had chosen. Eight days later, it was France that Canada were facing, in their opening fixture of the 1986 World Cup.

In cold, black-and-white terms, Canada went to Mexico, where they played three, lost three and failed to register a goal to call their own. Going into the tournament, they were widely viewed as one of the most disproportionate visitors the World Cup finals had ever welcomed. While a nation as illustrious as the Netherlands were forced to watch the 1986 World Cup from afar, the Canadian national team were aboard their team coach, being goaded by the locals as they approached the Estadio Nou Camp in León to face the European champions, France.

Canada were given little chance of anything more than a sound pasting. As they trawled towards the stadium, hand gestures of derision were made by those at the roadside to denote how many goals Michel Platini and his enigmatic team-mates were going to put past them. Six, seven, eight goals were fully expected.

A short few hours later, during a press conference within the bowels of the stadium, the assembled press pack were relentlessly grilling Platini and his coach Henri Michel about how they had conjured up a situation where they had needed a late Jean-Pierre Papin goal to clinch a narrow 1-0 victory against their inferior opponents. Bearing witness to this spectacle, were Waiters and his captain, Bruce Wilson. Only minimally interacted with throughout the press conference, they took great satisfaction when Platini, with his head in his hands, weary and frustrated, tried to get his message across to the blinkered journalists before him that they had to give Canada great credit for the way they had played. While Canada were crudely ignored by the members of the press, Caesar himself was delivering praise.

Canadian football had reached its very zenith in León. Their next two matches resulted in back-to-back 2-0 defeats at the hands of Hungary and the Soviet Union, both in Irapuato. The match against a regressing Hungary was a missed opportunity, conceding a goal within two minutes and compounding that with a late red card for substitute Mike Sweeney. It was a major disappointment after the positives taken against France five days earlier.

Regardless, it had been an unforgiving group in which Canada had found themselves placed, and they had acquitted themselves admirably throughout their debut World Cup campaign. A bright future of further World Cup appearances wasn't necessarily outlandish.

By September that same year, however, the entire fabric of a national team that had enjoyed a near club-like ethos had begun to unravel. Waiters stood down as Canada's head coach after Mexico, passing the baton on to his assistant, another Englishman, Bob Bearpark. Less than three months beyond the 1986 World Cup finals, Bearpark took a partially experimental Canadian squad to Singapore to take part in the Merlion Cup, an invitational tournament. The new head coach took an array of youth and shadow players, along with a small selection of members from the squad that had travelled to the World Cup, inclusive of Vrablic, along with Dolan, James, Sweeney, Randy Ragan, Dave Norman and Jamie Lowrey.

A six-team, round-robin tournament, with the top four advancing to the semi-finals, Canada were deemed the favourites. In the last four, they faced North Korea, who they had drawn 0-0 with during the group stages.

It was during an idle game of cards that the future direction of the Canadian national team dramatically changed direction. Vrablic and Norman had been joined by Hector Marinaro and Chris Chueden. James was also invited to take part. Ulterior motives were eventually floated, as James soon found himself to be the recipient of a tempting offer, yet also a moral dilemma. A share of $100,000 had been offered to those sitting around the table to throw the match against North Korea.

With precarious club futures, all members of the card school accepted the offer. The match was lost 2-0, but James had had second thoughts. After the match, he returned the money to the other players, and later confided in his teammate Ragan about what had happened.

On returning to Canada a snowball effect took hold. Having approached the now-retired captain, Wilson, Ragan then took the allegations to Waiters, and onward to the Canadian Soccer Association itself. A criminal investigation sprang into action, and the Royal Canadian Mounted Police charged Vrablic, Norman, Marinaro and Chueden with accepting bribes. A protracted investigation then took place before the criminal proceedings were eventually dropped, deemed to be out of Canadian jurisdiction. The Canadian

Soccer Association, however, implemented playing bans on the four players involved.

James, in a bid to distance himself from the others, was open and transparent about the incident, and came away without sanctions. In time, Norman eventually came clean on his involvement, and he even made a return to the national team some years later, as did Marinaro. Chueden never played for Canada again.

Vrablic, too, never returned to the national team, and within a few short years he'd completely vanished from the game. Aged only 21 at the time and having moved on to Olympiacos after the 1986 World Cup, his career swiftly evaporated, having been the man who could have carried the flag for the Canadian national team towards the new millennium. A promising career was lost, and so was Canada's optimistic future.

It was a sour end to a wonderful rise; the hope can only be that by 2026, when Canada is to co-host the World Cup finals, the Canadian football authorities can perhaps reconcile with those players of the 1986 World Cup squad that remain ostracised.

Chapter Five

Eastenders

FOLLOWING CANADA and Hungary's exits from Group C, Groups A and B spat South Korea and Iraq out of the tournament, respectively, both having qualified for Mexico via the Asian Football Confederation (AFC).

It had taken the AFC an indecently protracted amount of time to reach the point it had, with two berths being allotted solely to them for the 1986 finals. This came after decades of suppression at the hands of FIFA, during which a path to the finals of previous World Cups had generally either been littered with inordinately high hurdles to clear, in the shape of one-sided play-off matches against UEFA members, or later being unacceptably clustered together with the Confederation of African Football (CAF) and the Oceania Football Confederation (OFC).

While the 1966 boycott by the CAF had finally resulted in Africa being handed a qualification berth to call their own from 1970 onwards, increased to two for the 1982 finals, it had left the AFC and OFC to duke it out for one between the two. However, 1986 was marked by a new landscape, in which the AFC now possessed two qualification berths of their own, with the OFC cast off into its new position of a perpetual state of uncertainty, where emerging as their top nation only brought with it what amounted to a far too regular inter-continental play-off failure, a situation that's only projected to come to an end when the 2026 expansion to a 48-nation tournament affords the OFC its very first automatic World Cup qualifying team.

Despite the new system beyond 1966, between 1970 and 1982 the AFC still suffered through self-inflicted wounds when it came to their attempts at World Cup evolution. In 1970, Israel prevailed, whose divisive presence within the AFC eventually led to them being ostracised from the federation in 1974, from where they shuttled back and forth between UEFA and the OFC, until gaining full UEFA membership 20 years later.

With Australia qualifying narrowly ahead of South Korea in 1974, thus no Asian nation being present in West Germany, and New Zealand taking one of the two places on offer to the AFC and OFC in 1982, it meant that by the time the 1986 World Cup finals came into view, beyond Israel only Iran in 1978 and Kuwait four years later had reached the World Cup finals from Asia since the unexpected heroics of North Korea in England in 1966. North Korea themselves had been only the second-ever Asian qualifiers for a World Cup, and the first since Indonesia, who had taken part in the 1938 finals in France under the flag of the Dutch East Indies.

As Africa undertook a wonderful education that saw their World Cup qualifying nations largely improve tournament on tournament from the defensively organised Morocco of 1970 to the massively unfortunate Algeria and Cameroon of 1982, via the misunderstood Zaire of 1974, and the ground-breaking Tunisia of 1978, who became the first African nation to win a match at a World Cup finals tournament, by comparison Asia had shuddered forward in fits and starts.

Unwanted they might have been by their fellow AFC bedfellows, but Israel departed the 1970 World Cup having far from shamed themselves, responding to being outclassed by Uruguay in their opening match by taking highly creditable draws against both Sweden and eventual runners-up Italy.

Eight years later, in Argentina, Iran offset their magnificent, magical spell of restraint and frustration, which they cast upon an almost hypnotised Scotland, with a pair of semi-heavy defeats to the Netherlands and Peru, both by three-goal margins, results that only went to amplify the stunning lack of Scottish preparation for 1978.

Finally, in Spain in 1982, Kuwait's efforts went heavily shaded by the rancour of their 4-1 loss to France, during which Sheikh Fahad Al-Ahmed Al-Jaber Al-Sabah, at the time the head of the Kuwait Football Association, implored his players to walk from the pitch in protest against what had appeared to be a perfectly legitimate fourth French goal during their match in Valladolid. Amazingly, Myroslav Stupar, the Soviet referee, agreed to disallow the goal, only for France to score again in the final minutes. One of the World Cup's greatest oddities, it was an event that distracted from this having been the best national side yet to emerge from the Arab region, a team that had gained a well-deserved draw against Czechoslovakia and would go on to restrict England to a narrow 1-0 win.

It was within the wake of such volatile AFC variables that Iraq and South Korea headed to Mexico, one as a first-time qualifier, the other for only the second time, and their first World Cup for 32 years.

For Iraq, their route was one that had been taken entirely on the road, as the Iran–Iraq War raged towards its seventh year. Drawn into Group 1B, in Zone A, in the Western side of the split, there were two halves to each group, A and B, from which the winners would face one another, in a two-legged play-off. They would then go on to contest a place in a final play-off against the prevailing nation from Group 2's two groups, for a trip to the 1986 World Cup finals. As part of this, Iran were diplomatically placed in Group 2B, as far away from Iraq as bureaucratically possible, until they withdrew entirely before a ball was kicked in anger.

It's a format that was mirrored in Zone B, with two versions of Group 3 and 4, which was deemed to be the Eastern side of AFC qualifying, from where South Korea would pick their way through to Mexico.

Forced away from Baghdad, Iraq's 'home' matches in Group 1B were to take place in Kuwait, Qatar and India, against Lebanon, Jordan and Qatar, respectively, although the two matches against Lebanon were to eventually be annulled after their withdrawal from qualification, having lost their first four matches to an aggregate of 27-0.

With the number of Group 1B results suddenly reduced by a third, Iraq undertook all four of their remaining fixtures in just over five weeks, edging through to the play-offs only after obtaining a nervous, yet vital, 2-1 victory over Qatar in Kolkata, in the group-deciding encounter.

In what were essentially play-off semi-finals, in September 1985 Iraq went head to head with the United Arab Emirates, who themselves would go on to qualify for the 1990 World Cup. Two wonderfully dramatic matches ensued, with Iraq departing the first leg in Dubai with a stunning 3-2 victory, procured by a late winner from Haris Mohammed Hassan, after his team had pulled themselves back from 1-0 and 2-1 deficits. Iraqi legend Hussein Saeed had scored both equalisers, firstly with a perfectly timed run and beautifully weighted lob over the advancing UAE goalkeeper. Saeed's second goal was driven home low, when capitalising on a flick-on from a free kick that had been speculatively aimed from just inside Iraq's own half of the pitch. Supremely opportunistic, the prolific striker laid the foundations for Hassan to snatch the winning goal, as the play became stretched, and the home team searched for a decisive goal of their own.

A week later, in a match hosted by Saudi Arabia in Ta'if, Iraq nervously came to within two minutes of elimination, seemingly struggling with the weight of their situation, as the World Cup must have loomed frighteningly large on the horizon. Added to this, the potential ramifications of failure would have been terrifyingly unthinkable, as the far from tolerant and understanding Uday Hussein, son of the Iraqi leader Saddam, was the president of the Iraq Football Association in September 1985.

It will have been with a pronounced sigh of relief from their players and coaching staff that fate smiled kindly on Iraq, as with the match petering out and the UAE counting down the seconds towards the final whistle, a long, speculative ball forward was badly defended, allowing Karim Saddam Menshid to guide home a wonderful finish, having only entered the fray as a substitute a few minutes earlier.

Progression snatched from the jaws of elimination, seven weeks later Iraq headed to Damascus to face Syria in the first leg of the Zone A final play-off. An uneventful goalless draw set the second leg up nicely as a winner-take-all event, in a match that again was to take place in Ta'if.

Led by the former Shakhtar Donetsk defender, Valeriy Yaremchenko, Syria had unexpectedly reached such dizzying heights largely on the back of a strong defensive ethos, shockingly knocking out Kuwait along the way. Having conceded only one goal in their previous six qualifiers, Ta'if was to be something of a culture shock for Syria, as Iraq overpowered them in a match that was played out in front of not just Uday but also his father, Saddam.

An intelligently worked first-half opener converted by Saeed was built upon early in the second half when Shaker Mahmoud Hamza was the beneficiary of another move that had Syria off balance, doubling Iraq's lead. Within five minutes, however, Iraq had given away a penalty, which was coolly dispatched by Walid Abu Al-Sel, leaving the tie delicately positioned, until Khalil Mohammed Allawi was the surprise scorer of a finely crafted free-kick routine with 18 minutes left to play.

Utopia reached, Iraq's build-up to the 1986 World Cup finals leaned heavily on their Gulf Cup fixtures during March and April, which conjured up a set of results that offered little in the way of insight for their future Group B rivals. Six matches, in which only one win was achieved, Iraq drew three and lost two, with all six outcomes being closely contested ones.

Aside from their Gulf Cup fixtures, which had been crammed into a 16-day span, prior to heading off to Mexico, Iraq had lost to Denmark's Under-21s in January, drawn two back-to-back matches against Romania in March, and narrowly beaten a League of Ireland representative team in April, all encounters that had taken place in Baghdad.

A stark juxtaposition, while the Iran–Iraq War raged on, Iraq's national team was being led by the former Brazilian international and Barcelona star striker, Evaristo, while the rewards that his players were lavished with for qualification included a house and car.

As usual with teams that come from nations that are controlled by a dictatorship, Iraq weren't without their peculiar tales of discipline. While threats for underachievement or even for failure to deliver results that are frankly beyond the smaller teams at a World Cup are all too common throughout the history of the tournament, Uday Hussein's shaving of the heads of his players is one of the more esoteric occurrences. Once in Mexico, Iraq mirrored Canada in losing all three of their group matches. Again, however, there were mitigating variables at play, and they remained defensively stubborn throughout, beaten only by a single-goal margin in each. In fact, they were the better team in the first half of their opening match against Paraguay in Toluca. Falling behind to a Julio César Romero goal, which arrived largely against the run of play, the tipping point came on the stroke of half-time when the referee, Sydney Picon, contentiously disallowed an Ahmed Radhi equaliser.

Fast out of the blocks, Iraq had begun the match with a stunning air of confidence and composure; a spectacular Haris Mohammed volley came as a shot across Paraguay's bows, while Alfredo Mendoza came close for the South American team, sending an effort over the top of the Iraq crossbar when well-placed and it being easier to hit the target.

As a match, this was one of the hidden gems of the tournament, a wonderfully open and entertaining encounter that swept from one end to the other, with Iraq looking the more likely to make the breakthrough. Promisingly, neither team was short on high technical ability, Evaristo having implemented a clear mandate to his players to enjoy the ball and keep the passes short and simple.

In the 35th minute, however, Iraq were undone by an unusual lack of concentration in defence, as Nadhim Shaker failed to follow the high line of the rest of his defensive colleagues, finding himself isolated and far deeper than he should have been, allowing Romero the freedom of the final third, to spring forth and loft the ball over the advancing Raad Hammoudi, Iraq's goalkeeper and captain.

Rather than hit the self-destruct button, Iraq upped their commitment to attack, and Allawi forced Roberto Fernández into a smart save from a free kick. From the resultant corner came the pivotal moment as, when it was arrowed over, Radhi powered a header into the back of the Paraguay net for what would have been a fully deserved equaliser. It was the last act of the first half.

However, with a striking similarity to the Clive Thomas incident at the 1978 World Cup match between Brazil and Sweden, Picon blew his whistle for the half-time interval just as the ball was in mid-flight, thus ruling out Iraq's goal, despite the strong opinions of Evaristo's players. A ludicrous incident, and one that FIFA were far from pleased to have to revisit for a second time in eight years. Picon's World Cup would go no further.

Spirits bruised, Iraq were overrun in the second half, but remained defiant enough to keep Paraguay out, with the game drifting towards a 1-0 scoreline, despite a succession of near-misses. This included César Zabala hitting the inside of the Iraq post from a ridiculous distance, Buenaventura Ferreira having a goalbound effort denied when headed clear by Samir Shaker, after he'd rounded the goalkeeper, and Mendoza also hitting a post when on the counter-attack, as Iraq pushed forward late on.

Much to be upbeat about when it had come to their first-ever match at a World Cup, the wound of that disallowed goal still stung, and the Iraq players once again voiced their complaints upon the final whistle. It was a mood shared by many of those in the stands, who greeted the approach of Picon to the Estadio Nemesio Díez tunnel with a shower of paper cups.

Four days later, at the same venue, Evaristo made just one change against Belgium, as Saeed stepped down, to be replaced by Karim Saddam, Iraq's hero against the UAE in qualifying. Saeed had struggled with injury prior to the tournament and there had been doubts that he would make it to Mexico, but whether through pressure applied from upon high or not, he was eventually an 11th-hour inclusion in not only Evaristo's squad but his starting line-up against Paraguay too.

Despite Saeed having completed the full 90 minutes against Paraguay, the physical demands had proved too much and he wouldn't play another minute of the finals. It was a turn of events that for almost an hour against Belgium had looked to have knocked the wheels off Iraq's highly likeable bandwagon. With only 20 minutes on the clock, Belgium had rocketed into a 2-0 lead, Enzo Scifo finishing wonderfully after excellent work from the magnificent Jan Ceulemans, before Nico Claesen converted a penalty that had been unconvincingly procured by the scorer of the opening goal.

From then on, Scifo became the target of repetitive reprisals from Iraq's players, as the yellow-card count ticked steadily upward, Basil Gorgis earning himself two, and with them the accompanying red card, in the 57th minute. Yet, instead of descending into chaos for Iraq, this was where the match moved towards them, as Belgium, unaccustomed to have broken out of their counter-attacking persona to take early control of the match, now struggled to deal with the determination of the ten men they were suddenly up against.

Two minutes after losing Gorgis, Iraq had a goal back, as Radhi lashed one in from a similar part of the pitch that Scifo had scored his. An equaliser would be beyond Evaristo's side, however, and a second successive narrow loss was absorbed.

Three days later, Iraq's World Cup came to an end at the Estadio Azteca against the host nation, on a day when Evaristo was forced into a change of goalkeeper. In came Abdul-Fatah Nsaief, and for 54 minutes he defied footballing gravity as Mexico mounted attack after attack, only to be frustrated by a combination of both unorthodox and textbook saves, along with the frame of the goal proving problematic.

Fernando Quirarte finally broke the precarious deadlock with a beautifully timed run and finish, but despite the balance of play predominantly leaning towards the Iraq penalty area, the match remained on a knife-edge until the final whistle.

A brave campaign at an end, stories have been floated of the sinister treatment that Uday Hussein administered on the Iraq players after their return home, and it's unsurprising that the fortunes of the national team diminished afterwards. The man in control had reputedly expected his inexperienced underdogs to challenge for the ultimate glory, with the reasoning being that Adidas had been impressed enough to supply their kits, which at the whim of a dictator's son had undergone a change in colour for the World Cup.

A form of redemption did eventually fall the way of Iraq's 1986 World Cup squad after the demise of their old boss, when Saeed, the best player the country ever produced, was handed the presidency of the Iraq Football Association in 2004, albeit a rise to power that came with its own accusations of wrongdoing along the way.

From the other side of the AFC qualification coin, South Korea also took to the tournament with a wondrous, infectious enthusiasm, but unlike Iraq, it was an adventure that came without sinister shadows pulling the strings. There was a refreshing innocence to the approach of South Korea, and their football matched their sense of spirit.

Emerging from Group 3A, in Zone B, South Korea had backed themselves into a bit of a corner in the first round of qualification, finding they needed a win in the last group match, in Seoul against Malaysia, having earlier lost to them in Kuala Lumpur. By the time the two teams faced one another again, at the Olympic Stadium, South Korea's task was a simple one. Win to progress to the next stage, as while they had beaten Nepal both home and away, Malaysia had contrived to be held to an unexpected draw in Kathmandu, and the combination of results left South Korea one point adrift, come the crucial final group fixture.

Amid an incredible atmosphere, South Korea burst into a 2-0 lead within 20 minutes, as Park Chang-sun venomously converted a penalty, and Cho Min-kook guided in a fine header to give the home team the perfect start.

In need of only a draw to progress, Malaysia had gone into the match with the intention of absorbing the South Korea offensive and aiming to catch their hosts on the counter-attack, but the first 20 minutes had destroyed that plan. Forced forward, Malaysia did find the back of the South Korea net twice, only for both efforts to be disallowed, events that launched a thousand conspiracy theories in Kuala Lumpur.

Pitted against Indonesia in the two-legged second round, South Korea were way too strong as World Cup fever gripped eastern Asia. In matches watched by a combined attendance of 160,000 spectators in Seoul and Jakarta, a 6-1 aggregate victory set South Korea up with a final two-legged showdown with Japan.

Producing some wonderful football, South Korea had picked Indonesia apart with smart interchanges of passes, technically adept one-touch football and a fine array of skill in procuring their goals. It made for an effervescent style of play for a team that was to be classed as South Korea's golden generation. Indonesia had, however, frustrated South Korea until they made the breakthrough in the 73rd minute, and would have had high hopes of putting pressure on in the second leg if they could just snatch the first goal.

Byun Byung-joo and Kim Joo-sung had been the first-leg heroes in Seoul, and nine days later they would be among the scorers again in the return leg in the Indonesian capital, where South Korea blew away the last vestiges of hope for the hosts within the first ten minutes with two quick goals, to which they had added two more by the 47th minute, meaning that Indonesia's 87th-minute reply was most definitely too little, too late. The scoring bookended by Byun Byung-joo and Kim Joo-sung, the second and third goals had come from Choi Soon-ho and Huh Jung-moo, as the generosity of the Indonesia defence seemed to know no limitations.

To reach the final round, Japan had swept North Korea, Singapore and Hong Kong aside, without any pronounced sense of jeopardy. South Korea were to be an entirely different matter, however, as their great rival's speedier development told. When the first leg of their clash took place in Tokyo, it was the team in all red that grabbed the initiative, as Chung Yong-hwan struck emphatically from distance, and Lee Tae-ho guided in the second with great subtlety, to give South Korea a 2-0 lead that they looked set to take into the interval, only for Kazushi Kimura to score for Japan with a magnificent free kick just before the break.

With no further goals, South Korea took their 2-1 lead into the second leg in Seoul, a match that remained on edge until Huh Jung-moo settled the escalating nerves of the crowd just beyond the hour mark, to take his nation to their first World Cup for 32 years.

South Korea ended 1985 with a spree of acclimatisation matches as they headed off to Mexico, via Los Angeles, where they faced the World Cup hosts twice, firstly in LA, and then again in Guadalajara. They took on Hungary and Algeria for good measure, in Irapuato and Nezahualcóyotl, respectively. A cluster of closely contested matches, South Korea lost the first three, before overcoming Algeria on what was a useful dry run for the World Cup to come. Compared with their busy end to 1985, they then undertook only one official pre-tournament warm-up match, losing to Paraguay in Hong Kong.

Drawn into an unforgiving group at the 1986 World Cup, South Korea were up against the holders, Italy, the 1978 winners, Argentina, plus Bulgaria, a nation that had qualified for four successive World Cups between 1962 and 1974. Faced with three monumental tasks, what South Korea offered in return was a generous helping of the unknown and a complete lack of fear.

South Korea had been beaten emphatically during their previous World Cup finals experience when they travelled to Switzerland in 1954. They had suffered not only the indignities of 9-0 and 7-0 losses at the hands of Hungary and Turkey, respectively, but also a pariahs' welcome home for their efforts, amid a shower of rotten tomatoes.

What South Korea lacked in official friendlies as they entered World Cup year, they more than made up for in terms of meticulous preparation. On the back of their trip to the USA and Mexico towards the end of 1985, the following year had begun with a month-long tour of Europe to play in a series of unofficial friendlies against high-profile club teams, the standout performance being their comeback from 2-0 down to defeat a star-studded Anderlecht in Brussels.

They were led by Kim Jung-nam, a former international with an intermittent coaching association with the national team that stretched back for over a decade. He ensured that nothing was left to chance, and South Korea arrived at the 1986 World Cup finals as arguably the truest of collectives, having reaped a club-squad atmosphere and a set of players that were eager to avoid the embarrassments of 1954, and instead leave a positive legacy.

Opportunism was also a key element of the South Korea team, and when crossing paths with the England squad in

Colorado prior to the tournament, a delegation was sent to enquire whether Bobby Robson would be willing to field a team against them in an impromptu match on a local school playing field. With an agreement reached, South Korea went down 4-1, but not before dominating the first 20 minutes and shocking England with the extent of their technical abilities. Robson's team had been forced to produce something special to overcome the perceived minnows.

A collection of players that combined experience and youth, apart from the magnificent Cha Bum-kun, the entirety of South Korea's squad was drawn from the domestic club game. Even then, with only five fully professional teams in operation in 1986 within a six-team national league that had only been born in 1983, it meant that some players were recruited from the semi-professional and amateur ranks. As part of this, three members of the squad came directly from their university teams.

Conversely, Cha Bum-kun was the undisputed South Korean footballing legend, and even at the age of 33 was still more than capable of dictating play. For over a decade he'd starred in the Bundesliga for Eintracht Frankfurt and Bayer Leverkusen, winning the UEFA Cup with both. Hugely consistent and blessed with impressive longevity of career, he was the benchmark by which all other South Korean players were measured, and the shining example of just how far footballing dreams could take a player from their reputedly modest nation.

No one-man outfit, however, South Korea had other worldly-wise players too. Cho Young-jeung, a central defender of great footballing intelligence, had played in the NASL with the Portland Timbers, while the highly adaptable midfielder Huh Jung-moo had enjoyed three years with PSV Eindhoven, where he was predominantly deployed in a deep-lying role, from where he was to become a compelling nemesis of the ageing Johan Cruyff after his return to Ajax.

Even among those who had only domestic club experience, there was also the high potential of Choi Soon-ho of the steel industry derivative side, the POSCO Atoms. A 24-year-old striker and occasional attacking midfield of great fluidity, Juventus harboured serious designs on signing him as a prospective future attacking option to supplement Ian Rush and Michael Laudrup, in a post-Michel Platini landscape in Turin.

Choi Soon-ho was a player who was fast, balanced, skilful and capable of taking defenders on. He would have been the ideal foil to Rush, whose one year in Serie A would ultimately be one of isolated frustration. It was to be a missed opportunity for more than just the rising South Korean star himself when his club ultimately dug their heels in and refused to part with their prized asset. It also had a huge knock-on effect that reverberated seismically for Rush and Juventus, as well as South Korean football development. As a result, it would be another 14 years before Serie A embraced its first South Korean player.

As slow burning a force for change as it proved to be, for South Korea this squad of players in 1986, which ranged from UEFA Cup winners and arch-enemies of Cruyff himself to university students, via the centre ground of the pioneers of organised professional league football in their homeland, meant that there was now a clear path along which South Korean players could progress as far as their natural talent could take them. The glass ceiling had been removed for those who could negotiate their freedom and for the South Korean global stars of generations to come.

In Mexico City, at the Estadio Olímpico Universitario, with only seconds of the second half of their opening match having elapsed, the World Cup must have felt like an unforgiving temptress to South Korea. Argentina had just scored their third goal, a second of the afternoon for Jorge Valdano, and much of the punishment was self-inflicted on a day when South Korea opted for a physical approach in their attempts to contain Diego Maradona. It was a performance that gave a plentiful supply of ammunition to those who still believed that Asia shouldn't be allotted a guaranteed place at the World Cup.

Collecting just two yellow cards, it certainly hadn't been for the want of trying that it wasn't more. It wasn't until Maradona had been on the receiving end of a seventh foul that South Korea belatedly elicited their first caution of the match from the Spanish referee, Victoriano Sánchez Arminio, a sanction earned by Huh Jung-moo, just before the interval, after suffering the indignity of being nutmegged by the Argentine No. 10.

With all three of Argentina's goals being created by Maradona, and the realisation that a negative approach isn't all that much fun, in the latter stages South Korea opted to venture forward. It was their captain, Park Chang-sun, who struck their only goal of the match, one that was undeniably the best of the afternoon. Catching his shot perfectly and using the thinness of the altitude, he sent in a shot from distance, which whipped past a startled Nery Pumpido and hit the back of the net via the underside of the crossbar.

Three days later, at the same venue, on a pitch that had sustained a heavy downpour, it was within the spirit of the last 20 minutes of their performance against Argentina that South Korea flew at Bulgaria in a match they had clearly earmarked as the one they had a reasonable chance of winning.

This still didn't stop them from falling behind to a Plamen Getov opener, when he lobbed in an excellent finish from the edge of the penalty area, after South Korea couldn't clear a cross, and their goalkeeper, Oh Yun-kyo, failed to connect strongly enough with his attempted punch.

A match in which the biggest moments seemed to be dictated by the two goalkeepers, South Korea threw themselves into attack, and had it not been for the brilliance of Borislav Mihaylov, Bulgaria would have buckled long before the equaliser was eventually obtained. Kept at bay until the 70th minute, South Korea's perseverance finally paid off when the half-time substitute, Kim Jong-boo, coolly turned the ball in, leaving the dismayed Mihaylov trying to claim an utterly unconvincing infringement. The match then meandered to a share of the points.

Kim Jong-boo, along with Yoo Byung-ok, had already played international tournament football in Mexico, when part of South Korea's squad for the 1983 FIFA World Youth Championship, where they helped their nation in their wonderful run to the semi-finals. It had been a tournament where South Korea had responded to their opening defeat to Scotland by brushing aside their Mexican hosts, followed by Australia. In the quarter-final they defeated Uruguay, powered by José Perdomo, José Luis Zalazar, Ruben Sosa and Carlos Aguilera, before narrowly falling in the last four to Brazil, in extra time, in a match where Kim Jong-boo had had the temerity to score the opening goal.

An underappreciated depth of talent, it's quite shocking that only two players from South Korea's squad of 18 for the 1983 FIFA World Youth Championship also made the return visit for the 1986 World Cup finals, given how magnificently they had played that summer.

A vast improvement on their overall performance against Argentina, South Korea had even won a few admirers for their efforts against Bulgaria, yet they still remained largely patronised, the outcome of the match having tied into a narrative of how their opponents were forever labouring to procure themselves a first World Cup finals win.

Five days beyond the mud and partial glory of the Bulgaria match, it was off to Puebla that South Korea went, to face Italy in their last group fixture at the Estadio Cuauhtémoc. A build-up that mixed little being given in the way of realistic hope for a South Korean success and plentiful reminders of Italian failure against North Korea 20 years earlier, it was a fixture that omitted a subtle pre-match ambiguity.

For South Korea, this represented a free hit. The World Cup holders had everything to lose in terms of their continued involvement in the tournament, yet little to gain in the way of confidence and momentum moving on to the knockout stages. Due to the prejudicial nature of the traditional chasm between the two nations, it meant that the underdogs couldn't be held to account for a wholly expected defeat. Conversely, the favourites would receive no plaudits for winning. For Italy, it was a guaranteed thankless task, whether they won, lost or drew; for South Korea, apart from the result, no matter what was to unfold, it was a no-lose situation.

In the early exchanges, Italy struck the image of a team defiantly stuck in a rut, throwing a platoon of white-shirted players forward in what was, at times, an eight-man attack force. Although moving up in high numbers, Enzo Bearzot's team still laboured in the final third, consistently thwarted by the enthusiasm, appetite and speed of the South Korea defence, plus the agility of their goalkeeper.

Having survived a few initial scares, South Korea gradually began to break out of defence to launch an attack or two of their own, much to the discomfort of the Italian psyche. An intriguing game of football started to unfold, despite Alessandro Altobelli opening the scoring in the 17th minute with a cute little dink over Oh Yun-kyo, when going to ground towards the back post. This came after a chain of events where the South Korean goalkeeper had again made heavy weather of getting a punch on the ball, and Giuseppe Galderisi had a compelling case for a penalty when brought down by Cho Young-jeung.

Partly returning to the physical approach they had taken to Argentina, by now South Korea's confidence in the tournament had grown enough for them to play the ball more than the opposing player, and it was threatening to pay dividends as the influence of Cha Bum-kun began to grow.

Italy should have scored again before the interval, however, as Altobelli hit the foot of the post from 12 yards when his team were awarded a generous penalty ten minutes prior to the break. It was a miss that was loudly celebrated by most of the spectators, as they willed South Korea on in their endeavours to make it a close match.

Into the second half, those in attendance got their wish, and just beyond the hour mark the scores were level, although not before South Korea had ridden their luck during the first 15 minutes after the resumption.

This was Choi Soon-ho's big moment, and having worked brilliantly to create the angle, he let loose with a thunderous shot that ripped past Giovanni Galli and into his top right-hand corner. It was one of the best goals of the tournament and certainly the aesthetic equal of the goal Park Chang-sun had scored against Argentina. It was a goal that the sharpshooting Soviet Union would have been proud to call their own, and given its relevancy to the game, in levelling the scoreline in a match against the reigning world champions, it made for the greatest moment in South Korean football history at that point in time.

An impossible dream that was in danger of turning into reality, for the next ten minutes it was South Korea who looked the more likely to score again, to the point that when the identity of the next goalscorer proved to be Altobelli it came as something of a surprise.

Then with eight minutes to go the match appeared to be over, and Altobelli was again pivotal, this time in forcing Cho Kwang-rae to roll the ball over his own goal line. Yet, within 60 seconds, the classic South Korean anti-hero, Huh Jung-moo, had guided in a beautifully worked goal for 3-2, making the remainder of the match a marvellously uncomfortable one for Italy.

South Korea's World Cup campaign might have ended in Puebla, but they had left a huge impression on the watching world, to go along with the strong foundations they had now laid for themselves in future tournaments, as they became a notable part of the World Cup furniture.

Of course, greater achievements were to come for South Korea in reaching the semi-finals of the 2002 finals as co-hosts, and during their run to the last 16 in South Africa in 2010, yet in terms of 1986 they were arguably the tournament's ultimate cult heroes. They destroyed a lot of European and South American prejudices, and they created a blueprint that other Asian nations would follow.

Chapter Six

DEF Jam

IN GROUPS D, E and F, Algeria, Northern Ireland, Scotland and Portugal were eliminated. In the first two cases it was all about them not being able to repeat the unexpected heroics of four years earlier, slowed down by ageing squads in the same group, a group they had to share with Brazil and Spain. For the latter two it was a combination of self-destruction, frustration and unfulfilled potential.

Algeria, as a nation, was subjugated under French colonisation between 1830 and 1962, a 132-year stretch of enforced rule that ended after the brutal Algerian War of Independence. A complex relationship has continued to rumble on, both politically and in sporting terms, with the two respective national teams having fielded players born on the soil of the other, along with a spate of French nationals that have been born of Algerian heritage going on to conquer the world, the most remarkable being the imperious Zinedine Zidane.

By 1986, just shy of a quarter of a century beyond gaining their independence, Algeria were setting off for their second successive World Cup, having qualified for the first time four years earlier in Spain.

Brushing aside Angola, Zambia and Tunisia on their way to qualification, Algeria had progressively got stronger throughout their campaign of two-legged ties to reach Mexico, with aggregate victories of 3-2, 3-0 and 7-1.

At the 1982 World Cup, Algeria had won the hearts, admiration and sympathies of a hugely impressed global audience, which had been stunned by two matches that had taken place in Gijón, separated by nine days, the second of which Algeria hadn't even taken part in, yet suffered the reverberations of for decades to come.

An incredible, iconic victory against West Germany had been undone by a result of convenience between Algeria's beaten opponents and Austria in the last match of Group 2. The North Africans had played their last fixture a day earlier, where they had picked up a 3-2 victory over Chile. Algeria could only watch on 24 hours later, abhorred by the spectacle of a heavily choreographed 1-0 win for West Germany, a result that saw the two-times World Cup winners through, along with Austria.

Algeria had become the first African nation to win two matches at a World Cup, and their manipulated exit in Spain was a shameful and bitter blow to both themselves and the tournament's integrity. At their first World Cup of asking, Algeria had significantly enhanced the global opinion of African teams and forced FIFA to belatedly implement final group fixtures finishing simultaneously from 1986 onward, to have the best opportunity possible to avoid further unscrupulous puppeteering of outcomes.

Four years later, in Mexico, while Algeria went into their second World Cup with greater experience under their belts, they were also an older squad. In 1982, only two members of their 22 were in their 30s, and the average age was 26.5. In Spain, they were in the perfect place in terms of squad demographic, and they were at the peak of their powers. By no means the only team in Mexico to be over the edge, the 1986 vintage of Algeria was like the talented boxer who has taken on a fight or two too many. This time around, only six members of their squad were under the age of 27, and six were in their 30s, while the average age skimmed in at just a shade under 28.

However, 1982 had piqued immense interest in Algerian players, and half of their squad were playing club football in Europe by the time of the 1986 World Cup. Most of these players were plying their trade in France, but there were also presences in Belgium, England and Portugal. So, while they were undeniably older in the legs, Algeria's players were also wiser in the head.

They were led by Rabah Saâdane, whose own playing career was prematurely ended due to injuries he sustained in a road traffic accident. As a coach he'd been involved with the Algerian national team in one capacity or another since 1978, filling roles as assistant coach at various levels, and serving on the technical committee. Saâdane had helped Algeria to their very first major global international tournament, at the 1979 World Youth Championship in Japan, and then led their Olympic team to Moscow a year later, before assuming a technical role with the senior team at the 1982 World Cup. Having broken away for new challenges beyond the summer of 1982, he was coaxed back in 1984 to take on the role of head coach.

Captained by the veteran Mahmoud Guendouz, he formed a solid defensive line that also comprised his 1982 World Cup compatriots Noureddine Kourichi and the Tunisian-born Faouzi Mansouri. This consistency of defensive presence was, however, offset by goalkeeping frailties, as the first-choice stopper, Nacerdine Drid, wouldn't be fit enough to play the opening match, nor would he be able to complete their last one. This meant that his understudy, Larbi El Hadi, would play more World Cup minutes in 1986 than Drid.

In midfield, the magnificent Lakhdar Belloumi was still the all-encompassing hero. The man classed as Algeria's greatest-ever player, and the scorer of the winning goal against West Germany four years earlier, he was once again supported by Djamel Zidane, where they were joined by Mohamed Kaci-Saïd and Karim Maroc.

Up front, Algeria were spoilt for choice, as FC Porto's Rabah Madjer and the dependable Salah Assad were backed up by the consistent Djamel Menad, and the talents of the Chelsea-born, Notts County striker Rachid Harkouk, who had been persuaded to join the cause.

Between clinching World Cup qualification and setting off for the finals, Algeria's form was poor. A four-team warm-up tournament in December 1985, in Mexico, had ended with three successive defeats, and disconcertingly the last of those came against the perceived weak opposition of South Korea. Moving into World Cup year, Algeria's only pre-tournament victory was obtained against Mozambique, and other than that there were back-to-back draws against Saudi Arabia, and four failures to pick up a win in the 1986 Africa Cup of Nations, albeit with an experimental squad. It wasn't an auspicious build-up.

Added to this, Belloumi wasn't fully fit going into the tournament, and Algeria were no longer a surprise package. Northern Ireland, Brazil and Spain knew what they were coming up against and largely what to expect.

Algeria's hopes rested heavily on their opening match in Guadalajara, at the Estadio Tres de Marzo. Northern Ireland represented their easiest opponent on paper, despite how well Billy Bingham's team had done at the 1982 World Cup. With Brazil the pivotal middle match and Spain at the conclusion, it was crucial that Algeria got off to a fast start.

The 1-1 stalemate was a damaging result for both teams, Zidane's second-half equaliser cancelling out Norman

Whiteside's early opening goal. It was a game that had many varying plotlines, including Northern Ireland failing to extend their lead on multiple occasions, Algeria losing Madjer just after the half hour after a shocking clash of heads with Mal Donaghy, and periods of a baking-hot afternoon where both teams struggled to maintain their composure and discipline.

There had also been a touch of the surreal when Madjer and Donaghy were down, the latter with blood pouring from his head, as they received treatment. As this was taking place, news of Mexico's first goal of the tournament filtered through from the Azteca Stadium, which for Mexicans in the crowd in Guadalajara was cause for intense celebrations.

It was a match that shapeshifted dramatically, as Algeria went from hanging on desperately, to levelling proceedings, to being the more likely of the two to snatch the winning goal. Yes, it was a final scoreline that did neither side any favours, but it was a wonderfully entertaining way they got there.

Three days later, still in Guadalajara, but now over at the Estadio Jalisco, Algeria went up against the might of Telê Santana's Brazil, in what was an intriguing game of cat-and-mouse football. Only one goal was scored, and Brazil were denied obtaining it until the 66th minute, when Careca finally broke the deadlock after a protracted series of near-misses, inclusive of a disallowed own goal, the frame of the goal being struck and Drid enjoying an inspired performance in goal.

Yet it wasn't entirely one-way traffic. For the first 15 minutes of the second half Algeria had their boldest period of the match, with Belloumi largely pulling the strings, the man billed as the Algerian Platini. The closest the underdogs came was when Edinho was forced to clear from the Brazilian goal line. And even when they fell behind, Algeria remained a threat.

Moving on to the Estadio Tecnológico in Monterrey, six days beyond their narrow loss to Brazil, Algeria were left with a hope and a prayer going into their clash with the talented, yet unpredictable Spain, a nation that had capitulated as hosts of the previous World Cup yet gone on to reach the European Championship Final in 1984. The classic double-sided coin, Spain could just as easily crumble as they could excel.

On this occasion, Spain's Dr Jekyll prevailed, and unable to match the skill of their opponents, Algeria were left with nothing more than an overly physical approach at their disposal, from which the match regularly drifted into rancour. This wasn't helped by the leniency of the Japanese referee, Shizuo Takada, nor the retribution-seeking Andoni Goikoetxea and his uncompromising Bilbao-style footballing butchery.

A day when the treatment meted out to Emilio Butragueño ensured that he didn't return for the second half, and Míchel was withdrawn for his own protection just beyond the hour, it was a credit to Spain that their responses were predominantly made with artistry of the ball, as they ran out 3-0 winners. The result saw them progress to the last 16 with the type of ease that shouldn't have been possible.

This isn't to say that Spain didn't get their punches and kicks in too, as Drid lasted for only 20 minutes until he had to be replaced by El Hadi. Drid departed with a collection of injuries to his ribs, shoulder, head and spine. Another casualty was Harkouk, who failed to end the match, suffering a knee injury that ultimately ended his career.

With their 1986 World Cup campaign offering a very stark contrast to the way they had captivated watching audiences four years earlier, this was unwittingly the end of an era for Algeria. It would be 24 years before they again qualified for a World Cup, the first of two successive qualifications, where they even went on to reach the knockout stages in 2014 in Brazil, and where they admirably took the eventual champions, Germany, to 120 minutes in the last 16.

Groundbreaking as an African team, in 1982 Algeria played an integral part in opening minds towards teams from their all-too-derided continent, yet 1986 did leave a sour taste in the mouth, due to their physical approach to the game, when they certainly had the talent to let their football do the talking again.

Over in Group F, another story of what might have been unfolded for a team that played in red, for a team that also opted to hit the self-destruct button, except in a far more spectacular manner than Algeria had.

On one hand, 1986 represented Portugal's first World Cup finals for 20 years, but on the other, it was a tournament that arrived just two years after they had come to within minutes of reaching the 1984 European Championship Final. Holding their nerve in UEFA qualifying Group 2, Portugal had booked their place in Mexico as runners-up, thanks to a shock 1-0 victory over the already qualified group winners, West Germany, in Stuttgart, due to a goal from Carlos Manuel. It was a result that inflicted a first-ever defeat in qualifying upon the two-times World Cup winners.

Combined with Sweden slipping to a 2-1 loss in Prague against Czechoslovakia on the very same day, in a match they had initially led, this represented a get-out-of-jail-free card for Portugal, who in their two previous qualifiers had lost in Prague themselves, and then laboured to a 3-2 victory over Malta in Lisbon, where the hosts had twice relinquished the lead.

Any feel-good factor over qualifying was soon exchanged for rancour, however, as what became known as the 'Saltillo Affair' erupted. A series of damaging events occurred that included a failed doping test, power plays between the dominant Portuguese clubs over player inclusion in the squad, arguments over sponsorship endorsements and direction of payments, plus the lack of quality in security measures at the team hotel, and the poor condition of the training pitches.

Added to this, stories of indiscipline within the Portugal squad emerged, and the negative press this brought turned a nation against its players, especially after news broke of the players' intention to strike. It was a crisis that escalated exponentially, and the mood was highly visible when the players took to training with their kits turned inside out, so as not to display the sponsor's logo. It was complete and utter brinkmanship, and it wasn't until the eve of the tournament that an uneasy truce was reached.

All of this ran alongside the common-or-garden issues that regularly make for a bumpy World Cup build-up, which included Portugal's coach, José Torres, falling out with the veteran Sporting striker Manuel Fernandes, a player who had just enjoyed the season of his life, scoring 30 league goals in 29 matches to end the campaign as his nation's top scorer, claiming the *Bola de Prata* within the process. With coach and player unable to bury their differences, Fernandes would watch the World Cup from afar.

Fernandes's long-term Sporting strike partner Rui Jordão also missed out on the trip to Mexico, coming as it did at the end of a season where he'd been ostracised at his club. Another blow was the loss to injury of the skilled Benfica winger Fernando Chalana, who had been such an important part of the team that had made it to the European Championship semi-finals, while his team-mate, the prolific

Nené, had retired from international football after Portugal's heroics in France.

With Torres himself having been a player of huge purpose with Benfica, Vitória de Setúbal, Estoril and for the national team, he brought with him a massive amount of experience. Nine times a Primeira Liga champion, and having played in three European Cup finals, he'd also been an integral part of Portugal's team at the 1966 World Cup, where he scored three goals. He'd also played under the footballing visionaries Béla Guttmann and Otto Glória.

Portugal were a team that had so much going for them as the 1986 World Cup loomed, yet they were utterly dysfunctional. If they weren't falling out with one another, they were playing to their own insecurities. For instance, Torres's reaction to news that Bobby Robson was coming to watch one of their last warm-up matches prior to departing for Mexico was to name a team that excluded most of his best players.

A draw, a win and a defeat, against Finland, Luxembourg and East Germany, respectively, were Portugal's last official friendlies leading up to the World Cup finals, and these were done and dusted before the end of February, as the demands that Benfica, FC Porto and Sporting were under made it stunningly difficult for Torres to pull his players together for a more extensive preparation for the tournament ahead.

Despite the tumultuous nature of their preparations, Portugal got off to a flyer, defeating England 1-0 in Monterrey, Manuel the hero, just as he'd been in Stuttgart. He was left in a ludicrous amount of space at the back post when receiving and converting the ball past Peter Shilton, after some wonderful work down the right by Diamantino. It was an afternoon when England had been startlingly profligate. Mark Hateley, Bryan Robson and Gary Lineker had all spurned multiple, reasonable opportunities when well-positioned. Apart from António Oliveira clearing one goalbound Lineker effort, the rest of the efforts were wayward.

Having taken a glass-half-empty view of their situation as the World Cup began, Portugal had plenty to be optimistic about, as they were spearheaded by the prolific FC Porto striker Fernando Gomes while his 20-year-old club teammate Paulo Futre was called from the bench just a couple of minutes before the only goal of the match. While confidence and togetherness might have been in short supply, there was no shortage of talent at Torres's disposal.

Towards the end of the match Portugal had a serious shout for a penalty waved away, and after all the negativity prior to the kick-off, for those watching at home Portugal swung into serious party mode in celebration of their success in their opening fixture. One more point would now likely be enough to see them through to the knockout stages.

Portugal's newly sourced confidence was still a fragile one, however, and the loss of their goalkeeper and captain, Manuel Bento, was a blow that they failed to properly absorb. Sustaining a broken leg when training at the Estadio Universitario in preparation for their next group match, against Poland, Bento had been playing as an outfield player when he landed awkwardly after challenging for an aerial ball. It meant that Torres now had to turn to Sporting's 38-year-old back-up goalkeeper, Vítor Damas.

In the match itself, luck remained elusive for Portugal, and this time it was they who couldn't take their chances, one of which came to within half an inch of getting them the point that would have ultimately prolonged their tournament, when the ball was hooked off the line and on to the post. Włodzimierz Smolarek netted the only goal for Poland in a deceptively entertaining match.

Four days later, Portugal were still in with a big chance of progression as they walked on to the pitch at the Estadio Tres de Marzo to face a stubborn Morocco team that had been content to accept goalless draws in their opening two matches, leaning on the preconceived limitations that the rest of Group F had presumed they had.

With Torres still uncertain of his best approach, he omitted Diamantino from his starting line-up and instead fielded Futre, who had impressed during the second half against Poland, to add to the 17 minutes he'd been given at the end of the England encounter.

While not an exact science at this point, given the other results throughout Group F, for Portugal the likelihood was still that if they could avoid defeat against Morocco in Zapopan, they would be heading into the knockout stages. With goals elusive for their opponents so far, there were certainly reasons for optimism, while a victory would even result in them winning the group if England avoided defeat against Poland.

Absolutely anything was possible as Group F's final matches got underway, yet of all the possible permutations, nobody foresaw what was to unfold. Having shown no goalscoring threat in their first two matches, Morocco let loose against Portugal in the most spectacular manner imaginable. With just over an hour on the clock, Portugal trailed 3-0, caught within the eye of an incredible African storm. After keeping the full extent of their cards up their sleeve for their first two matches, Morocco finally unveiled the true extent of their talents, blowing not only Torres's team away, but also the entrenched opinions of a watching world, who were still seemingly reluctant to take African football seriously.

When Diamantino looped in a beautiful goal for Portugal with ten minutes left to play, it was to be no more than a consolation, and with England defeating Poland in Monterrey, it meant that Torres's team had conspired to finish bottom of Group F, having sat atop of it after the first round of fixtures and having been handily placed in second position as the final round of matches kicked off.

Portugal were left to rue their errors as they made their exit from the tournament within the unique situation of finishing bottom of their group, despite having a win to their name. This compared to two teams from other groups progressing to the knockout stage without having picked up a victory.

With recriminations ringing long and loud in Portugal, the fallout was monumental, as Torres departed the role of head coach and a glut of their star players were declared persona non grata, and initially cast into the international wilderness, before sentiments began to soften due to a run of poor results in their absence.

As this international feud played itself out, a year later FC Porto were on their way to European Cup glory against Bayern Munich, a glory that was wildly celebrated, yet also served to display the talents that could have helped Portugal in their forlorn and unsuccessful efforts to qualify for the 1988 European Championship finals.

While many of the exiles did eventually return to international football, cohesion was elusive, as the divisions between the various factions of the squad were difficult to overcome; this despite, Benfica following FC Porto's European Cup success by reaching losing finals in 1988 and 1990.

A lost opportunity, in spite of themselves, Portugal had shown flashes of what they were capable of, in Mexico at the 1986 World Cup, two years on from a wonderful campaign in the European Championship finals, and had they progressed to the knockout stages, they might well have gained some momentum. Instead, despite the emergence of a talented crop of youth players, they would remain frustratingly absent from major international tournaments for a decade beyond the 1986 World Cup, and even when making their long-awaited return they would still prove to be startlingly adept at hitting the self-destruct button when they appeared to be in a good position to strike for glory.

Skilled, yet flawed, in many respects, when international success finally did come for Portugal at the 2016 European Championship finals in France, it was ironic that it came via a more pragmatic style of football and with a squad that had cultivated a type of togetherness and siege mentality that wasn't previously associated with their national teams of the past. But 1986 was arguably the starting point of a 30-year odyssey that took them to that 2016 glory.

Chapter Seven

Northern Lights

NORTHERN IRELAND were one of the biggest success stories of the 1982 World Cup. Drifting in from left field, finding themselves in a difficult group with Spain, a dangerous Yugoslavia and the talented unknowns of Honduras, they stunned everyone when they beat the hosts in Valencia, before exiting in the second-round group stage, where they were overpowered by the France of Michel Platini, Alain Giresse and Dominique Rocheteau.

It had been their first major international tournament since the 1958 World Cup, and with only six members of their squad having played their football in the English First Division in 1981/82, one of those making only two appearances, much of the talk in the build-up to the finals had centred on whether the Northern Ireland manager, Billy Bingham, would bow to pressure and name the ageing legend George Best in his squad. With Best's last cap now distant five years previous, Bingham opted not to take the mercurial genius to Spain, and his decision was vindicated as an eclectic collection of players excelled in a way that hadn't been expected of them.

Four years later, Northern Ireland were no longer the great mystery that would be able to blindside their group rivals. Since 1982, they had come perilously close to reaching the 1984 European Championship finals at the expense of West Germany, they had won the last British Home Championship and they had impressively qualified for the 1986 World Cup from a group that had contained England, Romania, Finland and Turkey. They had grown as a collective, and they now boasted 14 First Division players and one player who had enjoyed a fruitful spell in LaLiga.

A sluggish start was made to qualifying, however, and when beaten by Finland in Pori in their opening Group 3 match, a fixture that was meant to represent a sedate start to their campaign, it was a result that didn't bode well for Northern Ireland's hopes. England would pose obvious difficulties, while Romania had just taken part in the 1984 European Championship finals and could boast the presence of a precocious 19-year-old by the name of Gheorghe Hagi. Home and away, these were expected to be the four matches that would make or break Northern Ireland's ambitions. The loss to Finland was a massive setback.

Luckily for Bingham, he was in possession of a young midfield talent of his own who looked every inch the world-beater, a player who was three months younger than Hagi, and one who already had a World Cup under his belt.

When Norman Whiteside travelled to the 1982 World Cup at 17 years and 41 days old, he was to become the youngest player to appear in the entire history of the tournament, beating a record that had been held by Pelé. As a 16-year-old and still a few weeks away from being able to sign his first professional contract, Whiteside had made his Manchester United debut as a substitute, away at Brighton and Hove Albion. Within eight weeks he was taking to the field at La Romareda, in Zaragoza, to face Yugoslavia in the World Cup. By the time the tournament ended, he had more than double the number of World Cup finals appearances to his name compared to his senior club appearances. It was a startling rise to global prominence, and it was around Whiteside that Bingham built a revamped team, one that could reach a second successive World Cup finals and then aim to prosper once there.

By the time the 1986 World Cup qualifiers began, Whiteside had an FA Cup winners' medal to his name and had attracted the interest of the great and the good of Serie A. In September 1984, Romania arrived at Windsor Park, and Northern Ireland could afford no mistakes.

Using his tried and trusted traditional British approach, Bingham went for an aerial attack and a physical nature to winning the ball in midfield. Romania, in reply, tried to play the ball on the floor and stuck to their technically superior style. It made for a fascinating spectacle of football, as two very different footballing cultures went head to head.

It was a match that Northern Ireland edged 3-2, and the outcome sounds a closely run one, yet Romania's best football was reserved for the last ten minutes, as they searched desperately for a second equaliser. Bingham's side had enjoyed the measure of their opponents for most of an evening during which Whiteside and Martin O'Neill found the back of the net.

Back on track by the time 1984 had drawn to a close, Northern Ireland had picked off another victory at Windsor Park, this one in their return match against Finland. Bingham's team had fallen behind midway through the first half, and it took a goal either side of the interval from John O'Neill and Gerry Armstrong to give them the points.

A surprisingly difficult opponent, aside from a 5-0 loss to England at Wembley, Finland offered stubborn resistance in all their other matches, not only against Northern Ireland. They held both England and Romania to draws in Helsinki and picked off two wins against Turkey. Had it not been for a defeat in Bucharest, they would have been a serious contender for qualification.

Next up, Northern Ireland welcomed England to Belfast in February 1985, and they were now without their captain, Martin O'Neill, who had succumbed to a knee injury that would ultimately end his playing career. Armband handed to Sammy McIlroy, this was a match where if a draw wasn't to be the outcome then something had to give. During his five years in charge of Northern Ireland, Bingham had only lost at home once, while England hadn't lost at Windsor Park for 58 years going into this one.

An international derby encounter, it made for an evening of blood and thunder, Mark Hateley scoring the only goal with 13 minutes remaining. It was scant reward for Northern Ireland's efforts, and Bobby Robson was magnanimous enough to admit as much at the final whistle, Bingham's team having been without their own imposing target man, Billy Hamilton.

Just over two months later, Northern Ireland welcomed Turkey to Windsor Park for a must-win match. With half of their qualifying campaign now complete, Bingham's team had won two and lost two, while this fixture was to be their last at home, meaning that their run-in would consist of three successive away missions, to İzmir, Bucharest and London.

Everything was on the line against Turkey simply just to give Northern Ireland a fighting chance in the group, rather than any guarantees. A goal in each half from Whiteside, forced to play as an emergency striker, galvanised Bingham's hopes on an evening when Martin O'Neill remained absent, joined on the sidelines by both Armstrong and Hamilton.

With Romania and England having played out a goalless draw earlier in the day in Bucharest, it was a win that moved Northern Ireland into second place in Group 3, although having played two matches more than the eastern

Europeans, who lay in fourth place, three points adrift, in a format where a win was still only worth two points.

By the time Northern Ireland took to a World Cup qualifying pitch again, in İzmir, to face Turkey in September, Romania had played catch-up on their matches in hand and were now level on points with Bingham's team, with the joker in their hand being that Bucharest still awaited their visit.

Carelessly, Northern Ireland were held to a goalless draw in Turkey, on the same day that Romania were taking a valuable point at Wembley against England. Two matches, identical outcomes, but one draw was infinitely more valuable than the other.

Two fixtures now remaining, away to Romania and England, the odds were heavily stacked against Northern Ireland. When facing Turkey, they had again been without the services of Martin O'Neill and Hamilton, while Whiteside was also absent due to suspension. The talented winger Ian Stewart was a late withdrawal, and McIlroy played through the pain barrier. Added to it all, the legendary Pat Jennings had come perilously close to retirement in the summer of 1985, after Arsenal had made the decision to release him, only to be coaxed back to Tottenham Hotspur as cover for Ray Clemence and Tony Parks.

A muted collective performance from a patchwork side in attacking terms, the Turkey draw was played out a day after the tragic and shocking death of the Scotland manager Jock Stein at Ninian Park. It was a frustrating occasion, where Turkey came the closer of the two teams to making the breakthrough, denied only by the brilliance of Jennings.

Two points separated the top three teams, and even fourth-placed Finland weren't mathematically out of the reckoning yet. England held all the cards with two home matches to come, a two-point cushion and Turkey visiting

Wembley. The pivotal event was to be Northern Ireland's trip to Bucharest, to face Romania.

Ill at ease with having been in the role of the favourites against Turkey, Northern Ireland were back on more comfortable territory in being the underdogs heading to Romania. Still bedevilled by injuries, Bingham could at least take solace in the fact that his counterpart, Mircea Lucescu, was also without some important players of his own. Costică Ştefănescu, the veteran sweeper, was suspended, while the prolific Rodion Cămătaru, who had scored at Wembley, was nursing a broken leg.

Prior to the match, outside the Northern Ireland squad, few considered anything other than a win for Romania. A victory for the home team would mean only an improbable series of events in the last round of fixtures could deny them passage to Mexico. Within this, the message to Northern Ireland was crystal clear. Nothing but a win would suffice.

By half-time, Northern Ireland would have been good value for a 3-0 lead. Instead, they had to make do with a one-goal advantage, Jimmy Quinn finishing smartly after excellent work by McIlroy and overcoming the ball initially getting stuck between his legs.

Romania, having frozen for much of the first half, sprang to life after the interval and Northern Ireland had the heroics of Jennings and the cool defending of a debutant Alan McDonald to thank for the clean sheet that now put fate back in their own hands.

Just 72 Northern Ireland supporters had made the trip to Bucharest, yet the noise they made at full time would never have suggested they had been restricted to such numbers. Bingham had opted for a 4-5-1 formation, Quinn as the lone striker, supplemented by Whiteside breaking from midfield and support from the wings. As the match developed throughout a fraught second half, however, Whiteside was bound by more defensive duties, while Northern Ireland's wingers couldn't get on the ball. Bingham countered this by introducing Nigel Worthington to add a more combative element to midfield and Armstrong, who offered extra support to Quinn.

It was one of the truly great away World Cup qualifying performances by any British team, and it set up the final round of fixtures perfectly, given that this result, combined with England's comfortable victory over Turkey, meant that Bobby Robson's team had already booked their place in Mexico, so would have nothing other than professional pride riding on the upcoming clash at Wembley.

Still with work to do, Northern Ireland's task was to avoid defeat against England, unable as they were to rely upon Romania stumbling against Turkey. With England already assured of their place at the 1986 World Cup, and Bingham's team needing only one point, the obvious line of questioning prior to the match had been just how serious Bobby Robson's players would take it.

Unwilling to end up cast in a similar light to West Germany and Austria on the back of their 1982 result of convenience, England's remit was to win. Yet, with no peril attached to the evening from their perspective, they struggled to move through the gears, as the understandably more motivated Northern Ireland players made space in and around their penalty area a rarity.

After tentative early exchanges, Glenn Hoddle was the first to test Northern Ireland's nerve, cutting in from the right before sending a magnificently arrowed left-foot shot towards Jennings's top right-hand corner. He pushed it away with a wonderful one-handed save.

Hoddle was to be at the hub of whatever promising football England could muster, only to be let down by his largely uninspired team-mates. A marvellous ball into the penalty area by the Tottenham Hotspur man was shockingly squandered by Kerry Dixon, who suffered an off-night, leading the attack alongside Gary Lineker. The Everton striker was culpable next, when put through on goal by a lovely piece of vision from Ray Wilkins, only to be off target with his shot, putting it wide of the post, with Jennings exposed.

Sharp intake of breath after sharp intake of breath, the saving grace for Bingham and his players was that England's supporters began to turn on their players, especially after McDonald cleared the ball off the Northern Ireland line when a looping Gary Stevens cross dropped over the desperate reach of Jennings early in the second half.

It certainly wasn't a case of England being unwilling to score the goal that would deny Northern Ireland qualification for the World Cup, it was just that they seemed utterly intent upon being unable to procure it.

Dixon did up his game as the second half wore on, and Jennings had to be alert when using his legs to stop a deflected effort, and then pulled off an incredible save beneath his crossbar to deny the Chelsea striker's looping header.

Even Jimmy Nicholl, the Northern Ireland right-back, came close for England, when directing a Hoddle cross low and to Jennings's right, after it had been flicked on by Dixon, in what was arguably the closest moment a player in a green shirt came to scoring.

Dixon then missed the chance of the evening, as he miskicked badly when the ball dropped to him from height on the edge of the Northern Ireland six-yard-box, after they had struggled to clear a corner.

There was certainly nothing pedestrian about the home team's efforts, and even in the final minutes Mark Wright and Terry Fenwick were being sent forward for set pieces, so eager were England to obtain a winner.

As a final scare, there was a hint of handball from Whiteside when the ball bounced close to his hand as he ushered it away from the Northern Ireland penalty area from a corner that John O'Neill and McDonald had battled one another to concede, in what were escalating desperate measures.

However, Northern Ireland finally got themselves over the finish line after 90 nervous minutes of football at Wembley, taking the point they did ultimately need, as Romania picked up their expected victory over Turkey in İzmir. Upon the final whistle, there was a peculiar combination of jubilation from the Northern Ireland supporters, who were clearly large in number, offset by the boos of England supporters.

Into World Cup year there was good reason for Northern Ireland to be bullish, despite the difficult group they were drawn in for the finals. An unbeaten run of friendlies against France, Denmark and Morocco had been impressive, and on each occasion the opposition went with strong line-ups.

The match against the reigning European champions France had even been played in Paris, and Bingham's men had acquitted themselves well, while it wasn't until the latter stages of the Denmark match that Sepp Piontek's team managed to sneak an equaliser. Meanwhile, when it came to the Morocco match, it was only retrospectively that Northern Ireland's 2-1 victory could be valued as highly as it should.

As Mexico loomed, Northern Ireland's biggest problems rested up front, as Quinn would travel yet fail to play a single minute of the tournament, Hamilton was still struggling for fitness, and Armstrong was no longer capable of reproducing the magic of old on a prolonged basis. On the plus side, Colin Clarke had emerged after two high-scoring seasons in Division Three with Tranmere Rovers and Bournemouth, and he was now on the brink of a transfer to Southampton, forsaking reputed interest in him from Torino.

Other plusses included Bingham persuading Jennings to postpone his retirement until the end of the World Cup, the continued rise of McDonald, ensuring that there was no shortage of options in central defence, and the impressive form of the Nottingham Forest midfielder David Campbell, who had come through on the blindside during the second half of the 1985/86 season and would be an option that could allow Whiteside to be pushed forward.

No shortage of tactical options, once in Mexico, Bingham put his players through intensive altitude training, inclusive of demanding 3,000-metre runs during the highest heat of the day, at descending altitudes of 7,000, 6,000 and 5,000ft. Ultimate fitness was the name of the preparation game, an admirable approach, yet one that might have sacrificed more time on the training pitch with the ball at the players' feet, although two 40-minute warm-up sessions were played against Scotland, within a no-tackles pact.

Nods towards the need for mental well-being included wives and girlfriends accompanying the squad, although as the serious business began to get closer, they were kept at increasing arm's length. Bingham insisted upon strict divisions by the hotel pool, with players over one side, wives and girlfriends on the other, something that was of great frustration to the players, yet high amusement to Ron Atkinson, who happened to be a guest in the same hotel.

Subterfuge being played to the very last, it wasn't until an hour before kick-off of Northern Ireland's opening match, against Algeria, that Bingham revealed his starting line-up, having led the media to believe that neither Nicholl, McDonald nor Hamilton would start, only for their names to be on the team sheet.

It was, of course, a huge, missed opportunity in drawing with Algeria. Of the three home nations to travel to the 1986 World Cup, Northern Ireland had seemed the most well-prepared, and their first-half performance endorsed that line of thought. Yet the African team were allowed to come back into the picture in what was the classic game of two halves.

With Spain and Brazil to come, thoughts drifted to 1982. If Northern Ireland could beat Spain at a World Cup once, then maybe they could do it again?

The match at the Estadio Tres de Marzo in Guadalajara saw Northern Ireland take to the field with only one change to the team that had faced Algeria. In came Clarke for Hamilton, while Bingham resisted the temptation to start with either Stewart or Campbell.

Spain, off the back of losing their opening match to Brazil, and with the memories of Valencia hanging heavily over them, needed a fast start, and they got it. With less than one minute on the clock they had the lead, as Míchel perfectly picked out the run of his Real Madrid team-mate, Emilio Butragueño, who was through on goal to place the ball agonisingly out of Jennings's reach and into the bottom left-hand corner of the Northern Ireland net. A stunningly poor start to the match for Bingham and his players, by the 18th minute, Athletic Club's Julio Salinas had made it 2-0, sweeping the ball past Jennings from just inside the penalty area, when taking advantage of an error by McIlroy.

Unrepresentative of how the pattern of play had gone during the 17 minutes between the two goals Spain had scored, Northern Ireland had seemed to be working their way into the match until Salinas struck. Clarke had shown no signs of nerves on being handed a starting role and had tested the reflexes of Andoni Zubizarreta.

Trailing at the break, Northern Ireland began the second half positively, with McIlroy eager to make amends for the mistake that had led to Spain's second goal. Within seconds of the restart, Whiteside had a header cleared at the back post, when rising to meet a corner. With no time to dwell on the opportunity missed, Clarke soon had the ball in the back of the Spanish net in the most bizarre manner, as Zubizarreta needlessly came out of his penalty area to meet a speculative long ball forward, which he managed to slice high into the air towards Ricardo Gallego, who opted to head it back towards his goalkeeper. Fine in theory, but Gallego was horrified to then see the Barcelona-bound shot-stopper slip. This gave the loitering Clarke the chance to reach the ball first, and getting his head to it he directed it into the welcoming net.

An absolute gift of a goal, the remainder of the match was a torrid affair, as Spain tried to keep their composure and play to their superior technical abilities, while Northern Ireland leaned towards their strengths of tenacious pressing and the quick ball into the penalty area, something that increased with Stewart's introduction, when offering more width, and Hamilton being thrown into the mix with 20 minutes left to play.

Periods of intermittent panic broke out in the Spanish penalty area, and Northern Ireland were unlucky not to be awarded a penalty when the ball bounced up and struck Víctor on the hand, as the match began to take on an aura that was almost a prototype of the culmination of the Argentina vs England quarter-final. A test of character for Spain, they rode their luck at the back and probed on the break for a third goal that would kill the match off. Butragueño missed a golden opportunity to settle the fraying Spanish nerves when Jennings saved with his legs.

Northern Ireland were to run out of time, however. Despite having the fitness to continue long into the day, it was to be Spain's victory, albeit a precariously obtained one, in what tends to be forgotten as one of the best matches of the tournament.

Five days later, it was over to the Estadio Jalisco to face the frightening prospect of Brazil. With Steve Penney struggling with an ankle injury, Stewart was handed a start, while Campbell belatedly won a place in midfield, ahead of Worthington. Arguably, this was the team that Bingham should have started the World Cup with. That little more expansive, it could have opened the locks that Algeria and Spain managed to place on their first two matches, while the more conservative presence of Worthington might have better suited facing the fluidity and skill of Brazil.

At the Jalisco, results elsewhere across the tournament had left Northern Ireland with the slim possibility that a draw would be enough for them to advance to the knockout stages as one of the four best third-placed teams. As it was, two draws and a defeat would be good enough to carry two nations into the last 16, it's just that Bingham's team weren't to be one of them.

At major international tournaments, the order in which group fixtures are played is often of paramount importance, and facing the toughest opponents last is usually a thankless task, as by their third match, more often than not, they've very much found their stride. In the 1986 World Cup, this was very much the case with Brazil.

While Telê Santana's team had been lucky to close out for victory against Spain in their opening match and Algeria had only narrowly been overcome, despite Brazil being the better team, by the time that Northern Ireland rolled across their sightlines they were just entering the eye of a two-match storm in which they would play their best football of the tournament, scoring seven goals in the process without reply.

As Northern Ireland took to the pitch to face Brazil, it was an event that had a similar air to any boxing match that featured Mike Tyson at that point in time. There was a nervous excitement, yet also a sense of great foreboding. What an incredible opportunity it was, yet the punishment sustained might just ring in the ears of the defeated for weeks to come.

Four years earlier it had been Scotland who Brazil had picked apart; brave souls who had the foolhardy temerity to score first, something that only made it worse in the end. Yet there was such beauty, not just in those players in yellow shirts and their deeds with a football, but also in their vanquished opponents, who were glorious in their own right, simply by their association of defeated proximity.

Of course, just as in 1982, Santana's Brazil would fall short in Mexico, but that agonising exit was still nine days away. First there would be a two-part exhibition to enjoy, before we once again waved them a premature farewell from another World Cup.

It was Jennings's 41st birthday and he was collecting his 119th cap for Northern Ireland. Bingham had twisted his arm to continue turning out in international football, when the goalkeeper's instincts had told him to call it a day after his release from Arsenal in the summer of 1985. His last serious first-class competitive club match had been as far back as November 1984, from where John Lukic took permanent possession of the gloves at Highbury. Since then, Jennings had played just one more time for Arsenal, his own testimonial against Tottenham Hotspur. He went on to return to Tottenham for the 1985/86 season, making just one first-team appearance, against Liverpool at White Hart Lane in a January 1986 Screen Sport Super Cup fixture.

It was a demanding time for Jennings, despite what he'd thought had been the curtain coming down on his football career. Tottenham had needed goalkeeping cover and with it came a promise of reserve matches to help keep his senses sharp for the big Northern Ireland fixtures ahead. Having signed up to do a series of supermarket appearances in his homeland, it often meant him flying back and forth between Belfast and Heathrow.

Then came an unexpected call from Howard Kendall at Everton, who was in desperate need of experienced FA Cup cover, for both the 1986 semi-final and final. Neville Southall had picked up a serious ankle injury on international duty, and his understudy, Bobby Mimms, had stepped up to fill the void. Kendall, feeling his third-choice goalkeeper, Mike Stowell, was far too inexperienced to be the next in line for first-team football, went out and purchased Fred Barber from Darlington. The problem was that he'd already played in that season's FA Cup, so would be unavailable if anything were to happen to Mimms. So, Jennings was the answer, and with Tottenham's blessing, he signed forms for the Goodison Park outfit.

Continuing to train with Tottenham and heading off on Northern Ireland duties whenever the call went up, Jennings's only in-person dealings with Everton were to travel to Villa Park for the semi-final, and to Wembley for the final, where he sat in a cup final suit, watched the game with the Everton squad, and got to keep the tracksuit he was handed. It also meant that when he headed off to Mexico for the World Cup finals, he did so as an Everton player.

While not with the exact same set of personnel, Bingham took to the Jalisco and Brazil with the same tactics as he had the match at Wembley against England, which had taken them to Mexico. A deep-lying defence, five across midfield and a lone striker. Within 15 minutes those plans had been undone, as Careca opened the scoring, supplied by the skill of the excellent Müller, who himself had had the first compelling effort on goal saved by Jennings. With little room to manoeuvre towards the right-hand corner, the Torino winger whipped in a punishing cross, which the much-coveted São Paulo striker swept past a helpless Jennings.

As goals come, it was utterly brutal, a move in which Müller had received the ball from the enthusiastic and explosive Josimar, a player making his international debut in place of the injured Édson. It wouldn't be the right-back's only telling contribution to the match.

Regardless of the setback, as half-time approached, Northern Ireland were still operating under the context that one goal would be enough to send them through. Their best play flowed through Stewart and Campbell, while McIlroy squandered their best chance when snatching at a shot from the edge of the penalty area. Sighs of relief were heard when Jennings denied the legendary Júnior, while at the other end the unconvincing goalkeeping of Carlos did offer a little encouragement, and Clarke provoked a scare for the Brazilian defence.

Then, three minutes before the interval, came the moment. Brazil's second goal took the breath away. Northern Ireland were lulled into a false sense of security as the ball was stroked around from one player to the next, some 30 to 40 yards from goal. Júnior, Elzo and Alemão were all involved in moving the ball into the possession of Josimar, who let loose with a wondrous shot that flew into the top right-hand corner of Jennings's net. Broadest of shoulders and the most telescopic of legs, Josimar was away to celebrate, while Jennings was left to stagger around, as if caught flush on the chin in Las Vegas by Tyson. Everything about it was a work of art, and it became one of the most indelible moments of the 1986 World Cup.

What tends to be forgotten, however, is that within seconds Whiteside missed a golden opportunity to strike back, planting a free header wide of the post when unmarked, having been beautifully picked out by Stewart. It was a miss that was arguably more demoralising than Josimar's goal, and even for the most optimistic of Irishmen, realistically the gig was up, despite there still being 45 minutes left to play.

Still, Northern Ireland embraced the second half with a wonderful sense of bravery. McIlroy again tested the concentration of Carlos from distance, as the Brazilian goalkeeper fumbled and then reclaimed one effort. Set pieces also became a bit of a concern for Brazil, especially after Hamilton's arrival from the bench.

For a spell, the match became an end-to-end affair. Emboldened by the freedom of the worst having already happened, Northern Ireland just went for it, and the ball again fell invitingly to McIlroy. Catching it sweetly, Carlos was forced into a save that Jennings would have been proud to call his own.

There was no danger, however, of Jennings's thunder being stolen by his counterpart, as he pulled off yet another fine save, from Careca, and denied Wálter Casagrande, who had entered the fray as a substitute with less than half an hour on the clock after Müller's match ended prematurely. It was a true exhibition of goalkeeping from Jennings, and a beautifully fitting way to head into retirement.

One more goal was conceded, as Careca struck a third for Brazil in the final minutes, but it took something magical to breach again, with Zico part of the support cast, having made a late cameo. If you could choose to concede one last goal, this was the perfect one, and despite having initially been reluctant to continue playing beyond his departure from Arsenal, it was an emotional Jennings that walked from the pitch at the end of the match.

A 3-0 defeat with greater depth than the scoreline could ever suggest, had this been the Northern Ireland approach to the matches against Algeria and Spain, they would have undoubtedly usurped Uruguay for a place in the knockout stages.

An era-ending tournament, it would be 30 years before Northern Ireland made it to the finals of another. It wasn't only the back of Jennings that they saw after the 1986 World Cup, as his long-time understudy, Jim Platt, also went into international retirement, as did Armstrong and Hamilton. McIlroy would carry on, but only for another year. These were all losses that were understandable when age and fitness were considered.

Starkly, however, and despite still only being 21 years old, Whiteside would only play nine more times for Northern Ireland beyond Mexico. A succession of injuries that stemmed from a persistent problem with his right knee eventually led to his retirement from football just five years later.

With the next generation of Northern Ireland player not living up to the one that it followed, Bingham remained at the helm until the end of their unsuccessful bid to qualify for the 1994 World Cup finals, the emerald baton for international footballing endeavour picked up in the south.

It had been a wild and unforgettable ride though, and while 1982 is rightly brandished as the peak of their powers, Northern Ireland provided a valuable and underappreciated layer of texture to the 1986 tournament too. Had the wind blown in a slightly different direction, then they might have even matched the heroics of four years earlier.

Chapter Eight

The Tragedy of Big Jock and the Unluckiness of the Draw

WALES AND Scotland foster the second-oldest international rivalry in football history, a rivalry that was born on 25 March 1876, at Hamilton Crescent, Partick, Glasgow. This hallowed patch of land also hosted the very first official international football match, when Scotland faced England three and a half years earlier.

In 1876, Hamilton Crescent was, and still is to this day, the home of the West of Scotland Cricket Club. Despite its place in football history – it's a venue that also hosted the three matches it took to decide the outcome of the 1877 Scottish Cup Final between Vale of Leven and Rangers – there's very little on show to suggest its relevance to the sport of the inflated round ball.

Marginally over a century later, at Anfield on 12 October 1977, this enduring but largely provincial Celtic rivalry took a global and controversial twist, when a legendary World Cup qualifier unfolded at the home of Liverpool Football Club. Not as close to qualifying for the 1978 World Cup finals as the myth insists, Wales were, however, massively hard done by as a 2-0 victory took Ally MacLeod's Scotland to Argentina. It was a tense and passionate evening when anything other than a defeat for Wales would have set up a group decider in Prague against the reigning European champions, Czechoslovakia.

The mountain that Wales would have still had to conquer to reach the 1978 World Cup finals is often lost in the translation of the controversy that surrounded Scotland's victory in Liverpool, on an evening when the Football Association of Wales (FAW) opted for the larger revenue stream on offer at a packed-out Anfield, rather than the tribal footballing advantages on offer at the Racecourse Ground, Wrexham, a venue that no nation looked forward to visiting when it came to facing Wales.

With just 11 minutes remaining, a cross was swung into the Welsh penalty area, which was challenged for by Scotland's Joe Jordan and David Jones of Wales. It was a closely contested ball and an arm was raised; the ball made connection with a hand and the French referee, Robert Wurtz, pointed to the Anfield Road end penalty spot.

Don Masson, of Derby County, converted, and seven minutes later Kenny Dalglish skilfully validated the win with the second goal. A largely one-way grudge was nurtured and eight years later Wales were presented with the opportunity for redemption.

The gap in talent between the Scotland and Wales teams of October 1977 was a marked one, but by September 1985 the distance hadn't just closed, Wales had arguably eclipsed Scotland. In possession of quite possibly the best goalkeeper in the world at that point in time, in the shape of Neville Southall, plus the lethal goalscoring instincts of Ian Rush, these two truly world-class components were added to by the spectacular Mark Hughes, the defensive magnificence of Kevin Ratcliffe, the European Cup-winning experience of Joey Jones, the talented, yet menacing edge of Pat Van Den Hauwe and the mercurial playmaking skills of Mickey Thomas.

While Scotland still had a strong squad, it was one that lacked the type of flair they had been spoilt with in previous years. When they made the trip to Ninian Park, Cardiff for the make-or-break Group 7 qualifier against Wales they were shorn of the ageing but still influential Kenny Dalglish, who was ruled out through a groin strain, plus the suspended Graeme Souness, after he picked up a careless yellow card in Reykjavik, during Scotland's previous qualifier away to Iceland. This was a match from which they escaped with a crucial but narrow 1-0 victory, thanks to a late winner from the Aberdeen midfielder Jim Bett. Barcelona's Steve Archibald was also absent against Wales due to a dose of influenza.

With what could be described as a line-up of very good players, it was still a team that was lacking the type of world-class elements that Wales could boast, yet conversely Scotland's team was perhaps the better balanced one.

Scotland were now led by the legendary Jock Stein, who took over from MacLeod shortly after the rancour of the 1978 World Cup, going on to qualify for Spain four years later. He'd previously held the job on a part-time basis during the qualifying campaign for the 1966 World Cup, when a place was denied Scotland only in a final group-deciding match against Edmondo Fabbri's Italy, in Naples.

The man responsible for Celtic collecting nine successive Scottish league titles between 1965/66 and 1973/74, plus owning the added distinction of being the first man to lead a British team to European Cup glory, when beating the mighty Internazionale in Lisbon in 1967, Stein had left Parkhead in the summer of 1978, after being persuaded to stand aside as manager during a difficult 1977/78 season, for what he believed to be a position on the board of directors.

When the position eventually offered proved to be a nominal one, Stein instead accepted an invitation to take over as the manager of Leeds United. A highly lucrative contract was handed to him at Elland Road, just days after a profitable testimonial had taken place in his honour at Celtic Park against Liverpool.

With echoes of Brian Clough's time in charge at the club, Stein lasted just 44 days in the Leeds job, jumping at the opportunity to succeed MacLeod as Scotland manager. Having initially ridden the storm of Scotland's failure to reach the latter stages of the 1978 World Cup, the much-derided incumbent was gone, after he presided over a 3-2 defeat to Austria in Vienna, which marked the start of Scotland's attempt to qualify for the 1980 European Championship.

Having instigated the move himself, via a quiet word to friends in the media, Stein and the Scottish Football Association (SFA) seemed to be the perfect union. However, Stein's time in charge was a polarising one to an extent. Scotland qualified for the 1982 World Cup with ease, bowing out of the tournament narrowly and with a degree of farce to the Soviet Union. They followed that with a poor run of results during the qualifying campaign for the 1984 European Championship, where they failed to pick up a victory after beating East Germany at Hampden Park in their opening match.

Group 7 in the UEFA section of the qualifiers was unforgiving. For Scotland and Stein, beyond Wales and an increasingly awkward Iceland, stood Spain, fresh from having reached the final of the 1984 European Championship against the host nation in Paris.

Scotland and Wales had very different starts to their bids to reach the 1986 World Cup finals. Wales crashed to back-to-back defeats in Reykjavik and Seville, in matches just five weeks apart in the autumn of 1984, while Scotland started their campaign with a win at home to Iceland on the very same evening that Wales were losing to Spain. A month later, Scotland pulled the perfect rabbit from the hat, when they destroyed Spain in Glasgow. Simultaneously, Wales were labouring to a narrow victory in Cardiff against Iceland. Stein's golden touch had apparently returned.

Blessed with a reputation that preceded him by a significant distance, lesser coaches might not have held on to their job in the same circumstances as Stein did, in the wake of Scotland's disappointing efforts in the 1984 European Championship qualifiers.

It was a masterclass of a performance from Dalglish that had picked Spain apart, scoring Scotland's third goal of the night with a spectacular run and finish. It was a victory that gave Stein control of the group, while Wales's win against Iceland could have easily been viewed as an insignificant one.

There Group 7 sat, until a two-month span between late February and late April 1985, which turned the race for Mexico on its head. Edged out narrowly by Spain, 1-0 in Seville, Scotland then prepared for the visit to Glasgow, of Wales. Having not won in Scotland since 1951, their opponents had themselves been unfortunate to lose in Spain, and the odds were stacked against Wales winning what was the 100th meeting of the two nations, at a sold-out Hampden Park.

Wales caught Scotland cold, however, the hosts completely underestimating not only the capabilities of the opposition, but their mental durability and desire. Rush, linking with Hughes in a way Stein had publicly doubted was possible during the build-up to the match, scored the only goal of the encounter, when arrowing a sweetly struck effort into the top corner of Jim Leighton's net.

It was a result that left Scotland staring at the unthinkable. Having looked so assured after defeating Spain at home, they had now handed the initiative to a Wales team who initially appeared to be out of the running, after losing their opening two fixtures.

Wales then tore Spain apart at the Racecourse Ground, winning in style, 3-0, on an evening when Rush scored twice, yet his strike partner, Hughes, took the headlines with a spectacular scissor-kick goal, sandwiched between Rush's two efforts. It was a goal that arguably cemented Hughes his transfer to Barcelona. Wales had never beaten Spain before.

Keen observers, Wales watched from the sidelines as first Scotland and then Spain chiselled out nervous and narrow victories in Reykjavik, which set up a stunning finish to Group 7. Wales's early defeat away to Iceland was now laid bare for the damaging result it was.

Ninian Park awaited its date with destiny, while Spain had the luxury of a fortnight to assimilate the events in Cardiff, before they faced Iceland once again, in the final match of the group in Seville.

Mike England, the Wales manager, would have been well within his rights to be disappointed with the FAW's decision to use Ninian Park for the match. The Racecourse Ground had become something of a fortress, and the memory of how they had dismantled Spain there was fresh in mind, as were other notable performances throughout the 1980s, inclusive of thrashing England, demolishing Romania and holding the mighty Brazil and Soviet Union to draws there. Since that fateful night at Anfield against Scotland, Wales had only lost in Wrexham once, that being a European Championship qualifier against West Germany over six years earlier.

Ultimately, the choice of Anfield in 1977 had played into Scottish hands. As far as the Wales manager was concerned his team needed to give themselves every advantage possible, yet Ninian Park felt like a concession of sorts. The FAW had even considered asking for use of the Cardiff Arms Park.

Three days prior to the match, Stein and Mike England took part in a television preview of the crucial upcoming qualifiers on the BBC's *Football Focus*, where they were joined by the England manager Bobby Robson and his Northern Ireland counterpart Billy Bingham, who themselves would face off against one another at Wembley in November, after alternating encounters with Romania and Turkey.

A wonderful display of mind games, it was with a mischievous glint in the eye that Stein attempted to use the issue of venue to unsettle Mike England, and he certainly seemed to provoke an only vaguely restrained ire from the Wales manager, which prompted him to stumble over the correct facts of how the 1977 match ended up at Anfield, erroneously claiming that it was a ban that took them into another country. All the while, Robson and Bingham sat back and enjoyed the verbal duel, having earlier tried to play devil's advocate in their opinions of the potential outcome of the clash in Cardiff.

Due to the stature of the match and the prize on offer, ITV readily took up their option to broadcast it live, at a point in time when the television blackout of English club football was at its peak. In comparison, England's qualifier at Wembley against Romania the following evening was only shown to the nation in the form of late-night highlights by the BBC.

With Scotland, Wales and Spain locked together on six points each, goal difference was everything. With Scotland in possession of this advantage and Wales only marginally ahead of Spain, it meant that Wales were realistically in need of a win. Given the performance Wales had put in at Hampden Park and given the calibre of the players that Scotland were deprived of, Stein found himself and his team cast in the role of the underdogs.

However, bullish noises were still made during the build-up. Stein had insisted that Scotland weren't playing for the draw that would likely send them into a two-legged play-off against the winner of the OFC section, instead insisting that he was looking for the win that would all but see them qualify automatically for the finals. The pressure on Stein to prevail was enormous. Scotland had qualified for the three previous World Cups, and although his job was effectively hanging on the outcome of the match, he'd privately contended that he planned to step down as manager beyond the World Cup finals, a tournament he was sure Scotland would take part in.

The focused Stein was suffering with poor health. On a course of diuretics to assist in a fight against heart failure, it's suggested that he stopped taking his medication in the build-up to the decisive match to avoid the related side-effects until the crucial fixture had passed. Retrospectively, opinions have been voiced that Stein didn't seem himself on the day of the match. His assistant Alex Ferguson and the midfielder Gordon Strachan both felt he appeared unwell before kick-off, while the broadcaster Roddy Forsyth, when conducting an interview with him that afternoon for BBC Scotland, noticed that he was pale and sweating.

To others, he seemed in fine form. During the warm-up, when the Scotland fans behind Southall's goal refused to give back the training balls when they went into the crowd, the Wales goalkeeper informed Stein, who in good humour went and asked the Tartan Army for the balls back. There are photos of the Scotland manager full of smiles as he rounds them up.

Wary of the damage that Hughes had done at Hampden Park in winning the ball for Rush to score, Stein deployed a five-man defence at Ninian Park. Regardless of the adjustment, Wales were 1-0 up within 13 minutes thanks to a low strike from Hughes, and the home team almost sneaked a second goal a short time later when Robbie James headed just over the bar. Scotland were on the back foot.

At the interval, the Scotland dressing room was a blizzard of commotion. Recriminations over how the goal had been conceded gave way to incredulity. Jim Leighton had completely misjudged a cross just before half-time, resulting in him desperately diving at the feet of Hughes to block another Welsh goalscoring opportunity. In the dressing room, Leighton confessed that the reason he'd missed the cross was because he'd lost one of his contact lenses. Totally unaware that Leighton wore contact lenses and incandescent that he wasn't equipped with a spare set, Stein turned to his back-up goalkeeper, Alan Rough, to whom his last reputed words imparted were, 'You are on, you fat bastard.'

The second half began as the first had ended, with Wales in ascendancy. Rush missed a golden opportunity to extend their lead and Stein took that as his cue to make his last change, when replacing Strachan with the exciting but sometimes anonymous Davie Cooper of Rangers.

The added threat that Scotland now posed forced Wales to drop deeper. Resorting to long balls for Rush and Hughes to chase, the match was delicately poised. Scotland increasingly dangerous, Wales capable of hitting on the break, and one goal for either team likely to eliminate the other. This was footballing drama at its finest, yet a watching nation was completely unaware of the tragedy in the making that was slowly unfolding on the Scotland bench.

With just nine minutes remaining, Steve Nicol lofted a cross from the right-hand side of the Scotland attack into the Wales penalty area. Slightly overhit, Graeme Sharp managed to head the ball back towards the penalty spot, where David Speedie instinctively tried to get on the end of it. Maintaining little in the way of control of the direction in which he could send the ball, Speedie struck it upwards and against the raised arm of David Phillips. The referee, Jan Keizer, who had also officiated when Wales defeated Spain, was left with little option but to point to the spot.

Cooper was later to claim that it was less of a case of him being brave enough to take the penalty and more that nobody else seemed willing to step up for the immense responsibility. He struck the ball cleanly, low to the left of Southall, where the Everton goalkeeper got a hand to it, yet one that was agonisingly not strong enough to keep the ball out. As the Scotland bench celebrated, Stein remained seated.

It was a devastating blow for Wales. Galling that it was once again a Scotland penalty that would deny them, it was tormenting for Wales that they hadn't put the result out of sight when they were clearly on top during the first hour.

A frantic final few minutes ticked by as Wales fought hard to find the goal they now needed. When the referee blew his whistle for a foul with just seconds remaining, Stein got to his feet, believing it to be the end of the match, intending to make his way to shake hands with England. Impeded by a photographer, part of a collective that Stein had had regular words with throughout the match when blocking his view of the pitch, it's said that he grappled with the photographer, pushing him out of the way. When he turned around, England could see that his Scottish counterpart was in distress. Stein dropped to his knees, where he was soon tended to by his coaching staff, the police and the Scottish team doctor, Stewart Hillis.

At the final whistle, an assortment of players, coaches, photographers and reporters invaded the pitch, mostly unaware of the developments down by the bench. As Stein was placed on a stretcher and carried through a chaotic tunnel to the Ninian Park medical room, scenes that went out live on television, Ferguson took to the pitch to keep the players from going back to the changing room, fearing that was where Stein had been taken.

One man who had witnessed events, however, was Souness, Stein's suspended captain, a man that the manager had struck up an unlikely friendship with. Two polarising characters, but both infused with a burning desire to win. Souness positioned himself outside the door of the medical room, acting as protector of his manager.

The worrying images that television viewers had seen of Stein on that stretcher was of a man who was conscious and lucid enough to be watchful of the direction he was being carried. The shock of his resultant death just minutes later was at odds with the visuals on offer. ITV's commentator that evening, Brian Moore, had surmised that Stein had simply been overcome by the tension of the dramatic finale to the match.

Scotland's supporters celebrated long and loud. Andy Gray, an unused substitute that night, was in the centre of the pitch, punching the air. The combination of events were utterly jarring, as two entirely different scenarios were unfolding. Soon, the severity of the situation became all too clear. Hillis worked tirelessly in his attempt to save Stein, but it was a forlorn Souness who broke the news, wandering along the corridor saying, 'He's gone.'

It was shocking, but at the same time it was something that blended into an era in which the British public was becoming accustomed to seeing tragedy as a staple part of their television diet. Bradford, Heysel and now 'Big Jock'. It wasn't just football, however, as time would occasionally freeze when a television programme would be interrupted for a newsflash. In an era before 24-hour news channels, the country would collectively hold its breath whenever one would break. Not much more than a year earlier, the nation had watched and even laughed as Tommy Cooper died on live television, the watching audience under the impression that his tragic on-stage collapse was part of the act.

There was a sad symmetry to the location of Stein's death, having played for a year with the ambitious non-league outfit Llanelli Town, a quarter of a century earlier, around 55 miles further along the Welsh south coast, a time of his career where he honed his game, from where he would go on to become Celtic's captain.

Three days later, Stein's funeral took place at the Linn crematorium in Glasgow. The wider game paid its respects with silences at football grounds around the country being immaculately observed. Football then dusted itself down once more and got on with the show. Ferguson was asked by the SFA to guide Scotland on a part-time basis through the two-legged play-off against Australia, and then onwards to Mexico for the World Cup finals.

After a sombre friendly against East Germany in October, a 2-0 victory at an electric Hampden Park in late November against the Socceroos was followed a fortnight later by a sterile goalless draw in the return match at the Olympic Park in Melbourne, the venue of the 1956 Olympic Games. Ferguson had pushed Stein's team over the finish line. They were two physical games of football, which came to an expected conclusion, that of Scotland qualifying, yet it was one that was far harder to come by than many anticipated.

The SFA was left with an impossible decision to make with regards to Stein's successor. They had wanted to appoint a full-time, permanent replacement, but Ferguson was unwilling to commit himself to the role on anything other than a part-time basis up to the end of the World Cup, before considering all options in the summer. Another path available to the SFA had been an alternative, permanent appointment, that of Billy McNeill of Manchester City. The man who had succeeded Stein at Celtic in 1978 was believed to be receptive to the idea of taking the job.

Ferguson was seen as the man who would ensure the continuation of Stein's work, however, and given the close working relationship they had forged throughout qualification, plus the respect that Ferguson held for Stein, it was quite likely a choice that the SFA weren't brave enough to go against. While far from ideal, a part-time Ferguson was viewed as better than no Ferguson at all.

Despite there appearing to be no adverse effects to having a part-time manager during the build-up to the 1986 World Cup finals, in retrospect, not having someone in charge who could be fully focused on the tournament in the months leading up to Mexico was perhaps a mistake. With his Aberdeen team fighting on all fronts, inclusive of harbouring designs on the European Cup, and Tottenham Hotspur making guarded overtures towards him, Ferguson had much to think about.

Beyond the play-off against Australia, Scotland had four pre-World Cup friendlies to navigate before heading to Mexico. A narrow 1-0 victory over Israel in Tel Aviv, a deceptive 3-0 win over Romania at Hampden Park on the night Dalglish won his 100th cap, a 2-1 loss at Wembley to England, and a hard-fought draw in Eindhoven against the Netherlands took Ferguson and Scotland to the end of the domestic season.

The win against Romania had been a stirring one. Opponents who had been narrowly edged out of a place in Mexico themselves by Northern Ireland, opponents who had reached the finals of the 1984 European Championship. It was an evening where Dalglish had been presented prior to kick-off with a trophy by the legendary Franz Beckenbauer to celebrate his landmark achievement in becoming the first and to this day only Scotland international to reach 100 caps.

In a high-tempo performance, Scotland overpowered a Romanian team that had only conceded one goal in their previous seven fixtures, that being a vital one, however, in Bucharest against Northern Ireland. They also boasted the presence of a 21-year-old Gheorghe Hagi, who was the source of their most dangerous moments, almost bringing his team back into the match with a near-miss, before Scotland confirmed the win with their third goal of the evening.

While undeniably a confidence-boosting victory and performance, it was also one that Scotland wouldn't realistically be able to project on to the World Cup finals. The heat and humidity of Mexico wouldn't be an environment suitable for such a high-tempo approach to the game of football. As a standalone endeavour it was a performance to be proud of, yet as an experiment of how to play against Denmark, West Germany and Uruguay in Mexico, it was a missed opportunity.

Faced with a 22-man squad to pick and only weeks remaining in the job, Ferguson didn't shy away from controversy in his selection. With a nod towards recognising that a subtle approach was required to playing under the Mexican sun, Ferguson left Speedie out of his final selection. So pivotal to Scotland getting their equaliser in Cardiff against Wales in September, it was a decision that rankled with the player, while his Chelsea team-mate, Pat Nevin, also suffered a similar fate.

Whereas Nevin took the news philosophically, Speedie's disappointment was only tempered by being assured he would be the first player called upon should there be any late withdrawals from the squad, if he would agree to be on Ferguson's standby list. When Speedie and Nevin arrived at Chelsea's training ground the following day, they both found the other had been placated with the very same promise.

They weren't alone in feeling hard done by. Ferguson also omitted Liverpool's captain Alan Hansen, on the brink of clinching the league and cup double and one of the most cultured centre-backs in world football. So often left out of the national team over the years and suffering with a constant suspicion about his fitness, the slower pace of the game in the heat of Mexico would have been perfect for what was the classical ball-carrying defender. In effect, Hansen essentially sat at the opposite end of the argument used for discarding Speedie. Given that Ferguson, understandably, opted for his club pairing of Willie Miller and Alex McLeish as his first-choice central-defensive picks, Hansen would have either been useful as part of a five-man defence or the ideal back-up to Miller and McLeish. Perhaps Hansen was instead viewed as too long of a shadow for Miller and McLeish to operate in.

When push came to World Cup shove, McLeish was indeed unavailable beyond Scotland's opening match due to a stomach bug, and it was instead left for David Narey to supply cover. A capable but not world-class replacement for McLeish, he'd been the unexpected scorer of that indelible goal against Brazil, which so provoked Telê Santana's finest into footballing perfection at the Benito Villamarín in Seville four years earlier, when Zico, Oscar, Éder, Falcão and Sócrates inspired their team-mates to run out 4-1 winners.

Other contentious omissions included Mo Johnston of Celtic, who had been so influential in his club snatching an unlikely league title on the final day of the season, when Heart of Midlothian inexplicably self-destructed with one hand on the trophy and basking in the prospect of what was ultimately an unrequited league and cup double of their own.

Sat on the outside looking in, Johnston was in good company. Archibald, with less than 24 hours to absorb the disappointment of a European Cup Final defeat with

Barcelona, was another to receive the dreaded consolation call from Ferguson, as was Ally McCoist, who having only just won his first cap in Eindhoven, against the Netherlands, was maybe less surprised than others, although he was the top scorer in the Scottish Premier Division in 1985/86, and had many advocates pressing for him to be given a place in the squad.

In the case of Archibald, there would be a reprieve, however, when Dalglish was cruelly ruled out of the tournament with a groin strain, thus missing out on what would have been a fourth World Cup. Speedie and Nevin both sat by the phone waiting for a call that never came. Archibald was the man who Ferguson turned to, subsequently removing the potential historical sensory overload of the concept of any Barcelona No. 10 not being able to work his way into a Scotland World Cup squad.

Over the years, a myth has been propagated that Dalglish pulled out of the squad because Hansen was left out. Hansen, however, accepted the decision with grace and agreed to be on the standby list for Ferguson. Hansen had often missed out when it came to Scotland, winning only 26 caps for his country over an eight-year span, even returning to represent them again beyond the 1986 World Cup, just as his club manager did on two more occasions.

Regardless, both Dalglish and Hansen would have brought some much-needed on-pitch breathing space for Scotland. When you look at the players who prospered the most in Mexico, this was, to all intents and purposes, the World Cup of the playmaker. The World Cup of the No. 10. The players who could see the game three, four, maybe five passes ahead of the game were god.

Dalglish, at the age of 35 by now, would have had to be used sporadically in Mexico, but he would have been the one player that Scotland possessed who could have regularly picked the defensive locks of Denmark, West Germany and Uruguay. Meanwhile, Hansen also had that third-eye effect to his reading of the game. The fact that Souness struggled in Mexico, to the extent that Ferguson dropped him in the final group match against Uruguay, speaks volumes of how he missed the cerebral presence of his former Liverpool team-mates.

Enslaved by questions to which answers may not have existed, Scotland were drawn into a stereotypical group of death, where under the rain clouds of Nezahualcóyotl and punishing heat of Querétaro, Dalglish and Hansen would only have been able to do so much in response to the hypnotism of Denmark, to the strength of body and mind of West Germany and to the ruthless brutality of Uruguay.

In Mexico, Ferguson found it to be too difficult a juggling act. Of his 22-man squad, 19 players made it on to the pitch, with Jim Bett the only outfield player not to feature. Indecision over his strongest line-up and which formation to opt for proved detrimental. At just the time when Scotland needed every advantage they could give themselves, they were ultimately found to be dysfunctional. Just how a more settled Wales team might have fared in comparison will always be open to conjecture.

Despite their underdog status – Denmark certainly viewed Scotland as the weakest team in the group going into their opening match – Mexico ended along similar lines to the World Cups of 1974, 1978 and 1982 for the Scots, in that they were eliminated at the group stages by the finest of margins.

Fielding Miller in the unfamiliar role of sweeper, Scotland successfully negated the threat of Piontek's Denmark during the first half of their opening fixture in Nezahualcóyotl. Paul Sturrock, having been a surprise inclusion in the squad, was subsequently the shock choice for the starting line-up ahead of Archibald. Scotland did such an effective job of subduing Preben Elkjær and Michael Laudrup in the first half that ITV's team of pundits were cautiously optimistic that they could gain a positive result. The passionate Scottish support at the Estadio Neza 86 agreed, and this match was blessed by the best atmosphere of the entire tournament.

Nicholas was Scotland's best performer, and the one player they could boast who wouldn't have looked out of place in the Denmark team. However, a devastating 15-minute second-half Danish masterclass settled the outcome, as Elkjær picked Scotland's defensive lock to roll in what proved to be the winning goal. Even then, Roy Aitken had what looked to be a perfectly legitimate equaliser wrongly ruled out for offside.

Such a promising display ended disappointingly though, not just in terms of the result, but also due to the sight of Nicholas being carried from the pitch in pain. Denmark, having dismissed the prospects of Scotland, found far easier pickings against Uruguay and West Germany. They breathed a very heavy sigh of relief at the end of this match.

Against West Germany in Querétaro, Scotland could again count themselves unlucky. Deprived of McLeish due to illness, shorn of Nicholas thanks to strained ankle ligaments, and without Sturrock, who failed to overcome an injury of his own, Ferguson was left with no option but to make changes to his line-up to face the beaten finalists of four years earlier and twice winners of the World Cup.

Ferguson had been of the mind to rotate his team regardless of the injury and illness problems he faced, but the loss of Nicholas was a big blow, after he'd been a constant worry to the Denmark defence. With Narey replacing McLeish, and Archibald coming in for Nicholas, in what were more or less like-for-like alterations, the third change brought with him a switch of formation, as Eamonn Bannon's introduction meant that Ferguson deployed a five-man midfield and returned to a flat back four. Archibald was expected to work alone up front, where he would be supplemented from the flanks whenever possible.

Archibald had missed out to Sturrock against Denmark purely on form shown in training, and Ferguson will have viewed the loss of the Dundee United man as big a blow as the loss of Nicholas was.

Strachan opening the scoring against West Germany was one of the shocks of the group stages, after Scotland had spent the opening exchanges in a desperate rearguard action. When the goal came, it was one of great beauty, and the sight of Strachan contemplating leaping over the advertising hoardings in celebration was one of the finest images of the tournament. It was also validation for a player whom many observers had felt was going to be replaced in the line-up by Cooper.

Scotland's lead lasted only five minutes, however, before Rudi Völler prodded the equaliser over the line. Understandably, nervousness set in for Scotland and Narey looked vulnerable, very nearly gifting Beckenbauer's men another goal before half-time.

Within minutes of the restart Scotland were behind when Klaus Allofs took advantage of a penalty-box deflection to sweep West Germany into the lead. From there, Scotland relaxed a little. As the free-scoring Frank McAvennie entered the fray, eventually followed by the arrival of the free-spirited Cooper, Scotland began to look dangerous once again. In a brief cameo that had shades of John Barnes's later appearance from the bench for England against Argentina, Cooper gave West Germany a restless last quarter of the match, providing McAvennie with a golden opportunity on the six-yard line that the West Ham United striker failed to take.

Again, Scotland's effort and endeavour won them admirers, yet left them bereft of points in Group E. Also, while there had been many plus points to the performance for Ferguson, there had been concerns too. Souness had struggled with the heat and humidity once more and had appeared a shadow of his usual self. West Germany had exploited Narey's hesitancy in the absence of McLeish. Added to this, Archibald had been relatively ineffective and Maurice Malpas had picked up an injury that would rule him out of the final group match against Uruguay. Being unable to retain the ball in defence for any prolonged period was telling and it left the absent Hansen looming over every defensive frailty.

Back in Nezahualcóyotl, during the build-up to the showdown with Uruguay, the Souness question was batted back and forth in the media. While most felt he would be deserving of dropping out of the team should Ferguson be bold enough to do it, not many thought he would do so. Even this semi-compliment of his decisiveness was turned against Ferguson in the final reckoning.

The Scotland line-up and formation had again been reshuffled. Not only had Souness been stepped down, but Malpas, Archibald and Bannon were also removed from the team that had faced West Germany. In came Paul McStay, Arthur Albiston, Sharp and the fit-again Sturrock. Nicholas was risked among the substitutes and a 4-4-2 formation was implemented. Souness didn't even make the bench. He might have proved to be the perfect man for the job of bringing an experienced mind to the centre of a chaotic midfield and might well have been in his element against Uruguay.

With Uruguayan belligerence at its peak with José Batista sent off in the very first minute for a reckless challenge on Strachan, Scotland were handed a one-man advantage for the remaining 89 minutes. Frustrated by their opponents, the match drifted to a depressingly predictable goalless draw. Nicholas and Cooper were thrown on for the last 20 minutes, yet to no discernible avail. Meanwhile, Nicol glaringly missed Scotland's best chance of the match.

All Scotland had needed was one goal. The introduction of four of the six third-placed teams reaching the newly reintroduced knockout stages of the tournament had given them hope of reaching the last 16. They had performed well in their two narrow losses to Denmark and West Germany, but the concept of being able to reach the latter stages of a World Cup when having lost their two opening group matches didn't feel right. It felt like a get-out-of-jail-free card, but one that Ferguson was unable to play.

Home Scotland flew, and before the year was over their manager had a new project on his hands at Old Trafford. He was succeeded by Andy Roxburgh, a man who had been part of the SFA coaching pyramid since 1975 and would go on to lead his nation not only to the next World Cup, but also their first European Championship finals in 1992. This would be achieved during an era in which the levels in natural talent of the players at his disposal were significantly lower than those his predecessors were able to enjoy.

Yet another case of what might have been for Scotland, by the 1986 World Cup a weariness had crept into the Scottish footballing psyche, one that arguably set off for Mexico already fearing the worst, only to be proved correct. Given the events of Cardiff, their supporters could hardly be blamed.

The fateful nature to Scotland's trip to Ninian Park in September 1985 sadly cast its shadow once again a decade later. Cooper, the man who coolly and calmly slotted home the crucial penalty that opened the door to Mexico for Scotland, also died unexpectedly, at the age of just 39, one day after suffering a brain haemorrhage at the recently built Broadwood Stadium, the new home of Clyde, while shooting scenes for a coaching programme called *Shoot* for Scottish Television.

Glasgow, an often-divided city, the wider nation of Scotland and beyond mourned another shocking and untimely loss.

Chapter Nine

We've Got the
Whole World at Our Feet

MID-1980S ENGLAND were massively uninspiring.
Dominated by the misguided concept that they couldn't cope
without the presence of Bryan Robson, there was an all-too-
often percentage-playing and conservative approach to their
football. Decked out in the type of unmemorable kits that
Umbro were churning out in the middle of the decade, it was
all an austere sartorial departure from the kitsch Admiral
offerings of the Don Revie and Ron Greenwood eras, and
four years away from the classic Italia '90 variations, when
Umbro significantly upped their game.

White V-neck shirts with faint vertical lines, navy-blue
shorts and white socks might have pleased the traditionalists,
but it was a kit that was as aesthetically dull as the style of
the football that was played by those wearing it. While the
red-and-white away version was certainly kinder on the eye,
up against the impressive kits of Adidas, Le Coq Sportif
and Hummel, they simply weren't kits to instil you with
optimism.

You can forgive poor football if it's played out in a
wonderful kit; you can forgive a poor kit, if the football
played in it is wonderful. Yet poor football played out in a

poor kit is unforgivable, and the mid-1980s England flirted with both of those concepts.

Then there was the music. 'We've Got the Whole World at Our Feet' was England's official musical offering for the 1986 World Cup. It reached a high of number 66 in the UK charts, as penned by Tony Hiller, the man behind the biggest hits of The Brotherhood of Man, inclusive of their 1976 Eurovision Song Contest-winning 'Save Your Kisses for Me'.

As part of the research for this book, I gave the song a listen. It's what can only be classed as 2min 55sec of abject awfulness. Sat in between the off to Benidorm feel of 'This Time (We'll Get It Right)', in 1982, which reached a mindboggling number two in the UK charts, and New Order's chart-topping 'World in Motion' of 1990, 'We've Got the Whole World at Our Feet' is of its time, both in terms of football-related musical quality and the general lack of public enthusiasm for it.

There's something of a sad feel to the front cover of the record. A squad picture that was meant to represent the players who were heading to Mexico. Trevor Francis, Dave Watson, Tony Woodcock, Mark Wright and Paul Bracewell wouldn't travel to the World Cup, but their faces peer at you from the front cover. Their places on the transatlantic flight instead went to Chris Woods, Steve Hodge, Peter Beardsley, Peter Reid and the Tottenham Hotspur version of Gary Stevens, all of whom are absent from the photograph.

As 1986 rolled into view, England were steady, if unspectacular. Football fans and music aficionados voted at their turntables and hi-fis. 'We've Got the Whole World at Our Feet' bombed.

Bobby Robson was somewhat hamstrung at the time. Marooned in a no-win situation to a degree. Damned for not being Brian Clough, he was under ever-intensifying scrutiny because of his failure to take England to the 1984 European Championship finals. The fluidity of his Ipswich Town team, which was powered by a midfield of Frans Thijssen, Arnold Mühren and John Wark – a midfield that was ahead of its time as far as club football in England was concerned – couldn't be transplanted into the England team. By rights, Glenn Hoddle, Ray Wilkins and Bryan Robson should have been the ideal players to replicate the Ipswich midfield, but despite his very best efforts, Bobby Robson's England consistently appeared to be far more rigid than his Ipswich ever looked.

On face value, when you look at the cold, black-and-white stats, England's qualification for the 1986 World Cup appears quite impressive. Unbeaten in their eight matches, they scored 21 goals and conceded only twice. Awkward international derbies against Northern Ireland were navigated, while the dangerous questions posed by Romania were also answered, although not in any overexcitable style.

Examined from an alternative perspective, however, 13 of those 21 goals were plundered against Turkey, 8-0 in Istanbul and 5-0 at Wembley. England opened their qualification campaign with another 5-0 victory, at home to Finland, and stumbled to a clumsy 1-1 draw in the return in Helsinki, making it a grand total of 19 of their 21 qualifying goals coming against the two undeniably weakest teams of Group 3. In the four collective matches played against Northern Ireland and Romania, England scored just twice.

They did a professional job, but they kept the risk-taking to a minimum. Of the eight matches, they won four and drew four. Winning their first three matches meant they had won only one of their last five qualifiers.

From the individually talented group of England players of the 1970s, who couldn't form a compelling enough collective to ensure qualification to the finals of a succession of major tournaments, the baton had been passed from Greenwood to Bobby Robson beyond the unfulfilled potential of the 1982 World Cup.

After an intense, but ultimately unsuccessful media and public clamour for Clough to get the job – having also been overlooked by the Football Association five years earlier – Bobby Robson was viewed from some perspectives as an unwelcome England manager. Over the course of the eight years of his leadership of the national team, he was hounded from perceived failure to perceived catastrophe, often punished for no greater sin than not being Brian Clough.

It was an ageing team that he inherited from Greenwood. The average age of the squad that the former England manager took to Spain in the summer of 1982 was 28. Nine of the 22-man squad were over the age of 30, while Terry Butcher was the youngest at 23.

Bobby Robson's approach to the England job was initially an expansive one, with his first match in charge being a European Championship qualifier in Copenhagen against Denmark. He recalled the Aston Villa winger Tony Morley, who was grossly unlucky not to make the squad for the 1982 World Cup, plus Russell Osman, another player who could count himself hard done by in missing the tournament. Beyond that, Robson largely stuck to the on-pitch players that Greenwood utilised in Spain.

A partial overhaul was still required, and Robson ended up dealing a little too head-on with the issue of Kevin Keegan's international future, publicly declaring he was wanting to go in a new direction but making the mistake of not talking to the England captain privately before informing journalists. It was a diplomacy faux pas.

An early scene had been caused and, when England failed to depart Copenhagen with a victory, the new manager was essentially denied that all-important early bounce that can be the difference between success or failure, something that was exacerbated when England lost a Wembley friendly to West Germany just three weeks after the draw against Denmark.

The boldness of those early days in the job soon eroded, to be replaced with a safety-first ethos, particularly after failure to qualify for the 1984 European Championship finals, and two sobering defeats in friendlies against France in Paris and to the Soviet Union at Wembley, with England looking light years behind both opponents.

It was under these darkening clouds that Robson elected to play the percentages during the qualifiers for the 1986 World Cup. It left the general feeling that it wasn't as important to him how he got England to Mexico, as long as he did get them to Mexico. Given the amount of media abuse he received throughout his time in charge of the national team, an embracing of a more pragmatic approach was an entirely predictable cause-and-effect situation, which was only really broken after the announcement was made, prior to the tournament, that he would be stepping down from the job at the end of the 1990 World Cup. Only then did Robson gingerly release the handbrake, when bowing to public demand to build his side around the outrageous talents of Paul Gascoigne.

There was also the breaking away from his strict 4-4-2 formation in Italy. He became more expansive in his bespoke approach to different opponents, something that hadn't always been the case before. The opening draw against Ireland and the negative and in some quarters vindictive media response provoked a rebirth of Robson, which made you wonder what could have been, both in terms of the eight years he'd had the job, plus what he might have been able to do with it moving on to the 1992 European Championship and the 1994 World Cup.

This was of course further down the line from the 1986 World Cup, yet there are parallels to be drawn. Just as in 1990, in 1986 Robson was essentially backed into a corner where he was left with little option but to throw caution to the wind after two initial adverse performances and results, plus added injury and suspension problems.

Back in the qualifiers, and still looking for the perfect composition of team, it's testament to how far Robson was from identifying a settled team that of the 13 players who played an on-pitch role in the opening qualifier against Finland at Wembley, only eight of them would travel to Mexico for the World Cup finals.

Another indicator of just how much Robson threw his side together on an ad hoc, game-to-game basis in the hope of finding elements that would gel, Gary Lineker, the man who would win the Golden Boot in Mexico, didn't start a World Cup qualifier until facing Romania at Wembley in September 1985, after his transfer from Leicester City to Everton. It's often forgotten that Lineker was a relative late-comer to the England team prior to the 1986 World Cup and that Mark Hateley was widely viewed to be England's most dangerous threat in front of goal.

Six different strike partnerships were tried out during the qualifiers, and the search for the perfect duo didn't end until the emergence of Peter Beardsley. The Newcastle United striker played no part during the qualifiers, while Tony Woodcock, Peter Withe, Paul Mariner and Trevor Francis all did, yet none of them made it to Mexico.

Woodcock had started the qualifying campaign as the main source of goals for England yet didn't even make the standby list for the finals. Withe and Mariner fell by the wayside in a gravitational manner, as age and fitness began to bite for both. Conversely, Robson had been eager to name Francis, but a dip in form, offset by the outstanding performances of Beardsley, left the England manager with little option but to omit him, especially after he failed to impress when he played at Wembley against Scotland just weeks before the squad was to be named.

Francis went into that match under no illusions, that it was essentially a make-or-break audition for a place in the squad, after Beardsley had put in a stunning performance alongside Lineker in Tbilisi during England's most impressive pre-World Cup display in defeating the excellent Soviet Union, ironically in a match where England proved they could click effectively without the services of the injured Bryan Robson.

Some positions did pick themselves, however. For instance, there was no compelling rival to put pressure on Peter Shilton, in the wake of the international retirement of Ray Clemence, while players such as Kenny Sansom, Terry Butcher, Bryan Robson and Ray Wilkins were also certainties, whenever available.

Shilton's back-ups in Mexico would be Chris Woods and Gary Bailey. Woods had spent the 1985/86 season in the Second Division with Norwich City as part of a successful promotion-winning campaign, while Bailey had been put under pressure at Manchester United by the signing of Chris Turner from Sunderland, thus playing only 25 of his club's 42 league matches that season, although injury also played its part in Bailey's absence. Bailey would sustain a serious knee injury in training during the build-up to the finals, which he never fully recovered from. Beyond the 1986 World Cup, he played only five further times for Manchester United and never represented England again.

Rumours did circulate that Robson had approached Clemence over the possibility of travelling to Mexico to provide experienced cover for Shilton, but having lost out to his great rival four years earlier, the Tottenham Hotspur goalkeeper was in no mood to give up his summer to watch another World Cup from the bench. The irony was that Clemence, along with Sheffield Wednesday's Martin Hodge, were the in-form English goalkeepers throughout the 1985/86 season, yet neither would travel to Mexico. While in the case of Clemence it was perceived to be by choice, Hodge was very much open to consideration and he had many sympathisers when he missed the final cut, instead finding himself on the standby list. Bailey's fitness problems only served to highlight Hodge's plight further.

In central defence, Robson was unfortunate to lose the services of Mark Wright, who played all but two of the qualifiers, yet missed out on Mexico after he suffered a broken leg in the FA Cup semi-final for Southampton against Liverpool, at White Hart Lane. Wright had been one of the biggest plus points of England's qualifying campaign, playing with a calm assurance that was almost Hansen-like, in terms of the composure he displayed on the ball. That underlying class was the perfect complement to Butcher's more Anglo-Saxon approach to the game.

It was a huge blow to Robson's plans to lose Wright. They made a complex, but beautifully balanced partnership. While Butcher was less refined than Wright in terms of style of play, the former had a grasp of self-control that the latter could only dream of. Wright was prone to volatile reactions when provoked at club level from time to time, and Butcher was a positive influence on him on the international scene.

When casting around for a replacement for Wright, Terry Fenwick proved a very different and uncompromising proposition, yet he was to be the chief beneficiary. Earmarked to provide cover for Kenny Sansom at left-back should it be needed, and to be an option for man-marking jobs in midfield, he was a provider of steel and had no qualms about stretching the boundaries of the game's laws.

Alvin Martin's fears of potentially missing out on another World Cup, having been one of the unlucky names to miss out four years earlier, were proved unfounded, while the Tottenham Gary Stevens could also cover central defence if required.

While Chris Waddle and John Barnes were shoo-ins to contest the wide positions when it came to out-and-out wingers, Trevor Steven offered something different in the way that he would tuck in at times, narrowing the midfield so that the right-back could roam forward, a right-back who just happened to be a team-mate at club level too. The other Gary Stevens.

Centrally, the prospect of playing Bryan Robson, Ray Wilkins and Glenn Hoddle would eliminate one of the wingers, although the England manager had shown many times before that he wasn't averse to playing Hoddle out of position in a wide role. Yet, the growing suspicions that the England captain Robson wouldn't be fit enough to play a major role brought others into play. Steve Hodge impressed immediately, while Gordon Cowans briefly came back into contention.

In qualifying for the 1986 World Cup, Robson used 27 different players. Of those, 18 made the World Cup squad. Beyond Woods and Bailey, the back-up goalkeepers who played no on-pitch role during the qualifiers, the two outfield wildcards in the squad were Beardsley and Hodge. Both players were there with a great deal of public enthusiasm, and they would have huge roles to play in Mexico.

Of the unfortunate nine to have taken part in the qualifiers but not to have made the squad, beyond the injured Wright, the most hard done by was quite possibly Everton's Paul Bracewell, the classy midfielder who had even had game-time at the Azteca Stadium in the summer of 1985 as part of an acclimatisation tournament that England took part in.

Going to Mexico, the myriad of questions Robson had faced for almost four years seemed to have been answered as England flew to Colorado to begin altitude training before the first of a cluster of warm-up fixtures prior to facing Portugal in their opening match of the tournament. The England manager was suddenly in possession of the most settled team he'd had since taking over from Greenwood, and it was the mid-1980s rise of Everton he had to thank for that. Pre-tournament, the biggest issue Robson appeared to encounter was setting off without his contingent of four Goodison Park-based players, who were still three days away from playing in the FA Cup Final.

While Liverpool were Everton's opponents, the red half of Merseyside walked on to the lush Wembley turf for the FA Cup Final with only one English-born player in their starting line-up, that being the Republic of Ireland international Mark Lawrenson. There wasn't one Liverpool player in the England squad for the 1986 World Cup. While Sammy Lee and Paul Walsh had England caps to their name collected under the current management, neither was playing on a week-to-week basis at Anfield, thus were nowhere near contention for the squad. Conversely, Steve McMahon had had an impressive first season with Liverpool, but he picked up an injury that ruled him out of the run-in to their double-winning campaign. An unused substitute at the FA Cup Final, he was yet to come into Robson's consideration, but his time with the national team would come.

England's preparations for Mexico seemed less regimented than Northern Ireland's. Beyond South Korea's wonderfully opportunistic request for an informal kickaround, an 11-0 win was procured against the Colorado Air Force, which offered little in the way of lessons, although Hoddle arguably validated his place in the starting line-up with a display that saw Robson compare his style of play to that of Johnny Haynes, an iconic former Fulham team-mate of the England manager.

In a foreboding turn of events, the injury-prone Bryan Robson managed to damage himself when on a gentle mountain walk. Robson the manager fretted about his captain and publicly pondered the hypothetical scenario of the Manchester United midfielder breaking down when the serious work began to kick in. It was as if the England manager could see what was coming, yet he appeared unable to stop himself from attempting to build a team around a player who could fall apart at a moment's notice.

Sedate run-outs against Mexico and Canada resulted in 3-0 and 1-0 wins, respectively, for England, at the Coliseum in Los Angeles and the Swangard Stadium in Burnaby. Beardsley netted his first goal at full international level against Mexico in what Robson felt was the Newcastle United striker's best performance in an England shirt so far, but Hateley averted any prospect of being usurped for his place in the starting line-up against Portugal by scoring twice at the Coliseum, followed by the only goal in Burnaby.

Bryan Robson played against Mexico, and he seemed to survive the experience. He was then wrapped in cotton wool to make sure he was available to face Portugal. Ever the all-action hero, however, the England captain threw himself into one challenge that left him clutching his problematic right shoulder. Portents of doom were noted down by pensive journalists, while disdainful observers who weren't of a Manchester United-centric mind rolled their eyes and dreamed of other possibilities.

In the heat of the Coliseum, milky-white Englishmen rejoiced in the victory, but counted the physical cost of the outing. Sansom lost eight pounds in weight during the match, Wilkins lost five pounds. Massive blisters to the soles of feet and facial wounds sustained from stray Mexican elbows

Bryan Robson sits on the sidelines and watches as his England team-mates take on a US Air Force side, in Colorado Springs in the build-up to the World Cup. His own tournament would be a short-lived one.

Bulgaria's Nasko Sirakov is sent sprawling by Italy's captain, Gaetano Scirea, in the opening game of the tournament. Both nations would progress from Group A but fall in the last 16.

Kim Pyung-seok brings down Diego Maradona. South Korea took a physical approach to their opening game, against Argentina, but stunned everyone with how good they were with the ball at their feet too.

Scotland's Gordon Strachan attempts to keep pace with Denmark's Michael Laudrup, on a wet and humid afternoon at the Estadio Neza 86, where Alex Ferguson's side were unlucky to lose.

The legendary Jock Stein, prior to Scotland's qualifier in Seville, against Spain. Tragically, he would die seven months later, at Ninian Park, in Cardiff, after his side gained a crucial draw with Wales.

The Soviet Union goalkeeper, Rinat Dasayev, commiserates with his overworked opposite number, Hungary's Péter Disztl, after conceding six majestic goals to Valeriy Lobanovskyi's rampant side.

Before their tournament descended into later rancour, Uruguay started out with a promising performance against West Germany, denied a win only by a late equaliser. Antonio Alzamendi duels it out with Harald Schumacher, in Querétaro.

Portugal's Frederico and António Sousa fend off the attentions of Poland's Jan Urban. Having beaten England in their opening game Portugal's campaign began to unravel after a 1-0 defeat, in Monterrey.

A pensive-looking Iraq team line up for the pre-match photos, prior to facing Mexico. Suffering three defeats in three group games, they would have to answer to a demanding head of the Iraqi Football Association, Uday Hussein.

Paraguay's Rogelio Delgardo and César Zabala watch on, as the English referee, George Courtney, brandishes a yellow card at Mexico's superstar striker, Hugo Sánchez.

Gerry Gray, Canada's Glasgow-born midfielder, in pursuit of the Soviet Union's Sergei Rodionov, in Irapuato, during their last group game. Canada's first World Cup, they would lose all three games.

In commanding form at the Estadio Jalisco, in Guadalajara, the legendary Pat Jennings bows out of football within the best company imaginable, against a bewitching Brazil.

Spain's Ramón Calderé, challenges Algeria's Mohamed Kaci-Saïd for the ball, in Monterrey. Four years earlier, Algeria had beaten West Germany, but this time around they couldn't repeat the magical formula.

Gary Lineker pounces to score his second goal, on his way to the hat-trick against Poland, in Monterrey, that completely transforms England's tournament, when on the brink of elimination.

And the holders are out. Yannick Stopyra turns in acclaim of scoring France's second goal, in their last 16 clash with Italy, at Mexico City's Estadio Olímpico Universitario. It is the end of the road for Enzo Bearzot.

The wonderful Mohamed Timoumi, of Morocco, is brought down by Lothar Matthäus, during their cagey last 16 fixture against West Germany, in Monterrey. Franz Beckenbauer's team narrowly edge through.

Andoni Goikoetxea powers home from the penalty spot to put Spain 3-1 up, during their incredible last 16 clash with the talented, yet flawed Denmark. Spain, trailing on the brink of half-time, go on to win 5-1, in Querétaro.

Michel Platini tries to shield the ball from Alemão, during France and Brazil's titanic quarter-final encounter at the Estadio Jalisco. The two teams could only be split in a dramatic penalty shootout.

In their quarter-final, at the Estadio Azteca, England's Terry Butcher tentatively tries to deal with Diego Maradona. Easier said than done, the Argentine scores twice via controversy and artistry.

Michel Platini is denied by Harald Schumacher, as West Germany defeat France in the semi-final at the Estadio Jalisco. The game is a rematch of their iconic clash four years earlier, in Seville.

Diego Maradona leads Belgium a merry dance, as he flashes the ball across a helpless Jean-Marie Pfaff and into the net for his second goal of their semi-final, at the Estadio Azteca.

Jorge Valdano wheels away in celebration, as he rolls the ball past Harald Schumacher to extend Argentina's lead in the final. Game seemingly over, little did anyone expect the drama to come.

Argentina are stunned, as Rudi Völler stoops to head home West Germany's equaliser in the final. Within three minutes, the game turns away from them once again.

From agony to ecstasy, Jorge Burruchaga latches on to a Diego Maradona through ball to win the World Cup Final, with just six minutes remaining. It is an incredible end to a magnificent tournament.

Diego Maradona riding high at the Estadio Azteca with the World Cup, as the celebrations get into full swing. Eight years earlier he had missed the cut for Argentina's squad for the 1978 finals, and this was his redemption.

were also dealt with, while Hodge, the projected understudy to Bryan Robson, was nursing an ankle injury, which was troublesome enough to float the idea that he might be sent home, to be replaced by Arsenal's Stewart Robson.

Burnaby was a more laid-back experience, although it was against Canada that Lineker picked up the wrist injury that required that light cast he wore throughout the World Cup finals. This was the most notable event during a tepid 1-0 victory.

As a final test, a very physical match was played against the Mexican champions, CF Monterrey. No quarter was spared by the hosts and the England manager kept Bryan Robson, Shilton and Lineker out of harm's way, positioning them up in the stands.

Mindful of the negative press that Sir Alf Ramsey and his squad received during the 1970 World Cup, Robson was on the front foot with a charm offensive that was designed to kill the assembled representatives of the media with kindness. Jovial press conferences and training sessions for public viewing were designed to promote openness and fun. An approachable England, as opposed to the abrasive version that was projected 16 years earlier, it also flew in the face of the negative experiences of Argentina and Italy, upon their arrivals in Mexico, which had descended into chaos.

The Estadio Tecnológico in Monterrey was now waiting, but the 1-0 defeat inflicted by Portugal didn't follow the script that Robson or his team had in mind.

Robson selected a predictable line-up to face Portugal, one he repeated three days later at the same venue, against Morocco: Shilton, Stevens, Sansom, Butcher, Fenwick, Robson, Wilkins, Hoddle, Waddle, Hateley and Lineker. It was a safe selection, which played the percentages and took no real risks, apart from those that were gambled on the fragility of the captain.

Beyond the question marks hovering over Bryan Robson, the biggest conundrum concerned England's central defence. Fenwick had looked comfortable in the warm-up matches and had filled in for Butcher, alongside Wright, in each of the last three World Cup qualifiers. Offsetting this, Butcher and Fenwick had only partnered one another on four occasions, and Martin, with greater longevity at international level, was fresh off the back of an excellent season with West Ham United, in which they had been involved in the First Division title race all the way up to the last weekend of the campaign and reached the FA Cup quarter-finals.

Aside from that, deploying Bryan Robson, Wilkins and Hoddle meant that the midfield balance was compromised against strong opponents. Hoddle was being asked to play on the right, when in Steven there was a player available to the England manager who fulfilled that very role for Everton every week. It was a case of square pegs into round holes, a concept that future England managers would also feel compelled to run with.

Accommodating Hoddle was appreciated by fans and the media alike, yet three central midfielders into two didn't really go. A brave decision was required, but Robson wouldn't countenance it, and it was only after the loss of Bryan Robson and Wilkins, beyond the Morocco match, that the puzzle was solved for him.

Against Portugal it had been an uninspiring performance by a team that had been led to believe by its manager that their World Cup task would be a hopeless one if it were to be undertaken without their captain. Prior to the loss of Bryan Robson and Wilkins, a degree of bravado and assertiveness would have been useful. By all means field the captain, but then choose either Wilkins or Hoddle, rather than both, freeing up the right-hand side for Steven or the fielding of two wingers rather than one.

Even had caution been erred upon and Bryan Robson been left on the sidelines against Portugal and Morocco, giving him the time to work on his fitness for the latter stages of the tournament, England had no shortage of midfield talent to compensate for his absence. Wilkins was a player ahead of his time, the purveyor of a perfectly weighted and timed pass. It was no surprise that he was the type of player that appealed to the heavy-hitting clubs of Europe, and he was instrumental in the rehabilitation of AC Milan from Serie B regulars into the all-conquering version of *I Rossoneri*, as powered by Ruud Gullit, Marco van Basten and Frank Rijkaard, towards the tail end of the decade, under Arrigo Sacchi.

There was a cerebral nature to Wilkins that was utterly unique to him among his English peers. In a bid to find a version of his own at Ipswich Town, Robson had signed Arnold Mühren. Like the visionary Dutchman, Wilkins could see all the angles on a football pitch, and he was adept at exploiting them.

Of course, Hoddle had skill in abundance. A dip of the shoulder here, a shift of the hips there, and he was gone. When he was in the mood it isn't outlandish to say he was the most aesthetically gifted English-born footballer of his generation. They were of the same artistic mindset, but totally different in the style with which they displayed a shared ethos. In theory, Wilkins and Hoddle should have been a perfect central-midfield partnership, but Bryan Robson was the alpha male who ensured it was an impossible union.

It's no coincidence that England's fortunes improved at the 1986 World Cup once that power struggle ended. Conversely, the loss of Wilkins, after his sending off against Morocco, was arguably more damaging than the loss of the captain. Wilkins could slow a game down, something that was of huge value in the Mexican heat, and he would have perhaps perfectly suited competing with Diego Maradona later in the tournament. Hoddle was undoubtedly the more skilful of the two, but Wilkins had the greater game intelligence, and his loss was an unconsidered slow puncture to England's hopes of winning the 1986 World Cup. At the point in time of the loss of Wilkins, a player like Gordon Cowans would have been invaluable.

Against Morocco, nothing but an England victory was expected, as that long-serving English sense of entitlement kicked in, accompanied as it was by the continuation of the great and good of football looking down their nose at African nations.

Bryan Robson's World Cup ended in the 40th minute of England's second group match, which again took place in Monterrey. He went to ground heavily in the Moroccan penalty area, towards the left of the goal, in a competitive, yet innocuous challenge for the ball, landing on his right shoulder. It was the third time in under 18 months that he'd dislocated the same shoulder, and it was immediately obvious that he wouldn't kick another ball in Mexico.

The first person to reach the England captain was the Morocco right-back Labid Khalifa, swiftly followed by Wilkins, who tended to his former Manchester United team-mate while he waited for the England physio to arrive on the scene. With the England No. 7 writhing in agony on the turf, Wilkins soon grew frustrated with the slow reaction of Gabriel González, the Paraguayan referee, who belatedly began motioning for a stretcher when medical assistance was a more pressing need, as opposed to transport off the pitch.

Just one minute earlier González had officiously brandished a yellow card at Wilkins, with a dramatic flourish, after a something and nothing tussle with Mohamed Timoumi. Omitting an uncharacteristic irritability, matters would swiftly escalate for Wilkins.

It was a hunched and forlorn Bryan Robson who exited the pitch in vast quantities of pain and under no real illusions that his World Cup was anything other than over. Within seconds of his departure, his midfield partner had joined him in an early end to not only their match but their tournament too. Pulled up for a borderline offside call, Wilkins picked up the ball towards the left-hand touchline and semi-aggressively threw it in the direction of González, with it bouncing off the feet of the official. It was an incident that stemmed from the corner that Bryan Robson won while dislocating his shoulder and it was a farcical passage of play, which represented the culmination of the most calamitous two minutes in England's World Cup history.

Within a split second of throwing the ball, Wilkins knew he was in trouble, as he turned on an equally uncharacteristic burst of speed to retrieve the ball. It was a careless thing to do and the level of frustration that he'd allowed to bubble away seemed to take even him by surprise, yet had clearly been building up way before the injury to Bryan Robson.

By the final whistle, England could count themselves lucky to have held Morocco to a goalless draw, and their campaign was now beginning to tentatively resemble Scotland's ludicrous mission of self-destruction to Argentina in 1978.

Enforced absentees through injury and suspension, respectively, for the final group match against Poland, while Bryan Robson's tournament was definitively over, despite misplaced initial notions that he could yet return, Wilkins would at least be available again once his two-match ban had been completed, just as long as England could turn their fortunes around and still be involved in the competition by the time the quarter-finals came into view.

Away from the drama that surrounded the Morocco match, there were other ponderable issues for manager

Robson to consider in naming his team to face Poland. Waddle, Hoddle and Hateley had all failed to deliver anything in the way of compelling creation, and each had reasonable questions to answer if they were to retain a place in the starting line-up for what was now a win or bust situation over at the Estadio Universitario.

Since Greenwood had taken over as the England manager just as the last of the 1977 summer wine was being poured, England had only taken to the field for a competitive international match without at least one of Bryan Robson or Wilkins in their midfield on four occasions, this from a span of 44 meaningful fixtures in either the qualifiers or the finals of a major tournament. Robson was now facing up to naming a line-up for what could quite feasibly be his last match in charge of the national team without being able to call on the services of either of those two long-standing mainstays of the England midfield. A new plan was required.

There's an infamous photo of a contemplative England manager standing on the balcony of his hotel room in Saltillo, England's remote base in the Sierra Madre mountains. He's looking into the ether, elbows planted on the balcony rail, hands comfortingly clasped to the sides of his head, covering his ears from the World Cup almost. Robson strikes the image of a man with the weight of a nation resting on his shoulders, a man in deep concentration, thoughtful, distant, maybe even a little bit resigned to a cursed fate.

It was a photo that found its way into countless publications. It represented a man under intense pressure, unable to break the spell of his mounting problems. When pressed later about what was going through his head at the time the photo was taken, Robson was more than happy to inform an expectant press pack that he'd simply been listening to his Walkman. It was a rare light-hearted moment, and a few of the dark clouds that were following the England squad began to drift away.

Despite the loss of his two senior central midfielders, Robson did have multiple options at his disposal when it came to choosing a team to face Poland. Hodge was the obvious choice to replace Bryan Robson, having won his place in the squad ahead of Bracewell due to his adaptability, combative nature and suitability as an understudy for the Manchester United man. Hodge had been the player thrown on as a substitute against Morocco as the England captain was guided away, but in terms of making a straight switch, the other alternatives were Reid, and the Tottenham variety of Stevens.

What came was a complete overhaul of Robson's midfield, however, as Waddle dropped down to the bench and Hoddle finally got a central role, where he was to be partnered by Reid. Taking up the right-hand side was Steven, while Hodge was moved across to the left, albeit with a roving remit. On such excursions, Beardsley would drop in to cover, having come in to replace Hateley.

Whether through an accidental revolution or not, the balance and expansion due to unforeseen circumstances saw the new England tear into Poland with a wonderfully destructive intent. Lineker was the chief profiteer, as he claimed himself a rapid-fire first-half hat-trick, while Hodge had one disallowed during a 25-minute span of the first half where England looked likely to score every time they went forward.

It could have been a very different scenario, however, had Zbigniew Boniek taken a golden opportunity that came his way after Fenwick carelessly gave the ball away in the middle of the pitch, resulting in Włodzimierz Smolarek playing a beautiful through ball for the Polish captain to run on to. A goal for Poland at this stage might have dented the growing confidence of Robson's rejigged team.

For those on the outside looking in, it had to make for a sweet-and-sour experience. England had been backed into a corner and they had come out fighting. Those on the pitch responsible for the upturn in fortunes of an England team that had previously looked incapable of inspiration wouldn't be relinquishing their places in the team now. At least not without a good reason.

As it was, Fenwick came up with such a reason after picking up a second yellow card in the group stages, so he would be forced to sit out the last-16 match against Paraguay at the Azteca Stadium in Mexico City, opening the door for Martin.

Against Poland, it was a performance that made a lethargic nation sit up and take notice. The inclusion of Beardsley had been a universally popular one and it had paid off. A new strike partnership had been born – and leaving the Estadio Tecnológico behind, the scene of the disastrous performances against Portugal and Morocco – had seemed to lift a weight from collective shoulders in the England camp. There had been an overriding sense of national foreboding going into the match. Poland, 13 years on from that infamous evening at Wembley when they spirited away a place at the 1974 World Cup finals, had been on the brink of knocking England out of a World Cup all over again, but now the curse was broken and England's fate was now their own business.

So much had been made of the importance of the presence, or non-presence as the case turned out to be, of Bryan Robson that in some quarters a win was completely unexpected. The England captain was undeniably a spectacular footballer, but the concept of trying to build a team around a player with such a tenuous grasp of fitness was badly flawed. It was also a concept that jarred with the way Robson the club manager had been viewed. His Ipswich

Town was very much a team, where the right components had been pulled together to form a balanced collective. Yes, he could boast a dominant player such as John Wark, but it was never a situation where one individual was feted to such an extent that it could arguably have alienated the rest of the squad.

At its most pronounced, England's capability to function without their captain was classed as non-existent. To players such as Hoddle, Wilkins, Waddle, Barnes, Hodge, Reid and Steven, it must have antagonised on one level or another. Not antagonised by Bryan Robson himself, or even by the hype that surrounded him, but the perceived wisdom of thought that nobody else could carry England forward other than him.

England's squad was inhabited by a set of very good players but forming them into a fluid team was far from simple. Dispossessed of the kitchen-sink drama that was the perpetual will he/won't he be fit question, once the distraction of Bryan Robson was settled once and for all, the Bobby Robson of Ipswich Town began to reappear, almost as a mirage in the hazy shimmer of the intense Mexican heat.

The England that faced Poland, Paraguay and eventually Argentina should have been in operation from the very beginning of the tournament. Leaving Monterrey behind, Robson and his players headed off to Mexico City with a spring in their step.

Again, just as against Poland, there was a nervousness to England in the early exchanges of the match against Paraguay. This time it was Butcher who threatened to give their opponents an early lead. Again, just as against Poland, central-defensive focus was sharper after that early scare had passed.

After that early scare, this was certainly England's best performance of the tournament. Whereas the first half against Poland had been a display of shock and awe, the performance against Paraguay was much more measured, confident and commanding. Against Poland it had been a desperate bludgeoning by a team fighting for its life, yet against Paraguay there was an enjoyment of football on display, an easing of the shoulders to go with the improved freedom of movement that had sprung forth against Poland. This was the eye of England's 1986 World Cup storm.

Lineker struck twice more against Paraguay, while Beardsley netted the other. In a World Cup that provoked some spectacular goals from outside the penalty area, thanks to a heady combination of the laws of high altitude and the outrageous skills on show, it's telling that all seven of England's goals in Mexico were scored in and around the six-yard box. Despite being in possession of several players who could produce something special from outside the penalty area, England proved it was unashamedly a nation of goalhangers.

There had been a strange mix of respect and thuggery towards England from Paraguay, as studs were up at times and elbows deployed at angles that could take an eye out. Indeed, when Beardsley was busy putting England 2-0 up, Lineker was off the pitch receiving treatment for an off-the-ball incident after a Paraguayan elbow had contacted his face.

Conversely, Cayetano Ré, the Paraguay coach, had made respectful noises during the build-up to the match about how huge an occasion it was for his nation, even declaring in *The Times* that it would be an honour to fall to the team that represents the cradle of football.

Momentum was everything, and England suddenly had plenty of it, having scored six goals in two matches without reply. Reid had played through the pain barrier against Paraguay for 58 minutes, exiting after England went 2-0 up, making him the biggest fitness doubt for the quarter-final against Argentina. Robson's decision was to stick or twist, while Fenwick and Wilkins were back from suspension.

The safest thing for Robson was to stick to a winning formula, and he knew it. It was in effect a way of playing the percentages in a situation he now had little control over. Reid was deemed fit enough to play, but a bolder option would have been to deploy the returning Wilkins, or even Tottenham's Stevens, who had played for over half an hour against Paraguay in place of the ailing Reid. Stevens could have been used as a man-marker on Maradona, while the bolder and the more controversial step would have been to field the returning Wilkins, who would have been eager to redress his foolishness against Morocco.

Of course, this would have tested the abilities of Wilkins and Hoddle to perform at a high standard together. In the event, the only change made was that of Fenwick replacing Martin alongside Butcher.

As discussed earlier in this book, Diego Maradona scored two goals at the Estadio Azteca in the World Cup quarter-final against England. Regardless of the moral and aesthetic manner of those goals, Argentina deserved to be in possession of a two-goal lead as the match approached the final 20 minutes. They were the better team by a comfortable margin.

As England hit the ball into the channels to be chased, Argentina played the short ball, conserving energy with as minimal excessive movement as possible. They positioned themselves in clusters, responsible for defined zones of the pitch, letting the ball do as much of the work as possible. In response, England sat back and played it long for three or four players to repetitively chase after. This approach fatigued the runners and put increased long-term pressure on those who remained static.

From the very start of the second half, it was clear that England had begun to visibly shrink, while Argentina were circling for the kill. Robson's players were skating on thin ice and Argentinian goals were inevitable. Even Hoddle had been drawn into the general Little Englander approach that his team was taking, and he was stood blinking into the thinnest of air after Maradona shot past him in the build-up to the first goal.

It's here where Wilkins's greater game intelligence might have given England a better chance, as there seemed to be little in the way of a bespoke approach to the dangers that Argentina posed. In a match where they seemed to want to let Argentina worry about them, rather than take the responsibility of stopping their opponents, there was only going to be one winner, and it wasn't the team in the uninspiring mid-1980s Umbro kit.

Argentina undeniably underestimated England's ability to mount a serious fightback from 2-0 down. With only caution left, Robson promptly threw it to the wind, and he introduced Waddle and Barnes. While the former continued to blow cold, the latter offered a cameo role that shamed his manager for restricting his entire 1986 World Cup participation to just 16 minutes. With just under ten minutes remaining, Barnes conjured England an unlikely way back into the match when producing the first piece of genuine skill of the quarter-final for his team. Lineker was on the end of it and Argentina began to worry, especially after Carlos Daniel Tapia only managed to strike the inside of Shilton's right-hand post just seconds after England had drawn back to within a one-goal deficit.

Then came the chance. Another piece of brilliance from Barnes and another opportunity for Lineker, who predictably found the back of the net, the problem being that it was his body that rolled over the line rather than the ball, after what appeared to be an impossible goal-line clearance.

And then, it was all over.

Having struggled to find their stride against Portugal and Morocco, England had responded brilliantly when backed into a corner against Poland, and this engendered a feel-good factor that helped them roll past Paraguay and onward to their date with destiny against Argentina. Once there, they arguably froze once again in the quarter-final, until they responded positively when finding themselves backed into another corner again at 2-0 down.

As spirited as their late flourish was against Argentina, ultimately England ran out of time, and all these years later it's still difficult to decipher whether the 1986 World Cup was a success or a failure for them. I suppose it was a little of both.

Of course, there's the classic question of what if? What if that late Lineker opportunity had found its way into the net? At 2-2, going into the final stages of the 90 minutes, or even onward to extra time, would we have been looking at something akin to England throwing away a 2-0 lead at the 1970 World Cup in the quarter-final against West Germany, except in reverse? Alternatively, in the final, Argentina would throw away a 2-0 lead, only to redeem themselves with a winning goal. They certainly had the spirit, the skill and the motivation to survive the England fightback.

England weren't the better team against Argentina, but the better team doesn't always win at football, as there are so many more variables at play. Had they gone on to face Belgium in the semi-final, what would the outcome have been? Lineker injured himself when going for that late chance and he's on record as saying he wouldn't have been fit to play in a hypothetical semi-final. What would Bobby Robson have done without Lineker? A return of the physical presence of Hateley? A chance for Dixon? Barnes through the middle? The clamour for Barnes to have played in the semi-final, had he assisted in a complete turnaround in the result against Argentina, would have been hard to resist, yet could England have coped centrally in the heat of Mexico City when opting for a stretched midfield? We'll never know, as the doors slid in another direction.

This was an England team that arguably went out of the 1986 World Cup where they deserved to. In the main, since the 1966 World Cup, when England have managed to qualify for the finals of a major tournament, they've usually gone out where they deserved to. There has been a natural conclusion at play. Mexico was no different to what had come before, nor to what would follow.

The stock of some England players went up due to the 1986 World Cup, while for others it went down. Wilkins never recovered from the experience in terms of his international career. He won only two more caps beyond his sending off against Morocco, his last international appearance coming that November against Yugoslavia. Fenwick, the occasional pantomime villain of the England team, was soon gone too, while Hateley went from England's number-one striker to a bit-part role. Reid drifted to the periphery, while Martin won only one more cap.

Those who came away from Mexico in a better position were Lineker, who blew away all pre-tournament doubts about having enough quality for the international stage, plus Beardsley, who found a near telepathic link with him. Barnes left the audience wanting more, while Bryan Robson maintained his position as a vulnerable national treasure.

England's manager was awarded a four-year contract extension by the FA, and he set out to add a little bit of expansion to his team. Robson's England qualified for the 1988 European Championship with a degree of style, only to capitulate upon their arrival at the finals. Then came the 1990 World Cup and another tournament where England's fortunes fluctuated in the group stages, before gaining momentum, at times riding their luck along the way.

With a great deal of talent at his disposal during his time in charge, Robson's legacy as England manager is one of unfulfilled potential, of lacking that little bit of bravado and stubbornness that can make all the difference between a quarter-final or semi-final being upgraded for a final. Yet, it could also be suggested that he overachieved rather than underachieved, given the teams and players that did win the tournaments he took England to.

Either way, England's fortunes dipped dramatically beyond Robson's departure as manager, to the point that they failed to qualify for the 1994 World Cup. This was something that would have been unimaginable under Robson's guidance, but his own personal well-being was probably better served by moving on to new challenges.

Chapter Ten

Sweet Last Sixteen?

THE LAST time a World Cup had broken into a straight knockout bun fight of 16 nations was back in 1938 in France. Of course, there were no group stages prior to this round in 1938, and despite the grumblings of discontent over four third-placed teams progressing beyond the group stages, the return of an extensive knockout stage for the first time in 16 years was very welcome. No second chances, this was sink or swim territory, and while some of the nations to tumble out of the 1986 World Cup at the last 16 were happily waved off, the departure of others was deeply mourned.

It's fair to say that not many tears were shed for Uruguay, Bulgaria, Paraguay and Poland when their World Cups came to an end at the first knockout hurdle, while on the other hand, Morocco had won many admirers, Italy are always value for money and Denmark and the Soviet Union's exits were massive blows for burgeoning football hipsters everywhere.

For Uruguay and Bulgaria, the gig being up as soon as possible was the only natural acceptable conclusion, given that they had both reached the knockout stages with a record of two draws and one defeat. In the case of Bulgaria, it wasn't just that they hadn't managed to pick up a win in these World Cup finals, it was also that they had never won a match at any of the four previous World Cup finals tournaments they had taken part in either. They simply had no right to be there. At least Uruguay could point to an illustrious history that not many nations had bettered.

Eight years away from their finest hour and their magical run to the semi-finals of the 1994 World Cup, the 1986 Bulgarian vintage remains a misunderstood one. They were led by Ivan Vutsov, a successful coach at Levski Sofia, and as a defender a member of Bulgaria's squad at the 1966 World Cup. Just being in Mexico was an incredible achievement for a team that hadn't reached the finals of a major tournament for 12 years and had dragged their way through a qualification group that included France, East Germany and Yugoslavia.

While the European champions France were the obvious favourites in Group 4, Bulgaria hadn't been expected to threaten Yugoslavia and East Germany in the battle for the second ticket to Mexico. Yugoslavia were fresh off the back of qualifying for both the 1982 World Cup and the 1984 European Championship finals, and while they fell at the group stages of both tournaments, they were the team with all the experience. Meanwhile, East Germany's last and only major international tournament had been the last one that Bulgaria had qualified for, the 1974 World Cup. Despite their failure to reach another, they had remained a feared presence in their various qualifying campaigns and had even blown qualification for the 1980 European Championship when on the brink of reaching those finals at the expense of the Netherlands.

Beginning their bid for qualification with a draw and a loss in Belgrade and Paris, respectively, didn't augur well for Bulgaria, and even when they closed out 1984 by inflicting the group makeweights, Luxembourg, with their heaviest defeat of the qualifiers, it wouldn't have been viewed as a statement of intent by their rivals. Even Bulgaria's supporters were low on enthusiasm, as only 15,000 spectators had bothered to tip up at the Vasil Levski National Stadium, a venue that could comfortably house four times that amount.

As 1985 swung into action, Bulgaria had five matches remaining, but by the time they welcomed East Germany to Sofia, both France and Yugoslavia had picked up three more points each, and as the match ticked towards the 87th minute the Bulgarian cause appeared to be a hopeless one. But a deflected free kick changed everything. With the match meandering towards a goalless draw that would do neither side any favours, a choreographed set-piece routine unfolded. Not exactly going to plan, Stoycho Mladenov's effort took a heavy deviation off the heels of one of his own team-mates, who was positioned at the end of the East German wall, totally wrongfooting the Lokomotive Leipzig goalkeeper, René Müller.

As the ball bounced towards the bottom right-hand corner of Müller's net, a magnificent Ealing farce of a chase to stop it erupted, as goalkeeper and defenders alike just failed to get there on time, while Bulgaria's players willed it over the line. Wild celebrations broke out, and as game-changers go, this one moment proved to be the ignition point for a team who would have qualification for Mexico already assured by the time the return match took place in Karl-Marx-Stadt seven months later.

Bulgaria went on to win their next three matches, defeating France and Yugoslavia within a month of one another in Sofia at the end of the 1984/85 season, before a September victory away to Luxembourg. France had been undone by a combination of set-piece situations and the volatile atmosphere, conceding twice from corners to the towering Georgi Dimitrov and the prolific Nasko Sirakov, while Yugoslavia had wilted to a wonderful free kick and a fine piece of penalty-area opportunism from the spectacular Plamen Getov.

These were results that were complemented by France picking up another loss in Leipzig against East Germany, while Yugoslavia contrived to lose their last three qualifiers. It was a combination of events that meant Bulgaria now sat at the top of the group, as Yugoslavia prepared to entertain East Germany just three days after Bulgaria's victory in Luxembourg.

Belatedly, East Germany had played themselves into contention for qualification, and an Andreas Thom-inspired performance led them to a 2-1 win at the JNA Stadium in Belgrade. It was a result that put immense pressure on France to win their last two fixtures, which they ultimately did, but it was also a result that clinched Bulgaria their place at the 1986 World Cup finals with a match to spare, that being their visit to East Germany. It had been a stunning turnaround in fortunes, and Bulgaria getting their trips to Belgrade and Paris out of the way at the start of the qualification campaign had proved to be an astute gamble.

Qualification celebrations having been long and loud, Bulgaria then observed something of a hangover period that included losing that last, now insignificant, qualifier, away to East Germany, followed by friendly losses either side of Christmas in Valencia, against Spain, and again to East Germany, when on an acclimatisation mission to Querétaro in February. Their travails in Mexico didn't end there, as they also slipped to a 1-0 defeat against Club Puebla, although they then took their frustrations out on a local junior team, winning 14-0. Ten days beyond the loss to East Germany, Bulgaria were in Rabat for a goalless draw against Morocco.

While the technical organisation was one of the most advanced of any nation heading to the 1986 World Cup, the results were a concern. As way of a confidence booster, Bulgaria ran four goals past a Romanian B team at the Stadion Ivaylo in Veliko Tarnovo at the beginning of March. It was a result that blew away the cobwebs, and across a three-week span in April, Bulgaria played a trio of fixtures, Sofia encounters against Denmark and North Korea bookending a trip to Brussels to face Belgium.

Bulgaria shockingly tore a strong Denmark line-up apart, 3-0, with a hypnotic second-half power play, before being beaten in Belgium, 2-0. A clever booking, in preparation to facing South Korea in Mexico, North Korea were overcome, 3-0, with all the goals coming in the first half.

When Bulgaria set off for Mexico, they couldn't have been more prepared. This very concept had seemed impossible a year earlier, not only due to their sluggish start to qualifying, but also because of a spectacular self-destruction both on the pitch and within the corridors of Bulgarian football power. Violent indiscipline had erupted at the 1985 Bulgarian Cup Final, a match that was played out two and a half weeks after Bulgaria's crucial World Cup qualifying victory over Yugoslavia, two matches that took place in the very same stadium.

A tinderbox relationship already simmering between the two teams, CSKA Sofia defeated Levski Sofia 2-1 on a day when any modicum of control was fleeting, be that the control of the referee, the players, those on the touchline or on the terraces. Georgi Slavkov opened the scoring for CSKA, but before the ball had even hit the back of the net there were Levski protests of handball. Defiant CSKA celebrations were the backdrop to the Levski players surrounding the referee, an under-siege Asparuh Yasenov.

Early in the second half, Iliya Voynov struck a beautiful free kick to extend CSKA's lead. It had looked a clear foul on the edge of the Levski penalty area, but within a growing sense of a wider perceived injustice, their players had again swamped the referee in protest.

Kept in the match by the wonderful goalkeeping of Borislav Mihaylov, Levski were fortunate not to fall further behind, and when it appeared that CSKA had won themselves a penalty by unfair means, the Levski No. 1 took his protests too far, repeatedly pushing and shoving the referee. Despite the injustice of the situation, Mihaylov was lucky not to be flashed a red card, and he added further fuel by saving Slavkov's spot kick.

The incendiary nature of the match would only escalate from there, and when CSKA's Kostadin Yanchev ruthlessly brought down Levski's Emil Spasov, the victim of the crude challenge opted to wrap his hands around the throat of his aggressor, which only prompted a 19-year-old Hristo Stoichkov to react on behalf of his CSKA team-mate. As a result, another mass brawl broke out and, once contained, Yanchev and Spasov were sent off, this after Levski's Plamen Nikolov had already received a red card.

Perhaps feeling he had to redress the balance, Yasenov then awarded Levski a penalty for the most blatant of dives by Sirakov, which he got to his feet and converted, although Krasimir Dossev, the Levski goalkeeper, came desperately close to keeping it out.

No shortage of further acrimony, but no further goals added, upon the full-time whistle Mihaylov ran half the length of the pitch to accost the referee once again. As passions continued to run high, the police had to get involved and the battle continued in the tunnel, where Yasenov's ribs were damaged, as was CSKA's trophy.

Recriminations were swift and far-reaching, with Mihaylov one of five players handed out initial lifetime or significant bans, inclusive of the teenage Stoichkov, whose sanction was essentially early national service. The clubs themselves were rebranded and stripped of their trophies, Levski having won the league title. In 1989, all punishments, both individual and collective, were quashed, while players of importance to the national team were reprieved long before the World Cup rolled around, the two teams supplying eight players to the Bulgaria squad.

It wasn't only on the pitch that Bulgarian football was consuming itself either, as the former president of the Bulgarian Football Union, Dimitar Nikolov, had been imprisoned, along with a couple of his leading officials, for sentences that ranged between 7 and 18 years for their parts in financial impropriety.

With no let-up in the uproarious way Bulgaria were heading towards their first World Cup since 1974, their head coach, Yutsov, had also had to work on taking the sting out of the physical side of his team's game. Startlingly, during their win over Yugoslavia in qualifying, there had been 92 fouls awarded by the referee.

None of this chaos sat naturally with the levels of organisation Bulgaria had displayed in their preparations for Mexico, and it made them one of the most interesting prospects going into the tournament, something that was only boosted when they procured themselves an 85th-minute equaliser in the very opening match, against the reigning holders, Italy, at the Estadio Azteca.

Sirakov, he of the massively unconvincing dive in the 1985 Bulgarian Cup Final, was the hero, cancelling out Alessandro Altobelli's volleyed opening goal. For 30 minutes, straddling either side of half-time, Italy were fluid and dangerous in a way that suggested they might just be in with a decent chance of retaining the World Cup. They didn't make the most of their domination, however, and Bulgaria punished Enzo Bearzot's team, Sirakov's downward header bouncing beyond the grasp of Giovanni Galli and shocking everyone involved, inclusive of the goalscorer, who set off on his own personal lap of honour.

A huge bonus of a result, Bulgaria were set up perfectly to face South Korea, where their expected victory would be a virtual guarantee of progression to the knockout stages. Kim Jong-boo had other ideas, though, and when he levelled off Plamen Getov's goal, Bulgaria were delivered a dose of the same medicine that they had administered to Italy.

Two matches, two draws, no team should go into their last group match in a major international tournament safe within the knowledge that if they don't concede half a dozen goals or so, they will be heading through to the knockout stages.

Due to results 24 hours earlier, this was the situation, however, and with Argentina already through, the two teams played out a human game of Subbuteo. Neither overly insistent on ploughing forward, Argentina's goals came via two rare thrusts of attacking intent – Jorge Valdano in the fourth minute, and Jorge Burruchaga with 13 minutes to play. Given the lack of peril for Bulgaria, this was a free swing for them, and it was a shame that they didn't take it.

It meant that Bulgaria would return to the Estadio Azteca, to be brushed aside by the hosts, where the first of the two goals they conceded would be Manuel Negrete's iconic scissor-kick. Technically adept, Bulgaria seemed to dare Mexico to do their worst, sticking their chin out and beckoning them to take a swing, and what a swing it was when it came, from opponents that were deploying a very progressive 3-4-3 formation that constricted to 3-6-1 when feeling under threat.

And under threat Mexico were at times, as Bulgaria struck with speed on the counter-attack, only to be woefully profligate when their chances did arise. It was a pattern of play that was repeated in the second half, making for a fascinating clash of styles, on a day when Mexico were playing their best football of the tournament.

As the match wore on, Bulgaria were becoming more and more intent to shoot from distance, only to be wayward with their efforts. Just beyond the hour, Raúl Servín headed home Mexico's second goal, from a Negrete corner, and the task for Vutsov and his players was increasingly insurmountable.

This was Bulgaria's 16th World Cup finals fixture and once more they had failed to come up with a victory. Another team arguably undone by that lack of a little self-belief, their exit from the tournament wasn't down to any shortfall in ability. They were certainly not underprepared or lacking in passion, and eight years later proved what they were truly capable of.

Just 24 hours later, at the Estadio Jalisco in Guadalajara, another Eastern European team bade farewell to the 1986 World Cup, a third in succession from behind the Iron Curtain to topple out of the tournament, and the last one standing.

Poland, named among the top seeds in the draw, never really recovered from the first half of their final group match against England. A goalless draw against Morocco, and a 1-0 victory against Portugal, three points accumulated and two clean sheets achieved. This might not have been a Poland team that could match the more stylish vintages of 1974, 1978 and 1982, but they did deal in an impressive sideline of stubborn pragmatism, which only served to make their ultimate capitulation so much more surprising.

In qualification, Poland finished top of UEFA qualifying Group 1, ahead of the eventual World Cup semi-finalists, Belgium, where they were joined by Albania and Greece. A dream draw, given that second place would lead to a play-off, it was going to be a difficult task for the two experienced campaigners to finish outside the top two.

By the end of May 1985, five months before the last qualification ball was kicked in anger in Group 1, Poland and Belgium had already been assured of finishing in the top two positions. The magnificent Zbigniew Boniek had scored the only goal when his nation had made the trip to Tirana to face Albania.

When Poland then welcomed Belgium to Chorzów, in September, all they needed to do was to avoid defeat to qualify automatically. A goalless draw saw them over the finish line in a group that had been low on drama and goals. In their six matches Poland had scored just ten times, despite there being two perceived minnows in the group. This was still three more goals than Belgium had managed. It was within this meagre spirit that Poland navigated their opening two matches of the 1986 World Cup.

Heading into the tournament, Poland's head coach had something of a misleading record. Antoni Piechniczek had been in the job since 1981 and had been in charge when they had reached the semi-finals of the 1982 World Cup, yet across all 50 matches he'd overseen, he'd won just 21. However, while friendlies had often been a bit of a blind spot, Piechniczek's Poland had a very healthy habit of winning the big matches. This meant that their build-up to Mexico was highly inconsistent, and even when taking on a couple of friendlies prior to the decisive qualifier against Belgium, Poland had lost to Sweden in Malmö, and to Czechoslovakia in Brno, matches where Piechniczek had named experimental line-ups.

Beyond confirming their qualification for the World Cup, Poland set out on a six-game warm-up campaign, where they won just once, drawing twice and losing three times. True to their penchant for excelling in the bigger matches, the one victory they did gain was against Italy.

As Poland staggered forth from their loss to England and to the Estadio Jalisco in Guadalajara for their last-16 fixture, their opponents couldn't have been any bigger, as they were handed a date with destiny against the three-times winners, Brazil.

Not exactly brimming with confidence, a flight home was already booked for the Polish squad before they took to the pitch at the Jalisco, while Piechniczek dealt with internal disciplinary issues by leaving five members of his squad back at the team hotel, inclusive of the talented midfielder, Andrzej Buncol, his second-choice goalkeeper, Józef Wandzik, and the future Aston Villa and Sunderland right-back, Dariusz Kubicki.

Both Piechniczek and his captain, Boniek, were honest in their pre-match assessments, ceding that Brazil were better than they were, both physically and mentally, but tempering those concessions with the warning that anything was still possible in knockout football.

In many respects, this was a Poland team that shouldn't have laboured for goals. On average, going into the tournament, Boniek had scored almost one goal in every three matches at international level from midfield, while his old Widzew Łódź team-mate, Włodzimierz Smolarek, was a consistent contributor, and the future Celtic striker, Dariusz Dziekanowski, was viewed by some as a player with the potential to surpass the achievements of Boniek. They worked beautifully as a triumvirate but were shackled by a largely defensive system.

Admirably, Poland flew at Brazil from the off, deciding that if they were to have any chance of remaining in the 1986 World Cup, then unbalancing their opponents was their best bet. In the early exchanges, a ball into the Brazil penalty area from Ryszard Tarasiewicz managed to evade players of both teams and strike the post, causing a frantic scramble before Smolarek chipped the ball into the grasp of the wide-eyed Carlos.

Encouraged, Poland continued to stress-test Brazilian nerves, and Jan Karaś crashed a shot against the underside of Carlos's crossbar, only to see the ball spirited away to safety. Dziekanowski was also a regular threat, and difficult to contain. Yet, after 30 productive minutes in which Poland failed to make the most of the string of chances they created, Brazil punished them, when Sócrates coolly converted from the penalty spot with a two-step run-up, after Tarasiewicz had carelessly brought down Careca.

Poland managed to get through to half-time without any more mistakes, but the match was to run away from them in the second half, as first Josimar produced another piece of explosive magic to put alongside his goal against Northern Ireland, and then Edinho made it three with a beautifully crafted goal, thanks to a heavy assist from Careca, to produce one of the finest goals of the tournament. Careca then went on to help himself to a penalty of his own for the fourth, as Polish frustration really took hold.

A 4-0 scoreline that wasn't entirely one-way traffic, Poland had their chances throughout the second half, none better than Boniek's bicycle-kick that went just wide. On another day, Piechniczek's team might well have scored four of their own.

With defeat now inevitable, Piechniczek bowed to sentimentality, and with Careca having just scored Brazil's fourth, the veteran sweeper, Władysław Żmuda, was thrown on for the final seven minutes to enable him to play in a fourth World Cup and to equal Uwe Seeler's record number of World Cup finals appearances.

Heavy margin of defeat it might have been, but Poland didn't disgrace themselves against Brazil, and conceding seven goals without reply across the stretch of their last two matches at the 1986 World Cup finals wasn't representative of a team that could defend. Only one goal scored by them across their four matches in Mexico was damning though, especially for a team with some talented attacking options.

Another era ending, it would be 16 years before Poland again graced the finals of a major tournament, when reaching the 2002 World Cup, going on to qualify for another two since then, along with three European Championships, powered by the rise of Robert Lewandowski in more contemporary times. Throughout this rebirth, the new Poland have struggled to live up to the standards of the old Poland, failing to emerge from the group stages of all but the 2016 European Championship finals, where they rolled back the years to reach the quarter-finals.

In 1986, however, Poland unwittingly marked the end of a glorious chapter in which they had finished third at the 1974 World Cup, and repeated the feat eight years later in Spain. While never matching the squads that had preceded them, nobody could have guessed that it would be over a decade and a half before Poland ventured into another World Cup.

Eastern Europe wasn't alone in having multiple fallers in the last 16. For all the World Cup familiarity that came with Uruguay, Paraguay brought an equal amount of unfamiliarity. Uruguay might not have qualified for a World Cup since 1974, but this was a nation that had twice won the tournament and were beaten semi-finalists the last time it had taken place in Mexico, just 16 years earlier.

Uruguay might fluff their qualification lines from time to time, but they were very much a part of the World Cup furniture and their return for the 1986 finals was a welcome one. Paraguay, meanwhile, were a mystery, a team with a name that sounded like Uruguay's, just without any of the iconic imagery that springs to mind when it came to their more illustrious South American cousins.

Paraguay hadn't qualified for a World Cup since 1958, which had been the only one in which they had successfully navigated a qualifying campaign to reach, as their other two appearances, in 1930 and 1950, had been by invitation. Beyond the South American staples of Brazil, Uruguay and Argentina, since Colombia had competed in the 1962 World Cup, the only other nations to qualify from CONMEBOL prior to Paraguay's surprise participation in 1986 had been Chile and Peru.

Across a five-tournament span from 1966 to 1982, it had very much been a closed shop when it came to clinching World Cup places for South America nations. Brazil were obviously as omnipresent a figure as ever, while Argentina were only absent for 1970. Uruguay had taken part in 1966, 1970 and 1974. Chile had qualified in 1966, 1974 and 1982, while Peru had been part of the 1970, 1978 and 1982 World Cups. So, Paraguay's appearance in Mexico in the summer of 1986 came as something of a culture shock, yet they would prove to be an inspiration to other marginalised South American nations, as they also kicked in the door for Colombia and Bolivia, who would qualify for the World Cups to follow.

Not the South American qualifying format that we've all become familiar with for the last quarter of a century, for the 1986 World Cup, CONMEBOL still operated with a system of three separate groups, with the winner of each qualifying automatically for the finals. One group of four teams and two of three teams, with fixtures played on a familiar home and away basis within the traditional round-robin format. With four qualification berths up for grabs, this meant a further round of play-offs, which encompassed the three group runners-up, plus the third-placed nation from the four-team Group 1.

To get to this point, a lot of football had been played just to eliminate the three weakest nations, as Bolivia, Ecuador and Venezuela all left the stage having been predictably vanquished, while Brazil, Argentina and Uruguay were able to put their feet up and crack open the popcorn. Peru and Chile were the obvious contenders in what would effectively be two two-legged semi-finals, followed by a two-legged final, to condense four teams into one qualifier.

In Group 1, Peru had come to within nine minutes of qualifying automatically at the expense of Argentina, having beaten them in Lima and having led them in Buenos Aires in the decisive last match of the group. Colombia had been the sticking point for Peru, taking only one point from their two matches against the deposed hosts, who followed them through to the play-offs in third place.

Group 2 had offered another dramatic and decisive final group match, where Uruguay had needed a victory against Chile in Montevideo to top the group, which they narrowly achieved at the iconic Estadio Centenario. Chile's carelessness had come in their opening group match when held to a draw in Ecuador.

Less considered was Group 3, where Brazil cruised through with a match to spare, despite drawing both of their home fixtures. A spirited 1-1 draw for Paraguay at the Maracanã in front of almost 140,000 spectators was enough to secure them their play-off spot, albeit from a group where they won just one of their four fixtures.

An unseeded draw for the play-offs, when Chile and Peru were paired together, it seemed set to be the de facto final, as the makeweights of Paraguay and Colombia went head to head in the other side of the draw.

While Chile and Peru duked it out in Santiago during a wonderful first leg, the home team emerging with a 4-2 victory, 24 hours earlier Paraguay had proved too strong for

Colombia in Asunción, when the attacking intent of Ramón Hicks, Romerito and Roberto Cabañas had proved too much for the Colombian defence to contain.

Paraguay saw the job through in Cali a week later when slipping to a 2-1 defeat, although having struck first, thanks to a Buenaventura Ferreira strike just before the hour. On the same day, in Lima, a strangely subdued Peru dropped out of the reckoning when beaten 1-0 by Chile.

No time to draw breath, the first leg of the final play-off came just seven days later, and given that Chile had only lost one of their previous ten matches against Paraguay, their hopes would have been high when travelling to Asunción.

A tale of the unexpected, however, Paraguay stunned Chile, as they streaked to a convincing 3-0 victory, striking twice via a near-post flick-on at set pieces, through Cabañas and the captain, Rogelio Delgado, the first with only nine minutes having elapsed, the second within seconds of the restart. Rounding off the scoring, Lizardo Garrido contrived to score a horrendous own goal with just five minutes remaining.

A week later, Paraguay passed their test of nerve in Santiago, as having conceded as early as the 13th minute to an opportunistic Hugo Rubio, goals from the unexpected source of Vladimiro Schettina and the highly expected Romerito handed a disbelieving Paraguay the half-time lead, and a 5-1 aggregate advantage with only 45 minutes to play.

With Paraguay's first goal benefiting from more Chilean defensive chaos via a set piece, for the second, Romerito was sent clean through on goal to roll the ball past the exposed Roberto Rojas. It was completely against the run of play, as the home team were drawn forward in their attempts to breach what was at times a seven-man Paraguayan back line.

Too much to fight back from, Jorge Muñoz's second-half goal for Chile was too little, too late, coming as it did with only ten minutes remaining. Paraguay's presence in the play-off might have been an initial surprise, but the outcome once they were there was a very one-sided shock.

Heading into World Cup year, Paraguay had the most exhaustive build-up to the tournament of any of the nations on their way to Mexico. Prior to the big kick-off, they took part in ten fixtures, encompassing invitationals to the Miami Cup, the Hong Kong Tournament and the Chinese New Year Cup, followed by a five-match tour of Indonesia, Qatar, Bahrain and Saudi Arabia, as part of their extensive preparations for facing Iraq in their opening match in Mexico. Overkill it might have been, but Paraguay's ten-match tour of duty was a huge confidence booster, as they remained unbeaten throughout, winning six and drawing four, although they peculiarly elected not to face European opponents.

Romerito was the scorer of the only goal in Toluca as Paraguay narrowly overcame Iraq in their opening match. Three days later, at the Estadio Azteca, Paraguay stood up to the hosts and came away with a point, thanks to another strike from the same goalscorer, a beautifully directed header, plus a heroic penalty save from Roberto Fernández with only seconds remaining. As a collective, Paraguay were growing in belief.

As unknown a quantity as Paraguay were going into the tournament, just on their pedigree alone of being a South American football-playing nation at a World Cup they had been expected to brush Iraq aside, and while their narrow victory had gained them the points, absolutely nothing had been deciphered about the reality of the quality, or lack of quality, of Ré's team.

However, they showed greatness of spirit against Mexico, Romerito proving to be one of the emerging stars of the World Cup. A place in the knockout stages was pretty much assured after two matches and Paraguay were looking like an understated natural, within a style that was very different from the stereotypical idea the rest of the world harboured about South American teams. They were tough and hard-working, fast and penetrative, without being flamboyantly skilful. Percentages were played and discipline was high. They were wonderfully organised and one of the most Europeanised South American teams seen at any World Cup up until 1986. They seemed entirely comfortable with their limitations, and instead embraced their strengths.

Retrospectively, it was no surprise that Paraguay had overcome Chile in the qualifiers. Traditionally lower than the likes of Chile and Peru in the CONMEBOL food chain, while their opponents had arguably believed in their own hype and sense of position, Paraguay had focused on doing what they were good at. Strong in defence, a disciplined midfield, fast attackers to hit on the break, and a threat at set pieces in a way that would have been frowned at by the purists, in essence Paraguay were a working-class team that rubbed the middle classes up the wrong way. They were unsettling and inspiring in equal measure, which made Mexico and Belgium the perfect opponents for them. Teams that had higher notions for themselves.

Back to Toluca they went, where they came from behind twice to take a 2-2 draw against a Belgian team with no shortage of talent but a surprising lack of drive. Beaten in the 1980 European Championship Final, and regular qualifiers for major international tournaments, Guy Thys's team had all the experience they needed to deal with Paraguay, but only if they could find the determination to do so.

Conversely, Paraguay were already through to the knockout stages, and it was Belgium who were doing all of the sweating. Roberto Cabañas was the hero this time, on a day when Ré's team had looked the more likely to break the deadlock, until Franky Vercauteren scored against the run of play, a magical goal that he lobbed over a helpless Fernández and just inside the post.

There was a touch of the route one about Cabañas's first equaliser just five minutes after the interval, but within ten minutes Belgium had reclaimed the lead when Daniel Veyt marvellously sprang the offside trap to nip through and finish neatly.

As the match moved towards its climax, Belgium thought that they had a third goal when Enzo Scifo struck a sweetly taken free kick, only to see it disallowed by the referee, Bogdan Dochev, the man who would go on to run the line during the Argentina vs England quarter-final and be central to the drama that was the 'Hand of God'. There were no ambiguities about this decision, however, as Dochev had clearly indicated an indirect free kick, only for Scifo to send the ball straight into the back of the Paraguay net. Belgium would pay the price, and there were 16 minutes remaining when Cabañas struck again, gifted an inordinate amount of space in the penalty area.

It was a series of events that had a pronounced effect on the landscape of the knockout stages. A win for Belgium would have sent them to the Estadio Azteca to face England, and Paraguay would have instead headed to León to go up against the Soviet Union. But at the Azteca, Paraguay proved to be the perfect opponents for England, as two Anglo-Saxon approaches went up against one another. Industrious and stubborn, the outcome was dictated by one team having a collection of players that were more worldly-wise than the other and had the capability to find a higher gear or two.

Paraguay had undeniably reached their glass ceiling, but they were walking away from their first World Cup in 28 years having excelled themselves and exceeded the expectations of the rest of their continent. Ré had created a blueprint that other traditionally weaker CONMEBOL nations could follow, and while the next two World Cups would take place without the presence of Paraguay, Colombia and Bolivia would break through, as would Ecuador, eventually, in 2002.

It was the Paraguay of 1986 that made the impossible seem possible for those that followed them from the shadows, and they did enjoy their own return to the World Cup in 1998, the first of four successive qualifications.

From the gruff positivity of Paraguay, Uruguay left an alternative legacy on the 1986 World Cup, one that also left stud marks and changed the global view of Uruguayan football for the worse for decades to come. Given the negativity that surrounded Uruguay at the 1986 World Cup, it's strange to consider how highly they were rated in the build-up, and that they were considered by many to be a dark horse to possibly win the tournament.

Uruguay's place at the 1986 World Cup finals was secured well over a year before the tournament began, having edged out Chile in qualifying. A first World Cup since 1974, and rated as third favourites to lift the trophy, they were the reigning champions of South America, as winners of the 1983 Copa América, where they defeated Brazil in a two-legged final after getting the better of Chile in the group stages and beating Peru in the semi-finals.

With Omar Borrás in charge since 1982, Uruguay had finally begun to realise much of the slumbering potential that they possessed. Prior to taking the job, Uruguay had won the *Mundialito* in January 1981 on home soil. A tournament with the more official-sounding name of the 1980 World Champions' Gold Cup, it had been an event to mark the 50th anniversary of the first World Cup, where in Montevideo Uruguay had swept aside the Netherlands, Italy and Brazil.

It was a huge minor success, which surprisingly failed to act as a springboard towards the 1982 World Cup, but when complemented by a talented emerging group of Uruguayan youngsters, who had finished third at the 1979 FIFA World Youth Championship in Japan, it made for an embarrassment of riches that arguably led to a degree of indecision over the best composition of players for the senior team.

This indecision rumbled on into the first couple of years of Borrás's spell at the helm of Uruguay. Of the 31 players involved in winning the 1983 Copa América, only 12 went to Mexico three years later. Of massive importance, however, was that among those 12 names were Enzo Francescoli and Carlos Aguilera, two outrageous talents that would have improved any team at the 1986 World Cup.

Borrás was spoilt for choice, but by the time Uruguay headed to Mexico they did have a relatively settled team, which had begun to cluster together at the business end of their Copa América success and was noticeably evident during World Cup qualifying. He might have been the oldest head coach in Mexico, but Borrás was a modern thinker. Part-time athletics coach and writer of training manuals, he'd been a member of Ondino Viera's supporting cast of coaches at the 1966 World Cup and doubled his training pitch and touchline duties with that of technical director.

Tactically astute, Borrás had much in common with the former Ajax coach, Ştefan Kovács, in how he was an advocate of handing high levels of responsibility and even autonomy to his players, from whom he would seek opinions on not only tactics but also team selections. By the time he was selecting the 22 players he would take to Mexico, he could have comfortably named his squad twice over.

For a nation of just three million people, their relationship with and achievements in football were utterly phenomenal. Aside from Copa América glory and World Cup qualification, Borrás had also overseen a 14-month unbeaten run during his time in charge, inclusive of high-profile victories over Argentina and England. When qualification was clinched, this was a team on the crest of a significant wave.

Uruguay's approach to the tournament did offer some alarm bells, however. In between securing qualification for the World Cup and beginning their finals campaign against West Germany at the Estadio Cuauhtémoc in Puebla, Uruguay had accumulated a mixed set of results across a spread of 13 matches when Borrás didn't always have his best players at his disposal. With so many of his players plying their club trade away from Uruguay, Borrás was only able to field his preferred line-up on a handful of occasions prior to the World Cup, and they won only three of those 13 friendlies over what was almost a 14-month wait for the finals to kick off. Had the World Cup started in June 1985, as opposed to June 1986, then they might well have won it.

As it was, Uruguay's World Cup peaked in their opening fixture, at least until West Germany sourced their equaliser with just five minutes remaining, in a match that offered glimpses of the aggression to come within just the 25 seconds that it took Nelson Gutiérrez to remorselessly bring down Rudi Völler. It was the first of a series of brutal challenges, which were closely matched by Víctor Diogo's borderline assault on Thomas Berthold, and flowing in the opposite direction, Klaus Augenthaler on Francescoli, the latter event not even provoking a yellow card.

Lothar Matthäus uncharacteristically gave away the gift of the opening goal with what turned out to be the perfectly weighted through ball to the much-travelled

Antonio Alzamendi, who rounded the unexpectedly exposed Harald Schumacher before almost providing the miss of the tournament when faced with the now open goal, as his effort struck the underside of the crossbar, only to bounce half a yard over the West German goal line.

Klaus Allofs procured West Germany's late but utterly deserved equaliser, brushing off not only the attentions of the Uruguay defence but also that of his team-mate, Völler. Between the two goals, the defender Diogo and substitute Mario Saralegui picked up yellow cards for Uruguay on an afternoon when it should have been so many more, yet the Czechoslovak referee, Vojtech Christov, opted to repeatedly turn a blind eye, prompting a second half where Franz Beckenbauer's team began to retaliate in kind and could have collected a few cautions of their own.

If West Germany were to take anything from the match, then they would need to rise above the escalating maelstrom, and this they did, threatening the equaliser long before it finally came. They had a succession of missed and repelled opportunities, the closest being when Augenthaler struck the angle of post and crossbar. Uruguay relied heavily upon the goalkeeping excellence of Peñarol's Fernando Álvez, who had been drafted in to replace the injured Rodolfo Rodríguez, and had it not been for him, then West Germany would have been cruising towards a comfortable win rather than sweating over a late equaliser.

In the end, both teams might have mellowed towards the point each gained, as West Germany had still been trailing as the 85th minute arrived, no matter how well they had been playing, while Uruguay had undoubtedly been riding their luck, as well as the disciplinary tightrope.

Demolished by Denmark in their next match in Nezahualcóyotl, at the same venue five days later Uruguay antagonised their way past Alex Ferguson's Scotland, during a goalless draw that was achieved with only ten men for the last 89 minutes.

A heavy fine handed out by FIFA, and Borrás banned from the touchline, when Uruguay limped onward to the last 16 to face Argentina, they nursed three suspensions and the ire of a watching world. However, they exited the World Cup not with the toxicity that had sadly become their trademark, but with a serious effort to match Argentina and Diego Maradona for skill and footballing endeavour.

Perhaps the alteration of ethos was down to the familiarity of their great rivals from across the Río de la Plata, along with the knowledge that subtlety would be required to prevail, rather than the physical approach they had taken to the stereotypical group of death, a phrase some are inclined to attribute the birth of to Borrás himself. Whatever prompted their change in approach, this was the closest the 1986 World Cup came to seeing the true version of Uruguay, which, of course, is one of the greatest disappointments this vintage of the tournament has to offer.

As Uruguay confirmed their much-speculated character shift to that of the World Cup pantomime villain, even though they departed Mexico at the same stage as Paraguay, the campaigns of the two nations couldn't have been anymore different. For Paraguay, the World Cup had been a huge success, as they not only returned to football's biggest stage for the first time since 1958 but were much more at ease with the experience than Uruguay were, themselves having been absent for 12 years, yet the bigger legacy was left by the underachievers, rather than the overachievers.

Neither overachievers nor underachievers, Morocco simply proved to be achievers in Mexico, when becoming the first African nation to go beyond the group stages of a World Cup. Not only that, but they advanced from Group F as winners, topping a section that included a previous

World Cup winner and two semi-finalists, all three nations having set sail from Europe, thus hideously sure-footed when it came to their sense of place within the international footballing food chain.

While not the first nation from their wonderful continent to compete in a World Cup, Morocco were the African trailblazers beyond the bold and brave stance of the CAF to boycott the 1966 tournament in protest of both the continued lack of an automatic qualification berth for the greatest football show on earth and FIFA's controversial readmission of South Africa in 1963.

By 1970, the winds of change had belatedly begun to blow, and it was Morocco who were the first to benefit from Africa's qualifying section now having a direct path to the finals. Once there, at Mexico's first spin at hosting a World Cup, they acquitted themselves well, scaring West Germany, who they led at half-time of their debut finals appearance, before losing narrowly. They then went on to pose a serious challenge to Peru until the last 25 minutes of their match, before ending their adventures when taking a deserved point against Bulgaria.

During the 16-year interlude between Morocco's first and second World Cup, they won the 1976 Africa Cup of Nations, going on to finish third in 1980, yet surprisingly fell short in World Cup qualification. After three successive failures to reach the World Cup finals, it would have been all too easy for Morocco to have missed out yet again in 1986, especially given they had shockingly failed to qualify for both the 1982 and 1984 Africa Cup of Nations.

However, 1983 was a turning point, as the appointment as head coach of José Faria brought with it greater vision and organisation. A product of Rio de Janeiro, Faria had been a useful winger and occasional striker for Bonsucesso, Fluminense and Bangu, before injury ended his playing days prematurely. Turning his attentions to studying the game from the sidelines, Faria became an erudite football thinker, eventually returning to Fluminense as a youth coach, where he oversaw the rise of a generation of youngsters, led by the magnificent Edinho, who went on to play in three World Cups with Brazil, the last of this trio in 1986 as captain.

Having turned down a spate of tempting offers from other Brazilian clubs to become a head coach in his own right, Faria was coaxed away from his homeland by an offer to coach the Qatar Under-20 team, swiftly impressing enough to be poached by Al-Sadd, who presented him with a contract he simply couldn't refuse, one that earned him more money in his three years with them than he'd accumulated throughout his three previous decades in the game.

Faria's relationship with Al-Sadd was also profitable in terms of trophies won, as together they twice swept up the Qatar Stars League, adding more glory with successes in the Emir of Qatar Cup and the Qatar Super Cup.

In 1982, FAR Rabat, the team of the Royal Moroccan Armed Forces, swooped to take Faria to its capital city, and before long he was asked to combine those duties with that of leading the Moroccan national team, in a similar manner to how Valeriy Lobanovskyi would coach the Soviet Union as a side project to run alongside his commitments to Dynamo Kyiv.

With FAR Rabat, Faria took his new employers to previously uncharted heights, not only ending a 14-year Moroccan championship drought, but also winning the African Cup of Champions Clubs in 1985, the precursor to what's now the CAF Champions League.

Morocco and Faria seemed to be made for each other, not just in terms of football but spiritually too, and it was a union cemented when he eventually converted to Islam, as well as him choosing to make Rabat his permanent home.

The 1986 World Cup qualifiers proved to be unsettlingly problem-free for Morocco, as in a two-legged knockout format they comfortably dispensed with Sierra Leone, Malawi, Egypt and Libya, not losing a match or even conceding a goal until the second leg of their final play-off. Even this was a result that proved an insignificant minor dent, given that Faria's team had already built up an ultimately unassailable 3-0 aggregate lead, which would be beyond Libyan capabilities in overturning.

Everything fell sweetly into place for Faria and Morocco. Four weeks prior to the first leg of their final World Cup qualifying play-off at the Stade Mohammed V in Casablanca, they were in Lubumbashi, grinding out the goalless draw against Zaire that secured them qualification for the 1986 Africa Cup of Nations. Joyous a turn of events as this was in its own right, it doubled as the perfect preparation for Morocco's crucial World Cup qualifiers. The feel-good factor was escalating and Faria was the conductor.

Often classed as Morocco's golden generation, the rise of Faria's team wasn't, however, fuelled by a crop of handily emerging youth products. It was instead brought about by the Brazilian coach's new-found skills of improvisation. Essentially, all the components were readily available to Faria, or any other coach come to that, it was just that they needed assembling in the most organised and effective way possible, then given clear guidance and defined goals to aim for.

Faria would use only 14 of the 22 players he took to Mexico, and the striking theme was experience. Four of the 14 were in their early 30s, and not one was under the age of 23. Ten of them were within that 23 to 28 sweet spot, and at the peak of their physical powers. There was a telling combination of optimum physicality and wisdom.

Abdelkrim Merry was Faria's biggest asset, a wondrous striker whose 13-year international career would be restricted to just 13 appearances, four of those coming in Mexico. With a talent for football that was identified while still a teenager, his senior club career was played out entirely in France, where he shared a pitch with some of the world's finest players, inclusive of Johnny Rep, Clade Papi, Jean-François Larios, Enzo Francescoli, Maxime Bossis and Luis Fernández to name but a few.

Not on his own, when it came to natural talent, Faria could also call on the man that made his FAR Rabat side tick, Mohamed Timoumi, surprisingly one of only five players called up for the World Cup from Faria's club side. A dangerous attacking midfielder, Timoumi's performances in Mexico would win him a transfer to LaLiga with Murcia, benefiting as he did from the presence of the veteran playmaker, Abdelmajid Dolmy, a player who was often referred to as the 'Maestro'.

Beautifully balanced going forward, Faria also called up Abderrazak Khairi, the youngest member of the squad, another striker of rich potential and an FAR Rabat team-mate of Timoumi. He scored twice against Portugal as part of a wonderfully disorientating 90 minutes of football that turned all preconceived notions on their head when it came to a game of World Cup football between one of Africa's finest teams and one that had come so stunningly close to a place in the 1984 European Championship Final.

With most of the players that Faria would use in Mexico making the trip to Egypt for the Africa Cup of Nations, just as with the way the qualifiers landed, the finals of Morocco's continental international tournament worked as the perfect dress rehearsal for the World Cup.

An eight-team tournament in 1986, the Africa Cup of Nations would greatly mirror the World Cup for Morocco. Three group matches, the first two ending in hard-fought draws, the last one a decisive victory to take them through, the tournament then ended at the first knockout hurdle, which in the case of the Africa Cup of Nations would be the semi-final against the hosts.

In Mexico, Morocco would embrace their three group matches with two hard-fought draws, followed by a decisive win to take them through to a narrow defeat in the first knockout round. On this occasion it would be West Germany that proved their undoing, in a match that almost went to extra time, and in which Faria played the percentages and refused to let his players veer from the austere plan to play for an extra 30 minutes, where he'd contended Morocco's best hope of victory lay. Against West Germany a sense of fear seemed to grip Faria, when a little bit of freedom might have made all the difference. Yet, they did get to within three minutes of the Morocco head coach being able to test his theory, a notion that as the game stretched and the legs grew weary, Morocco would be able to repeat the power play they had against Portugal.

A missed opportunity, yet also a glorious achievement, Morocco had become the first African nation to make it beyond the group stages of a World Cup, just 12 years after the performances of Zaire had set a negative tone that many football observers have never really let them quantify.

Morocco had played well 16 years earlier at the 1970 World Cup, Tunisia had produced a first African victory at a World Cup in 1978, while Algeria had been cheated of their just reward in 1982 in the same tournament as Cameroon had won huge admirers and come close to knocking out the eventual winners, Italy.

Now Morocco had returned for another go and they had raised the bar, a bar that Cameroon would lift again four years later in Italy, suddenly changing the topic of conversation from whether African nations should be allowed automatic berths at World Cups, a viewpoint that was still being aired on the eve of the tournament, to when will we see an African winner of the tournament.

Beyond Cameroon and all things 1990, Nigeria, Senegal and Ghana have all gone to World Cups with serious intent, signalling a shift in the balance of African footballing power at international level to the sub-Saharan nations. The glass ceiling of the quarter-finals is still to be smashed, though.

Whenever that day arrives, however, the Morocco team of 1986 should be given huge credit for being one of the biggest stepping stones towards the goal of seeing an African nation reach the semi-finals of a World Cup, of seeing an African nation go one step further and onward to a first final, and on that day maybe even the dawning of a team of African world champions.

The greatest legacy that the Morocco team of 1986 gave the world was that they made fools of many people, people who had been preprogrammed to disregard the threat they posed, and the skill, knowledge and wisdom they possessed.

Chapter Eleven

The Self-Preservation Society

ARGUABLY, THE 1986 World Cup was the home of the most un-Italian of all Italian World Cup campaigns. Have a long, hard think about what you expect from Italy at the finals of a major tournament, and I'll bet you that the image you conjure up looks nothing like their efforts at defending their crown as world champions in 1986.

When it comes to football, the concept of the classical Italy tends to fall within two very defined subsections when it comes to the World Cup. Given their failure to qualify for the 2018 tournament, you could even suggest there to be three subsections.

Italy are usually all or nothing at major international tournaments. There's very little in the way of middle ground, as either they're winning or at least threatening to win them, or they're capitulating in the group stages to dramatic effect. Their failure to reach the 2018 World Cup finals took the breath away, the first time this had occurred since 1958, but then they responded to the gargantuan setback by winning the belated 2020 European Championship, before swinging back the other way, as at the time of writing their presence at the 2022 World Cup is under severe threat.

Italy failing to qualify for a major tournament leaves an uneasy feeling; the 1984 European Championship finals took place without the presence of Italy, who at the time were the reigning world champions. The strength of the tournament at that stage was phenomenal; one designated host nation and seven qualifiers, all of which had to win their qualifying group to reach the finals. No runner-up, no best third-placed nation, no play-offs, no Italy. The *Azzurri* would find themselves in a similar situation eight years later, when failing to qualify for the 1992 European Championship.

Winners of the World Cup in 1934, 1938, 1982 and 2006, runners-up in 1970 and 1994, beaten semi-finalist, or equivalent, in 1978 and 1990, Italy owns an enviable track record in the great World Cup scheme of being there or thereabouts. At the other end of the spectrum, they've floundered at the initial group stages in 1950, 1954, 1962, 1966, 1974, 2010 and 2014. Turning down the invitation to take part in 1930, 2018 was only the second time that Italy had failed to qualify for a World Cup, with 1958 being that other occasion.

This leaves you with just three other Italian World Cups to consider: 1986, 1998 and 2002. Their only real mid-ranging World Cups, and even then, in 1998, they came to within a penalty shoot-out of reaching another semi-final, at the projected expense of France, the hosts and eventual winners of that year's tournament. Four years later, Italy went out deep into extra time in the last 16, via the polarising golden goal, amid controversy and rancour, to co-hosts South Korea in Daejeon. Uncharacteristic mid-ranging World Cups 1998 and 2002 might have been for Italy, but aesthetically they still went down in a blaze of near-operatic drama.

Within a heady combination of high-achieving success and spectacular face-planting failure, 1986 was a unique experience for Italy, as it was the one and only World Cup in which they could tick neither box.

Enzo Bearzot and his World Cup-winning team were joined on the outside, looking in at the 1984 European Championship by 1982 World Cup semi-finalists Poland, the twice-beaten World Cup finalist the Netherlands, another set of former world champions in the shape of England, and two previous European champions, the Soviet Union and Czechoslovakia.

Still within the era when a World Cup-winning nation automatically qualified for the following tournament, it was difficult to gauge what competitive condition Italy were in heading to Mexico. Caught between two eras, Bearzot was left with a two-and-a-half-year run to the 1986 World Cup, in which his side would only compete in friendlies.

Indecision hung in the air for Bearzot, and it could be suggested that he hung on to his World Cup-winning team for too long. Yet, in terms of numbers, he only took ten players to Mexico that had travelled to Spain with him in 1982. Numbers can be misleading, however, as of the 12 players of that squad who didn't make it to Mexico, retirement, advancing age and degradation of form accounted for nine of them, while only three were still under the age of 30. If he'd been given the ability to turn back the hands of time, Bearzot would probably have loved to have taken most of those 12 players to Mexico too.

Despite the changes forced upon him, elements of Bearzot's 1986 squad that had been present in Spain four years earlier had passed peak condition, but were selected in the hope that they could roll back the years and inspire another unlikely success.

Within this, Bearzot wasn't alone, as Brazil's Telê Santana also put his faith in many of the players who served him so well in 1982, inclusive of an injured Zico. Meanwhile, Henri Michel opted for not veering off the path that Michel Hidalgo had led France down to eventual glory at the 1984

European Championship. Nor were these the only instances, as Poland crossed their fingers that Zbigniew Boniek could pilot another wild ride into the depths of a World Cup.

The qualification campaign for the 1984 European Championship had been nothing short of calamitous for Bearzot and Italy. Eight matches played and only one win was garnered, which came on the final night, in Perugia against Cyprus. Romania qualified from a closely contested group, ahead of Sweden and Czechoslovakia, with Italy a shocking and very distant fourth. From World Cup winners to the wheels falling off, it was a dramatic dip in fortunes and by the standards of the Italian Football Federation, Bearzot was lucky to hold on to his job, despite the glory of 1982 being so fresh in mind. With a clear run on 1986 it was perhaps hoped that the old magic would reappear in time for the defence of their title.

Bearzot had been involved with the *Azzurri* since 1969, firstly in charge of the under-23 team, before graduating to assistant of the senior coach, Ferruccio Valcareggi, for the 1974 World Cup finals. It was under Valcareggi that the classic double-sided coin of the Italian national team was at its most finely illustrated.

Valcareggi led Italy to glory in the 1968 European Championship, and then two years later took them to that iconic 1970 World Cup Final. Conversely, this was followed by failure to reach the 1972 European Championship finals and then their capitulation during the group stages of the 1974 World Cup. Boom has traditionally followed bust, and vice versa, since the dawning of footballing time for the Italian national football team, and whichever end of that spectrum they tend to be hovering around, they're always value for money.

By 1975, Bearzot had assumed control of the top job and it was an attacking and positive team that he took to Argentina for the 1978 World Cup, where, with 45 minutes remaining in their de facto semi-final against the Netherlands, they had one foot in the final, before Ernst Happel's team came on strong.

Via the stepping stone of a more circumspect 1980 European Championship, which was played out on home soil but within the shadow of the *Totonero* scandal, the 1982 World Cup was won while Bearzot and his team were shrouded in a siege mentality. In fact, Italy often saves their best work for when they are shrouded within such a situation, and the *Totonero* scandal of 1980 still hung in the air, thanks to the inclusion in the squad of Paolo Rossi, freshly returned from his two-year ban from football for his perceived part in a match-fixing scandal that saw both AC Milan and Lazio demoted to Serie B, among a wave of sanctions to hit both individual players and a variety of clubs. Originally a three-year ban, this had been reduced to two years upon appeal, making the Juventus man conveniently available for selection for the World Cup in Spain.

When Rossi was unimpressive during the initial group stages, Bearzot came under intense pressure to drop his misfiring and widely untrusted star striker. The coach stuck by the player, however, and Rossi repaid Bearzot handsomely. By the time the 1986 World Cup had rolled around, the Italian peninsula was desperate to see him weave his goalscoring magic once again.

Two and a half years is a long time to go without meaningful competitive international football. While friendlies against fellow heavyweight nations can pique the interest of both players and fans alike, it can be difficult to raise the enthusiasm for matches against the perceived lesser lights.

Going into 1984, it was hugely important for Italy to shake the failures of their European Championship qualifying campaign from the system. It was also crucial that they identified the successor to Dino Zoff, their legendary goalkeeper and World Cup-winning captain, who finally retired from both the club and international game at the end of the 1982/83 season.

Inclusive of the win over Cyprus, which closed the door on their abject European Championship qualifying campaign, Italy set off on a 15-match run that carried them to the summer of 1985, during which they were beaten only once, a narrow loss to West Germany in Zürich in April 1984. During this run, ego-boosting victories were collected, against Poland, Portugal and England.

Rossi was involved and scoring sporadically, although he'd failed to build upon his heroics of 1982, proving to be something of an enigma in a Juventus shirt, to such an extent that the Turin giants were willing to allow him to move on in the summer of 1985 to what was still a partially dormant AC Milan. On the plus side, Alessandro Altobelli was finally rising in prominence, having been a support act four years earlier.

As Italy went into the World Cup season of 1985/86, hidden weaknesses began to emerge. Three successive defeats weren't the way Bearzot had envisaged the final stretch of his World Cup preparations to begin, as losses were incurred against Norway, Poland and once again West Germany. This left him with just two further serious fixtures in which to find the answers to some pretty searching questions. Narrow victories against Austria and China did little to alleviate deep-seated fears.

A successor to Zoff had still to be settled upon. Ivano Bordon, the man who had been the principal back-up goalkeeper at Italy's last three major international tournaments, had been given his chance yet had failed to convincingly grasp it. Bordon drifted from the reckoning, which left a straight fight between Giovanni Galli of Fiorentina and AS Roma's Franco Tancredi, who by and large had shared the goalkeeping duties during most of the matches Italy had played over the course of the previous 18 months. Added to this, the uncapped Walter Zenga was brought in as Bearzot's third goalkeeper. The dispute between Galli and Tancredi was only settled when the squad was officially named, as Galli found himself to be in possession of the No. 1 shirt, and Tancredi the No. 12.

It wasn't only in the goalkeeping department that Bearzot was being kept awake at night, however. Since the beginning of 1984 he'd fielded 32 different players in his bid to find the perfect combination that could offer a strong defence of the World Cup in Mexico. Leaning on the past, but casting an eye upon the future, Bearzot undeniably got several of the calls he had to make wrong. He left Franco Baresi out of his squad yet called up his brother Giuseppe, the Internazionale defensive midfielder. At the time, it wasn't the glaring error that history points it out to be, but the third-eye defending of Franco would have been a useful weapon in the heat of Mexico. He'd been an unused member of the 1982 World Cup-winning squad and, in the summer of 1986, AC Milan were still sat upon the eve of their late-1980s greatness. A crystal ball wasn't necessarily required, however, to see the benefits that Franco could have brought to a team that would ultimately be crying out for strong leadership.

Thorniest issue of all was the inclusion, or not as the case may be, of many of the players who had lifted the World Cup four years earlier. Zoff had called time himself, while Gabriele Oriali and Francesco Graziani were the highest-profile casualties of a night of the long knives-style cull in the aftermath of a 3-0 defeat in Naples against Sweden, during those fateful European Championship qualifiers.

One other member of the starting line-up from the 1982 World Cup Final who failed to make Bearzot's squad was the iconic Claudio Gentile, an omission that allowed Italy's opponents to breathe a collective sigh of relief, but proved to be an absence that was mourned by commentators and journalists alike, so wonderfully foreboding a character he'd been in previous tournaments. Still only 32, and a formidable presence, he'd drifted from the international scene in 1984 after his long association with Juventus had come to an end with a transfer to sworn enemies Fiorentina.

The move away from Turin took away the compulsion from Bearzot to make Gentile one of the first names on his team sheet. From there, intermittent injury problems during 1985/86 derailed any hope he might have harboured of a recall for the World Cup. Yet, having played fewer club matches than he was accustomed to, Gentile might have had greater reserves of energy than other Italian players possessed. His experience, especially beyond the group stages against Michel Platini, would have been invaluable.

Other names sadly absent from the ranks of the Italy squad included Giancarlo Antognoni, the attacking midfielder who had been so instrumental in the *Azzurri* reaching the 1982 World Cup Final, when playing every match up to the semi-final, before picking up an injury that ruled him out of the final itself. The hypnotic Franco Causio was another with whom time had finally caught up, a player who symbolically appeared in the last minute of the final in Madrid as a deserved reward for an international career where he'd so often been the most potent weapon at the disposal of both Valcareggi and Bearzot.

Of the legends of 1982 who did travel to Mexico, Rossi and Marco Tardelli had the biggest question marks over them. The two strongest elements beyond Zoff that most people associate with Italy prevailing in Spain were nursing injury problems and further worries over form. Like Rossi, Tardelli had departed Juventus in the summer of 1985 for the city of Milan. While Rossi had taken up the red and black stripes of AC Milan, it had been the blue and black stripes of Internazionale for Tardelli.

Tardelli was in Mexico as the Italian captain, but neither he nor Rossi would play a single minute of the tournament. In comparison, Antonio Cabrini, Gaetano Scirea, Bruno Conti, Giuseppe Bergomi and Fulvio Collovati all played active roles, as did Altobelli, who became the focal point in front of goal in the absence of Rossi. Bearzot rolled the dice and took these calculated risks in the name of experience.

As part of this, contentious decisions had also been made on the omissions of Pietro Fanna and Giuseppe Dossena. Both players had played extensively during the seemingly endless run of friendlies in the extended build-up to Mexico. Dossena had been an unused member of the squad in 1982, while Fanna had been an integral component of Verona's shock Serie A title win in 1984/85, earning himself a high-profile switch to Inter, with whom he would win another Scudetto in 1988/89. Both players were hugely unfortunate to miss Bearzot's final cut.

During the build-up to the 1986 World Cup, Bearzot also gave Roberto Mancini his introduction to international football, but was unmoved by the talent and potential on show, so the Sampdoria striker was to be another who missed out on a trip to Mexico. It was a decision that must have been painfully frustrating to Mancini, given that his club team-mate Gianluca Vialli did make the squad, despite Mancini outscoring him during the 1985/86 season.

On top of this, you also have the peculiar case of Daniele Massaro, an unused member of the 1982 World Cup-winning squad, who was given game-time during Bearzot's planning towards Mexico, only to also find himself discarded from the final squad. Massaro departed Fiorentina in the summer of 1986, joining AC Milan, where he would initially fail to see eye to eye with Arrigo Sacchi, even being packed off for a season on loan at AS Roma, before he returned to the San Siro to prove the doubts of his coach wrong to such an extent that he would be rewarded with an international renaissance when Sacchi later took control of the *Azzurri*. Massaro missed only one match of Italy's 1994 World Cup campaign, having failed to make the squad of any major tournament between the World Cups of 1982 and 1994, tournaments that bookended his international career.

On the opposite side of the coin, the intelligence of Carlo Ancelotti was a valuable, although unused, addition, and the late run made by Avellino's Fernando De Napoli proved that, contrary to popular belief, Bearzot did have a flexible bone in his body, while calling on Vialli was a move of classic foresight. Far from the prolific striker he would become, Vialli had yet to score ten goals in Serie A and there were certainly contenders of greater achievement to whom the Italy coach could have turned.

Roberto Pruzzo of AS Roma was that season's Serie A top scorer, yet Bearzot's stubbornness stopped him from calling upon the sharp-eyed marksman. Pruzzo would have been ideal as a partner to Altobelli, but it was instead Giuseppe Galderisi who won that role, with Vialli appearing from the bench in all of Italy's matches in Mexico.

Timing in football is everything and it was a tournament too soon for Vialli, however. While Altobelli grasped the opportunity to take on the starring role and Galderisi was a hard-working counterpart, the inexperience of Vialli was no compensation for the lack of a fully functioning Rossi, in the same way a player like Pruzzo could have been. Italy simply didn't have to be as blunt going forward as they were.

Bearzot left himself with a weakened alternative option to his plan A. Unable to deploy Rossi and Tardelli, he effectively went into the 1986 World Cup with a smaller and more inexperienced squad than most of his big rivals.

That careless draw against Bulgaria and their entertaining struggle against South Korea sandwiched a truly heavyweight clash at the Estadio Cuauhtémoc in Puebla, where two football giants collided. Italy faced Argentina and again it was Altobelli who opened the scoring, this time with an early penalty. For a spell, Italy cruised, perhaps buying into the train of public Argentinian thought that Carlos Bilardo was an accident waiting to happen.

But then Diego Maradona happened and it was 1-1. Maradona and Argentina then had Italy on the ropes for a prolonged period. This was the third successive World Cup where the *Azzurri* and *La Albiceleste* had faced one another, and this was the only period of play in those three matches where Italy had looked truly vulnerable.

The tide eventually turned again, however, as Bearzot's team came on strong once more, inclusive of hitting the post and they wouldn't have been undeserving had they procured a winning goal. It all meant that Argentina topped Group A, and for Bearzot and Italy the width of the goalpost ultimately made the difference between a last-16 match against France as opposed to Uruguay. Had they veered towards Uruguay instead, and had they navigated a way past them, England would have been lying in wait for them in the quarter-finals, and the whole 'Hand of God' scenario would never have happened.

As it was, it was back to Mexico City for Italy, this time at the Estadio Olímpico Universitario, the principal venue of the 1968 Summer Olympics, where they were comprehensively outplayed by France. Even had they somehow sneaked past *Les bleus*, Brazil would have been waiting to ambush Italy in the quarter-finals. It's hard to imagine anything other than Brazilian revenge for what happened at the Estadi de Sarrià four years earlier.

Defeat to France marked the end of an era for Italy. Their relatively limp abdication as world champions and the departure of Bearzot, the man who cured the *Azzurri* of their mid-1970s malaise to such a degree that they went on to win the World Cup for the third time in their history, was an unsatisfactory way in which to close such an otherwise stunning footballing epoch.

Beyond Mexico, there would be no more of Rossi and Tardelli. Conti, Scirea and Collovati would also follow suit, while Cabrini hung on until retiring at the tail end of the qualifiers for the 1988 European Championship, as Bearzot's successor, Azeglio Vicini, cast his eye towards the future, towards a World Cup on home soil.

Vicini was largely handed a blank sheet of paper with which to draw up his plans for the 1990 World Cup, via the 1988 European Championship, and Cabrini alongside Altobelli were the last of the ageing ghosts of 1982 with which he had to deal. Altobelli would take part in the 1988 European Championship, but he too bowed out once that tournament ended.

The returning Franco Baresi, along with Bergomi, Vierchowod and belatedly Massaro, all junior members of the 1982 World Cup-winning squad, were the last links to Bearzot's defining glory, and they would help form a team in which Vicini was brave enough to add the components that Bearzot was unwilling to trust in Mexico, as well as utilising the best of a new generation of players that emerged as the 1990s arrived.

Bearzot was left with difficult questions going into the 1986 World Cup finals, and he basically fudged the answers. The squad of players he selected was poorly balanced, and while he was willing to gamble on the likes of Rossi and Tardelli, he was unwilling to back younger talent such as Mancini, or even to select fully fit players who were in form, such as Franco Baresi, Pruzzo and Massaro.

Italy's 1986 World Cup campaign could have closer resembled those of Brazil and France in how they turned back the clock for one more stylish dance at the finals of a major tournament. That Bearzot unwittingly denied both himself and his nation that possibility is a massive shame.

Chapter Twelve

The Game that Refreshes the Parts Other Football Can't Reach

A VIBRANT, passionate and partisan home support, two fantastically evocative kits, two teams capable of very distinct and very beautiful football, a screamer from Oleg Protasov, an emphatic finish from Sergey Gotsmanov, the woodwork hit on multiple occasions, goal-line clearances, a wonderful example of how erratic Danish international goalkeepers used to be prior to the rise of Peter Schmeichel, and two goals apiece from Michael Laudrup and Preben Elkjær Larsen.

In Copenhagen on 5 June 1985, the greatest international football match of the lot was played. It was quite possibly the very plateau above cloud level when it comes to 1980s football hipsterism. It was also a match that could, arguably should, have been revisited in Mexico in the quarter-finals of the 1986 World Cup. As talented in their own rights as they were, Spain and Belgium had a lot to answer for.

Elkjær is a mystical figure. Widely overshadowed by Laudrup over the course of the last three and a half decades or so, but massively revered by those who witnessed his unique style of play, it's impossible to draw yourself away from the urge to compare with Laudrup when it comes to

Elkjær. However, when you do, it ends up being more a case of noticing the contrasts than drawing the parallels.

For the geometrical vision you got from Laudrup, Elkjær instead offered a bewitching free-spirited hypnotism. For the crystal-clear still waters that seemed to run through Laudrup, Elkjær gave you a passionate volatility. For Laudrup's honed physical condition and his intense professionalism, Elkjær was a heavy smoker, and renowned for nights out prior to big matches. For Laudrup's mastery of the ball, which almost appeared to be a preprogrammed concept, Elkjær often struck the image of a man trying to control a small and excitable dog beneath his feet, as he swept past all-comers with an unorthodox beauty.

While Laudrup's career path was entirely textbook for a man of his many outstanding talents, Elkjær instead undertook a wonderfully meandering route through his. Laudrup, with a career that took in a flirtation where he nearly signed for Liverpool, before spells with Juventus, Barcelona and Real Madrid, is offset by Elkjær, who spent his peak years with Lokeren and Hellas Verona.

Elkjær's formative years within the professional game probably go a long way in explaining why he later allowed his career to take a more sedate path. Fast-tracked into the Danish under-21 team at the age of 18, he quickly became one of Europe's most sought-after teenagers after scoring seven goals in just 15 outings for Vanløse IF.

By the age of 19, and during the early exchanges of the 1976/77 season, Elkjær was heading to the Bundesliga, with 1. FC Köln edging out VfB Stuttgart in a hotly contested battle for his services. His debut for the club came swiftly, as he was thrown into a second-round, second-leg UEFA Cup encounter with Grasshopper Club Zürich, making an explosive entrance for his new team, scoring twice in a 3-2 victory.

Within days, Elkjær had made his Bundesliga bow, during a defeat to Borussia Mönchengladbach, going on to score in the very next match against MSV Duisburg. The initial spotlight was a blinding one, and he was once more thrown into the starting line-up at Loftus Road, against Queens Park Rangers in the UEFA Cup. A chastening evening in West London ended in a 3-0 defeat, and he appeared only as a late substitute during the second leg, when Köln almost completed an unlikely comeback.

Under the disciplinarian regime of the legendary Hennes Weisweiler, Elkjær struggled to get to grips with the focused and often clinical West German approach to the game, and to life itself within a high-rolling Bundesliga club environment. The teenage Elkjær embraced life away from the club a little too much for the liking of Weisweiler. One infamous occurrence, when reports of the talented youngster being out on the town in the days leading up to an important match surfaced, brought a heated exchange of views between coach and player. When Weisweiler confronted him over having been seen in a nightclub with a bottle of whisky and a member of the opposite sex, Elkjær reassured his coach it wasn't true, instead confirming it was in fact a bottle of vodka and two women. Elkjær was soon off to Lokeren.

In comparison, Laudrup was the perfect specimen. Prodigious for both Kjøbenhavns Boldklub and Brøndby IF, the great and good of European football came calling for him in the summer of 1983, when still a teenager. A move to Liverpool fell through, due to a disagreement over the projected length of the contract, when publicity photos of him in a Liverpool shirt had already been taken. Instead, Laudrup joined Juventus, fresh from them having reached, and lost, the 1983 European Cup Final.

However, with Juventus enjoying the services of Michel Platini and Zbigniew Boniek, Laudrup's first two years of

Serie A football were spent on loan at Lazio. It wasn't until Boniek's transfer to AS Roma in the summer of 1985 that Laudrup finally found his way into those famous black and white stripes.

The insanity of this exceptional situation for Denmark and Sepp Piontek was that for a long time both Elkjær and Laudrup were cast within the shadow of another wondrous Danish footballer, Allan Simonsen.

When Denmark and the Soviet Union went head to head in Copenhagen in June 1985, it was with a sense of excitement and apprehension that the hosts went into the match. Denmark's track record against the Soviet Union up until that point was a poor one.

Blessed by the presence of their own evocative attacking talent, spearheaded by the wonderful Igor Belanov and Oleh Protasov, the Soviet Union's upward arc was just a pace or two behind that of Denmark, who had begun to show signs of purpose during their ultimately unsuccessful bid to qualify for the 1982 World Cup, before excelling at the 1984 European Championship, having reached the finals at the expense of England.

The Soviet Union had failed to qualify for the 1984 European Championship, having reached the 1982 World Cup finals with a largely different generation of players. Mexico and the summer of 1986 would be the springboard for them to go on to reach the 1988 European Championship Final, by which time Denmark's star had begun to wane. It meant that when the two teams collided in the qualifiers for the 1986 World Cup, it was the eye of a very beautiful storm.

In Copenhagen, Piontek's men lifted themselves to new levels of brilliance, throwing their historical inferiority complex to the wind; it was a match ahead of its time, played at an almost intolerable pace and intensity.

Jesper Olsen was withdrawn by Piontek at half-time to shore up the left-hand-side of his team. It was a substitution that to the naked eye seemed like a sacrifice of attacking intent, but the renewed balance of the introduction of Per Frimann was the winning turn of the card.

With Elkjær having scored both of Denmark's first-half goals, which helped give the home team a valuable, yet vulnerable, 2-1 half-time lead, it was left to Laudrup to net both of Denmark's second-half goals, within a four-minute span just beyond the hour mark, matching exactly what Elkjær had done during the first period.

Unwilling to buckle easily, after both braces of goals had been conceded the Soviet Union were swift to strike back. Protasov in reply to Elkjær, and Gotsmanov in riposte to Laudrup. It made for the most awe-inspiring spectacle that could easily have ended 8-4 rather than 4-2.

As football matches go, it wasn't just that it was a magnificent spectacle, packed with iconic players, great goals, wondrous skill and a relentless pace, set against a stunningly atmospheric backdrop, with vital World Cup qualifying points on offer, it was also that this was a game of football that had healing properties, coming as it did just seven days beyond the Heysel Stadium disaster. Football was desperately in need of something to cling to when Denmark and the Soviet Union set foot on to the Idrætsparken; it needed a glimmer of hope that beauty could still prevail, and the two teams gave it the boost it so badly required.

This wasn't even a match where the control of UEFA qualifying Group 6 was on immediate offer. These were two teams in third and fourth position at kick-off, within a wide-open group where all the teams seemed intent on beating everybody else. Up to this point, Denmark had defeated Norway and Ireland, but lost to Switzerland, while the Soviet Union had beaten and drawn with Switzerland, drawn with Norway and lost to Ireland. It was just as complex for everyone, as Ireland, Switzerland and Norway had achieved similarly erratic results where surprise wins and shuddering losses had occurred.

Just over three and a half months later, Denmark and the Soviet Union played one another again, this time at the Central Lenin Stadium in Moscow, which was also the primary venue for the 1980 Summer Olympics. In the rematch, the Soviet Union edged a more circumspect encounter in front of 100,000 spectators, 1-0, thanks to another goal from Protasov.

From here, Ireland, Switzerland and Norway were accommodating enough not to win any of their remaining fixtures, paving the way for Denmark and the Soviet Union to cruise through to Mexico with a level of ease they couldn't have expected. They were so belatedly domineering in their qualifying group that the two of them combined to score 30 goals on their way to reaching Mexico, while in contrast, Switzerland, Ireland and Norway managed just 14 goals between them. Denmark finished qualification one point ahead of the Soviet Union, after a final match masterclass from Piontek's team away to Ireland.

By the end of the 1985/86 season, Laudrup was winning the Serie A title with Juventus, in succession to Elkjær, who had shocked Italy and beyond when collecting that honour during the previous campaign with Hellas Verona. Meanwhile, Dynamo Kyiv, with a hefty number of the Soviet Union World Cup squad at their disposal, lifted their second European Cup Winners' Cup, when defeating Atlético Madrid in the final, Belanov eventually winning the Ballon d'Or for good measure.

While Denmark were blessed with the calm authority and long-term planning provided by Piontek, the Soviet Union opted for a change in coach during the build-up to the finals. Out went the footballing romantic, Eduard Malofeyev, with Valeriy Lobanovskyi returning to the role for the third time. He subsequently dispensed with the type of passion-play that had seen the Soviet Union qualify under Malofeyev. For Lobanovskyi it was out with the artist's easel and in with the compass, protractor and isograph pens. Technical football was now the mission statement.

Malofeyev had been given time to construct his team, his squad, but a succession of defeats in the run-up to the finals put him out of his job, virtually upon the eve of the tournament. In the five official friendlies they took part in from the turn of the World Cup year, the Soviet Union were beaten by Spain, Mexico, England and Romania, before being held to a draw by Finland.

Meanwhile, Denmark's preparations were only marginally better. A draw at Windsor Park against Northern Ireland was followed by defeats in Bulgaria and Norway. They at least rounded this poor run of results off with a 1-0 victory over Poland in Copenhagen to give themselves a more upbeat send-off to Mexico than the one the Soviet Union were experiencing.

There is an argument to suggest that if Denmark weren't exactly playing possum in the build-up to the tournament, then their players were perhaps guilty of enjoying the pre-World Cup notoriety a little too exuberantly. Piontek's men had had a similarly disjointed build-up to the 1984 European Championship two years earlier, to the point that members of the Danish press pack had suggested that the squad not travel to France at all, due to the fear of national embarrassment once there. Denmark, of course, went on to play wonderfully in France.

Outside of Denmark, the pre-tournament friendly results were largely ignored and their participation in their first-ever World Cup was eagerly anticipated. The heir to *totaalvoetbal* and widely seen as the very epitome of all that Rinus Michels and Johan Cruyff had created a generation earlier, Piontek's team were regarded alongside Brazil and France as the carriers of the remnants of the beautiful game. It was the Soviet Union who were first out of the blocks in Group C, however, and it was they who set the early tone for brilliance. In Irapuato, they swept aside Hungary with an almost obscene ease and ruthless brutality of ball use that was one of the most abiding images of the whole tournament. Running out 6-0 winners, while it wasn't a fixture that was adorned with the pre-match gravitas that Spain and Brazil were afforded 24 hours earlier, the Soviet Union did bestow the tournament with its first performance of substance.

Within two minutes of the start, Pavlo Yakovenko caught the Hungarian goalkeeper, Péter Disztl, at his near post. By the fourth minute, Sergei Aleinikov had added a second goal, struck from distance after a fast-paced passing movement. Belanov then thundered home a penalty 20 minutes later for 3-0, which miraculously remained the score by the time the interval arrived.

Any respite Hungary were afforded was a purely temporary situation, however. Midway through the second half Ivan Yaremchuk rolled in the fourth goal, swiftly followed by László Dajka tripping in an own goal for 5-0.

By now, Lobanovskyi had withdrawn Belanov to preserve him for other battles to come. Yet this meant that when the Soviet Union were awarded a second penalty with less than 15 minutes remaining, the scorer of the first one was no longer on the pitch. It was left to the substitute Vadym Yevtushenko to spoon his effort over the crossbar from 12 yards. A shockingly poor penalty, it was quickly scrubbed from most memories, as within a few minutes his fellow substitute, Sergei Rodionov, was pickpocketing the sixth goal of the afternoon from right under the nose of a stumbling Aleinikov. It had been a wonderfully impressive and expressive opening to the tournament for the Soviet Union. It was also completely at odds with the pre-tournament form that they had been showing.

Two days later, over in Group E, it was the turn of Denmark to get their World Cup underway in Nezahualcóyotl, with their 1-0 victory against Scotland, Preben Elkjær scoring the only goal shortly before the hour.

A day later, the Soviet Union were back in action, this time in León, up against the European champions, France, in one of the best matches of the tournament. With Michel Platini at his empirical best and the prompting and probing of Alain Giresse, it was France who took the game to Lobanovskyi's team, and the joyous thing about that situation was that Belanov and Aleinikov took it straight back to them.

Platini rattled Rinat Dasayev's left-hand post with a free kick of incredible power, while in the second half Vasyl Rats managed to arc a long-distance effort just inside the very same post, past Joël Bats, to put the Soviet Union ahead. A definitive case of Rats beating Bats, even the Brazilian referee, Romualdo Arppi Filho, was forced to jump out of the way of the ball. It was evasive action that came as part of an impressive display of refereeing that would lead to him overseeing the 1986 World Cup Final itself.

A masterpiece of a group match, the Soviet Union held their lead for just eight minutes. Giresse found Luis Fernández in space at the end of a fluid period of keep-ball from Henri Michel's side, from where the midfielder took one touch to control the ball and another to guide it effortlessly into Dasayev's bottom right-hand corner.

No further goals were added, yet the intent to score remained. This wasn't one of those group matches where an unspoken agreement to draw was in operation. Beautifully poised at 1-1, neither team would have refused the chance to strike the winning blow. Jean-Pierre Papin was denied by the quick reflexes of Dasayev, from what was almost a point-blank header on the six-yard line, after a swift turn and inch-perfect cross from Yannick Stopyra. For the Soviet Union, Rats came close again and Bats was forced into a smart stop at his near post from one of his own defenders, when Manuel Amoros was overstretched, attempting to defend a free kick that was curled in from the right-hand side of the French penalty area.

What was most startling about the Soviet Union was their incessant approach to the task. They were relentless in their bid to attack and win. Bats went on to fumble a corner under his own crossbar, perhaps caught by the glare of the sun, only to be rescued by the frantic clearance of Maxime Bossis at the back post. On the Soviet Union went, Belanov dispossessed Jean Tigana then rolled the ball to the veteran Oleh Blokhin, who in turn played in Yaremchuk, who should have done better when bearing down on goal.

The outcome of the match uncertain to the very final whistle, with two matches played the Soviet Union were undeniably the most impressive team so far, and all of this was without the services of the ailing Protasov, who had missed both the Hungary and France fixtures due to a stomach bug.

Three days later, back in Nezahualcóyotl, Piontek's Denmark were thrown together with the much-feared Uruguay, who had come to within six minutes of defeating West Germany in their opening match and were blessed by the presence of the wonderful Enzo Francescoli.

To negate the threat of Uruguay's attacking talents, Piontek stood Jesper Olsen down to the bench, bringing in an extra defender in the shape of Henrik Andersen. Seemingly a negative tactical move designed to protect themselves, Denmark fooled their opponents and the watching world as they put in a performance that was equally as impressive as the Soviet Union's dismantling of Hungary.

While on paper Uruguay were sterner opponents than Hungary, on the arid grass of the Estadio Neza 86 they were down to ten men with less than 20 minutes on the clock. Despite this, they remained committed to attacking football until the final quarter of the match.

Piontek's team found Uruguay to be stubborn and threatening opponents, only really being able to feel confident of victory after Elkjær scored Denmark's fourth goal. This match was where Elkjær and Laudrup attained near perfection. The opening goal was scored when Laudrup teed up Elkjær, when lesser players might have selfishly gone for goal themselves. It was the beginning of an exhibition in a selfless footballing beauty that was as close to *totaalvoetbal* as you could possibly imagine, without the hallmark of Johan Cruyff and Rinus Michels stamped upon it. That this Danish revolution was the brainchild of a West Germanic coach left an air that the laws of footballing gravity were somehow being defied.

It was here where Uruguay hit the self-destruct button, when just eight minutes beyond Denmark taking the lead, Miguel Bossio crudely brought down Frank Arnesen, sending the influential midfielder sprawling in the most unnecessary of ways. Having received a yellow card just minutes earlier, it was an inadvisable challenge that ended Bossio's afternoon and opened the door for Elkjær and Laudrup to run amok.

Uruguay initially shrugged off the loss of Bossio and it was Omar Borrás's team that arguably should have scored the next goal, when Francescoli almost capitalised on the uncertainty of Troels Rasmussen at a corner, only to see the

Denmark goalkeeper redeem himself by pushing the ball around his left-hand post.

Elkjær was then unlucky to have a second goal disallowed, when he got on the end of a wonderful flowing move. He also planted a golden opportunity over the Uruguay crossbar. The chances were coming, but not all of them were being taken.

This was simply a case of Uruguay delaying the inevitable, and yet again it was Elkjær who was key to Denmark extending their lead. Søren Lerby was the grateful recipient of a punishing cross from Piontek's prized asset, which swept along the Uruguay six-yard line for him to guide beyond Fernando Álvez.

Against all expectations, however, Uruguay found a foothold in the match on the very cusp of half-time, with Francescoli both winning and converting a penalty, after coaxing a textbook error from Søren Busk.

Into the second half, Uruguay threw themselves at Denmark, largely making a mockery of their one-man disadvantage. More uncertainty from Rasmussen afforded Uruguay the chance to equalise, but it was a chance that went to waste. They were soon regretting their profligacy, as Laudrup created one of the defining moments of the 1986 World Cup.

With Danish shoulders easing and Piontek's men warming to their prickly second-half task, Denmark spent a significant amount of time orbiting the Uruguay penalty area, with the ball switching from one player to another, creating a visual simplicity that was nothing short of hypnotic. Then came the magic, as Laudrup dipped his shoulder to the left, turning 180 degrees as he went, breezing past a dumbfounded Mario Saralegui, taking the ball into the penalty area at a subtle diagonal trajectory and drifting through the gap between Nelson Gutiérrez and

Víctor Diogo. Laudrup was so swift within this movement that it would be harsh to suggest the Uruguay defence froze.

A desperate lunge from Diogo, Álvez going to ground half a second too late and it was all over, as Laudrup rounded both defender and goalkeeper before rolling the ball into the net. Uruguay's captain, Eduardo Acevedo, was unable to stop it from crossing the line and fell into the billowing netting as a dubious reward for his efforts, from where he floundered spectacularly to get to his feet. It was a goal of style that was enhanced greatly by the swathe of victims Laudrup left in his slipstream.

To their eternal credit, Uruguay didn't give up at this point. Winning a spate of free kicks that were within shooting range, Rasmussen continued to be tested and there were periods where Denmark weren't as focused as they could have been, occasionally lapsing into a propensity to switch off, which would come back to haunt them in the last 16.

It was the introduction of Jan Mølby shortly before the hour mark with the scoreline at 3-1 that gave Denmark the extra impetus to run in another three goals. Elkjær got his second of the match when he prospered from a forceful run into the penalty area by Laudrup. This was the goal that finally subjugated Uruguay. With Arnesen regularly being gifted all the space in the world on the left-hand side, and Mølby spraying precision passes for fun, the opportunities for more goals were bountiful. Elkjær should have completed his hat-trick long before he did so in the 80th minute, while Arnesen himself squandered a free header.

Uruguay were still on the front foot when Denmark scored their fifth, and Elkjær's third. A remorseless breakaway ended with him drifting past Álvez to prod the ball into an empty net. Uruguayan frustration was evident when Laudrup was cynically kicked to the floor by Acevedo as he was running in support of Elkjær. It was petulant, unnecessary, and it went unpunished by the referee.

Denmark's sixth and final goal was converted by Jesper Olsen, who had entered the fray as a replacement for Laudrup after he departed the pitch as a precaution after sustaining that kick from Acevedo. The Manchester United winger's effort slowly rolled over the line but came at the end of another stunning counter-attacking move in which Elkjær was again pivotal. Had Olsen swept the ball beyond Álvez, then it would be remembered now as one of the goals of the tournament. Even in the case of Elkjær, his hat-trick and his all-round performance, the definitive image of this match is that of Laudrup's scene-stealing goal.

With two wins out of two, Denmark had their prized place in the knockout stages assured and the elbow room to rotate their team in the final group fixture to come, against West Germany.

Less than 24 hours later, the Soviet Union closed out their group stage in Irapuato, with that disjointed 2-0 victory over Canada. In a bid to allow his players to recuperate, Lobanovskyi made nine changes to the team that had played so exceptionally against France. Only Oleh Kuznetsov and Aleinikov retained their places in the starting line-up, while Protasov was available for his first appearance of the tournament.

Despite the number of changes made by Lobanovskyi, there was still plenty riding on the outcome of the match. Top of the group was there to be played for and a win would secure it for the Soviet Union. They were made to wait almost an hour for the breakthrough, however. Ominously for Protasov, the score was still goalless when he was replaced by Belanov, and the former had barely sat down on the bench when Blokhin broke the deadlock, assisted by Belanov.

For Protasov, it was more frustration. Having been expected to be one of the stars of the tournament, his World Cup was restricted to the 57 minutes he played against Canada, and he didn't share a pitch with Belanov at all. Added to this, Blokhin was injured as he scored and was replaced by Aleksandr Zavarov, who went on to score the Soviet Union's second goal.

The difference between winning Group C and finishing runners-up was that the Soviet Union avoided playing the holders, Italy, in the last 16, instead being paired with Belgium. In theory, this looked like a bullet dodged, but in the practical terms of June 1986 it was to be anything but.

Three days later in Querétaro, Denmark brought their group stage to an end with a 2-0 victory over a West Germany team that was struggling to find its rhythm consistently. A late equaliser against Uruguay had saved their blushes, while they had been forced to come from behind to defeat Scotland. By everybody else's standards it would have been viewed as a respectable start to the tournament, but by the exacting demands of a nation that had reached the final of five of the last seven major international tournaments it had competed in, it was beyond mildly concerning.

Piontek made four changes to the team that had brushed Uruguay aside. Mølby was given a starting role and Jesper Olsen was back in, with Berggreen stepping down, as did Nielsen in making way for John Sivebæk, all alterations that accentuated just how strong the Denmark squad was. Both Berggreen and Nielsen were also one booking away from being suspended for their last-16 match, so their omissions were admirably strategic. The final change was in goal. With Rasmussen in erratic form and Ole Qvist struggling with a stomach bug, Piontek opted to bring in his third-choice goalkeeper, Lars Høgh.

Høgh had made the squad ahead of the emerging prodigy, Peter Schmeichel, and suddenly found himself front and centre against West Germany. Rather than acting as temporary cover during a match in which Denmark couldn't exit the tournament, for Høgh it would essentially turn into an audition to face Spain. With a string of fine saves and a display of confidence, it was an audition he passed with flying colours. When Piontek finally had the choice of all three of his goalkeepers against Spain, it was Høgh that would be given the nod ahead of Rasmussen and Qvist.

Denmark outclassed West Germany in Querétaro, in a match where Piontek was up against the nation of his birth. Declaring himself to be Germanic of origin but Danish of heart, there was no split loyalties to be dealt with for him. He might have even felt an unexpected or unrecognised extra layer of satisfaction after missing out on the 1966 World Cup as a player.

West Germany made a collection of changes of their own, and those wandering into the Estadio Corregidora might have been forgiven for expecting something of a non-event, given that both teams had already progressed to the knockout stages.

Piontek's men threw themselves straight on to the front foot, however, totally taking West Germany by surprise amid footballing etiquette that was very different to that which was in operation during West Germany's final first-round group match four years earlier. A penalty from Jesper Olsen opened the scoring two minutes prior to the interval, after Morten Olsen was cynically brought down by Wolfgang Rolff.

Seemingly allowing West Germany a bit of a breather during the midsection of the match, it will have come as a bludgeoning shock to the two-times world champions when instead of allowing it to meander to an uneventful conclusion, Denmark again hit the accelerator during the final third of the match, with Frank Arnesen laying on their second goal for the substitute, John Eriksen, a half-time replacement for Elkjær.

Unable to be diplomatic in their approach to a match where the winner would draw the shorter straw in the last 16, Denmark's inherent joy for football meant that they simply couldn't stop themselves from toying with West Germany. They were there to be beaten, and Denmark showed no mercy.

A perfect afternoon came with a bitter aftertaste, however, as Arnesen was flashed a second yellow card by the Belgian referee, Alexis Ponnet with only a couple of minutes remaining, when he reacted to unchecked Machiavellian provocation from Lothar Matthäus. A moment of madness, Arnesen knew immediately the ramifications of his actions, thumping himself on the forehead as he took his leave of the pitch and ultimately the tournament too. While Denmark had the talent to absorb the blow of Arnesen's absence, it would come with a change of shape that set in motion a domino effect that led to their truly incredible exit.

Alongside Uruguay taking on Scotland, this was a match that marked the last acts of the group stages, and with only one day of rest, the knockout stages began. On the first day, the Soviet Union were in action against a so far underwhelming Belgium. Laced with a touch of controversy, the Soviet Union and Belgium played out one of the best matches of the tournament in León, as twice Lobanovskyi's team went ahead, and twice Guy Thys's team equalised.

Belanov ripped in the opening goal from outside the penalty area, struck with such power that it came back out again, a goal that could easily have been the first act in a performance to match the devastating one they had displayed against Hungary. Nine minutes later, Belanov struck the post, and the match found its pivot, as 11 minutes into the second half Enzo Scifo made it 1-1, when drifting in from the back post. The Soviet Union had been the better team by far up to this point, and despite Belgium showing flashes of danger, their goal had come against the run of play.

Belanov's second goal arrived with 20 minutes to play, set up after a determined run from Oleksandr Zavarov, a goal that might well have been the winner, had it not been for the events of the 77th minute, when Jan Ceulemans collected a long ball forward, controlled it beautifully and dispatched it low and to Dasayev's right, just inside the post. Linesman's flag having been raised and then lowered, uproar commenced. Ceulemans did indeed look to be offside at the business end of the goal, but the ball had travelled from almost the halfway line and the Soviet Union back line wasn't holding a uniform line. Rightly or wrongly, a goal was given, and the match drifted into extra time.

Three minutes before half-time of extra time, Belgium grabbed the lead, as the fate of the match shifted. Stéphane Demol was the unexpected goalscorer, with the only goal of his international career, heading past Dasayev from the angle of the six-yard box, as the Soviet Union failed to clear a corner.

Five minutes after the restart the Soviet Union conceded again, another goal that stemmed from a corner, volleyed home by Nico Claesen, after tired attempts were made to clear the ball. It was a goal that should have finished Lobanovskyi's players there and then, yet within a minute Belanov had completed his hat-trick from the penalty spot, to set up a wild finale in which it took an exceptional save from Jean-Marie Pfaff to avoid a penalty shoot-out.

So, the Soviet Union made their exit from the 1986 World Cup, where they had been one of the most impressive teams in the group stages, only to fumble their lines in the last 16, and three days later there was a heavy sense of déjà vu as Denmark repeated the feat, except in even more spectacular circumstances, against Spain.

It was a match that Piontek's side seemed to be very much in control of until the 43rd minute. Jesper Olsen had opened the scoring from the penalty spot just beyond the half-hour mark, only to unintentionally lay on the equaliser for Emilio Butragueño at the worst time imaginable. Had Denmark gone in at half-time without having conceded, then Spain would have likely begun to question themselves as the second half rumbled on. Instead, every time they ploughed forward, they looked capable of scoring, which they did on four more occasions across 45 minutes of football where Denmark swept forward at every opportunity too, another team that looked capable of scoring on multiple occasions, except contriving not to. It was the most evenly balanced 5-1 imaginable.

Emilio Butragueño, the man who had snared Spain their equaliser, added three more goals in the second half. Andoni Goikoetxea was the only other player to score in a Spanish shirt on one of the most stunning days of the tournament.

Whereas the Soviet Union were able to use their experiences at the 1986 World Cup to spring forth and come so very close to glory at the 1988 European Championship, for Denmark their capitulation against Spain was the undoubted fatal blow to the 'Danish Dynamite' era.

While success would swiftly come to them at the 1992 European Championship, it was within a very different post-Piontek ethos and squad, which neither Elkjær nor the older Laudrup brother were involved with, making for the peculiar phenomenon where a team that fell stylistically short of glory have forever been far more adored than the more pragmatic version that lifted a trophy.

Sharing much in common, albeit from different approaches to football, within three days of one another the best two European teams in Mexico had exited the 1986 World Cup, much to the devastation of an entire generation of 1980s hipsters, who have arguably never fully recovered from the disappointment.

Chapter Thirteen

Los Caballos Oscuros

SPAIN'S REHABILITATION at the 1984 European Championship finals, from inept World Cup host two years earlier to runners-up in France, was stunning, and it handed them the enduring role of the dark horses at every major international tournament they took part in for the next two and a half decades.

Denmark's conquerors moved onward to the quarter-finals, where they went up against the Soviet Union's vanquishers, Belgium. Not terrible as far as compensation goes in losing the sumptuous football of Sepp Piontek and Valeriy Lobanovskyi. At least in defeating Denmark and the Soviet Union, respectively, Spain and Belgium had proved they had substance and style of their own too. Combined, they had scored nine goals against their two beaten opponents.

Spain won the World Cup in 2010. Each side of that success sits the European Championship glories of 2008 and 2012. No nation had ever won three major international tournaments before, where a World Cup victory counted as part of the hat-trick. Spain thus cultivated for themselves a unique position within the history of the game.

The Spanish national team has always been a little bit different, whether that's within their outrageously stylish trophy-winning exploits of 2008 to 2012 or the way they've largely reverted to traditional underachieving type since they so impressively picked apart Italy in Kyiv in the final of the 2012 European Championship, this inclusive of the self-inflicted wounds they bestowed upon themselves on the very eve of the 2018 World Cup finals.

Prior to the 2008 European Championship, you couldn't really say that people widely expected Spain to win the tournament. Blessed with outrageously talented individuals, their squads for major international tournaments tended to mirror the national persona of their nation. A collection of autonomous clusters, for whom it was mooted that some component parts were more 'part of the project' than others. Spain had all the theoretical components to be successful at major international tournaments, but when it came to practical application, the recipe fell flat, generally because the decadent ingredients wouldn't bind well enough.

It's one thing being a talented collection of players, but it's an entirely different concept to be a successful collective. All too often the varying factions would be pulling in opposing directions. Getting the varying cliques within a Spanish national squad to pull in the same direction is as difficult as wallpapering a ceiling, simply because Spain, as a nation, isn't always pulling together in the same direction. Made up of 17 autonomous communities, with the complicated additions of two further autonomous cities, Ceuta and Melilla, located upon the coastline of Morocco, Spain isn't a nation that was built for unity.

The dividing lines were always there, but they were scorched to the earth during the 1936–39 Spanish Civil War, in which the left-wing Republicans fought for control against the right-wing Nationalists. In the bloody game of a Communist ideology vs a Fascist ethos, the demands of the centre ground were largely disregarded. If you approved of neither concept, it was either a case of siding with the lesser of two evils or simply keeping your head down and agreeing with the wider consensus of the population of whichever city, town or village you lived in.

With Joseph Stalin arming the Republicans and Adolf Hitler and Benito Mussolini actively assisting the Nationalists, sides were apportioned upon a region-to-region basis. Yet, with greater numerical strengths in personnel, aircraft, tanks and weaponry, a Nationalist victory was the most obvious outcome. Backed by the devastating support of the Luftwaffe, Francisco Franco benefited from the greater interest of Hitler and Mussolini in a Nationalist victory, than Stalin's interest in the Republicans prevailing. A theory remains that Stalin was simply intent on keeping Germany busy while the Soviet Union prepared for another war that was still to come.

To the north and geographically isolated by the Nationalist eastward advance, San Sebastián fell in September 1936. From there, it took over 16 months until the Nationalist forces reached the Mediterranean, when it split the link between Barcelona and Madrid. While resistance remained strong, Catalonia was overrun by the end of January 1939.

It tends to be an uncomfortable fact for the most militantly individual regions, which are more symbolically linked to the fight against Franco, that the last stand of the Republican cause was taken on the streets of Madrid, the city credited as the Nationalist centre of power. Madrid held on until the end of March 1939, but when Franco finally claimed it, of course it would be where he would place his generalissimo's throne.

Having kept their distance from the Second World War, Spain was shunned when plans for the rebuilding of Europe were put in place. The financial input that other nations gained didn't go the way of Spain, as Franco had been closely linked to the Axis powers, if not enough to actively participate in the conflict, then certainly enough to supply Germany and Italy with the use of Spanish ports, along with offering supplies of vital materials and even military support on the Eastern Front.

Franco allowed Spanish volunteers to join the fight against Stalin but wouldn't sanction their involvement in the Axis offensives against the Western Allies or against any Western European nations that were under occupation. He also refused the tempting proposition of officially joining with Germany and Italy in 1940 after the fall of France, inclusive of the symbolic concept of reclaiming Gibraltar from the British. Fearing that he wouldn't be able to defend the Canary Islands from invasion by the British in retaliation, Franco opted to cheer his fascist friends on from the sidelines, rather than get his nation's hands dirty overseas. He even stationed field armies in the Pyrenees to act as a deterrent in the event of Hitler deciding he would quite like to roll on to the Iberian Peninsula after all.

These flirtations with the Axis powers meant that Franco and Spain were ostracised internationally for a prolonged period, before finally joining the United Nations in 1955, also being classed as an ally of America, due to Franco's anti-communist stance in what was the Cold War era.

While the Second World War raged on, Franco instead set about eradicating his domestic enemies. An estimated 200,000 people died during the first two years of his dictatorship. Regional diversity was repressed in favour of a centrally defined nationalism. Regional languages were banned in public and removed from schools, road signs, advertising, basically anywhere of a public nature.

The definition of what was and what wasn't Spanish often rested on the whims of government. Flamenco dancing was deemed very Spanish indeed, as was bullfighting, thus your grandparents always came home from their fortnight in the Costa del Sol in possession of a tea towel with a bullfighter on it, a set of small ornamental plates with flamenco dancers upon them, or some wooden castanets and maracas.

By the dawning of the 1960s, economic stability had begun to attract a wave of foreign investment. Spain was somewhere that people wanted to visit for holidays that offered guaranteed sunshine. The evolution of Real Madrid was perfectly timed for this, as they morphed into what was perceived to be Franco's plaything. This was something of an opportunistic occurrence, as Franco sought to cultivate new ways in which to project a positive image of Spain to the rest of Europe and beyond. Football was perfect in this respect, and it acted as an artistic conduit for subconscious propaganda. The purity of the all-white Real Madrid kit and their collection of the first five European Cups to be handed out helped make Spain appear an attractive and talent-fuelled place.

If Franco had a long-standing fixation with Real Madrid, it hadn't been particularly visible during the 1940s. Despite winning the Copa del Generalísimo back-to-back in 1946 and 1947, when *Los Blancos* won the LaLiga title in 1953/54 it was the first time that they had been crowned champions for over two decades. Relegation had even been a very real possibility at one stage during the 1940s.

If it's regime favouritism you're looking for in the immediate years after the end of hostilities, then Atlético Madrid's post-war link-up with the air force would offer a more compelling argument, when, as Atlético Aviación, they won the first two post-Civil War Spanish titles.

In fact, during the 1940s and into the first half of the 1950s, there was little to suggest footballing suppression of the 'troublesome' regions. In the nine-season span between

1944/45 and 1952/53, Barcelona won LaLiga five times, with the fourth and fifth of those successes being as part of a league and cup double. Athletic Club also did the double in 1942/43.

In many respects, this situation suited Franco's needs quite well. Having taken away so many cultural and lifestyle liberties and freedoms from Catalonia and the Basque Country, allowing them glory on the football field instead was something that gave those subjugated regions a focus for identity and pride. In Bob Paisley terminology, Franco was likely to be quite happy to 'throw them a piece of toffee'.

The landscape then changed in the mid-1950s. The introduction of European club competition was a major opportunity and one that should have been perfectly timed for a dominant Barcelona. Had Alfredo Di Stéfano completed his projected move to the Catalan capital in 1953, then it likely would have been. Instead, Di Stéfano was spirited away to Real Madrid and a new path was taken. Within a year, they were champions for the first time in 21 years and two years later claimed the very first European Cup.

From the dawning of the 1960s, the game ran away from Barcelona. Between claiming the 1959/60 and the 1984/85 LaLiga titles, they were domestic champions on only one further occasion, in 1973/74, powered as they were by Rinus Michels and Johan Cruyff.

As Real Madrid took a stranglehold upon both the domestic and Continental game, the spectre of underhand manoeuvrings increased. Franco was deemed to be pulling the strings and Barcelona were insistent that they were being denied the rightful fruits of their labour. This is a spectre that stretches back long before the arrival of Di Stéfano, way back to the infamous 11-1 reversal that Barcelona suffered in 1943 in the Copa del Generalísimo semi-final second leg at the Estadio Chamartín.

Within this, mistrust and resentment festered. Between the beginning of the 1960s and the death of Franco in November 1975, the LaLiga title evaded the grasp of the city of Madrid only three times. While it was an environment in which rich pickings were collected on the club stage in Europe, it led to difficulties in creating a national team that could match those successes in the international arena.

Largely inspired by Internazionale's former Barcelona attacker, Luis Suárez, in 1964 Spain won the second edition of the European Championship, yet it was a success that seemed completely out of character. World Cup quarter-finalists in 1934, they had played no part in either 1930 or 1938, the latter of those absences due to the Civil War itself, the former due to European reticence in making the arduous journey to Uruguay.

Spain did finish fourth in the 1950 World Cup, but then failed to qualify for the 1954 and 1958 tournaments. A refusal by Franco to allow his nation to take on the Soviet Union in the two-legged quarter-finals of the inaugural European Championship, which culminated in 1960, was followed by group-stage elimination at the 1962 World Cup.

Beyond success on home soil in 1964, Spain were again eliminated from the World Cup at the group stages in 1966, before failing to reach the finals of the 1968 European Championship as holders. This was followed by further failures to reach the finals of the World Cups of 1970 and 1974, plus the European Championship finals of 1972 and 1976.

When Spain finally returned to the finals of major international tournaments, in Argentina in 1978, they made yet another early exit, something that they matched at the 1980 European Championship in Italy.

Then, 1982 happened. Awarded the hosting rights as far back as 1966, Spain delivered a World Cup of intense beauty in broad terms, even taking in their stride the insistence of FIFA to enlarge the event from 16 nations to 24, and increasing the commercialism exponentially. In footballing terms, however, Spain couldn't rise to the occasion. No international powerhouse has made a worse effort at competing in their own World Cup. Five matches played and just one won, they limped out of their own tournament having scored just four goals.

Miguel Muñoz was the man that Spain turned to in their hour of ignominy. Handed the job of piecing a new national team together, he essentially started with a blank sheet of paper in an era when the bar hadn't been set all that high by his predecessors, within an era when neither Real Madrid nor Barcelona were dominating the domestic scene. The rise of Real Sociedad had brought a sense of liberation to the Basque Country and Athletic Club were swift to follow suit.

The longest-serving Real Madrid head coach ever, and a legendary servant of the club as a player, Muñoz should have been a polarising figure, but he brought with him a surprising sense of unity to the Spanish national team. He'd departed the Santiago Bernabéu part way through a difficult 1973/74 season, after an incredible 14 years in charge in which he'd won nine LaLiga titles and two European Cups. Prior to that, in his playing days, he'd been a European champion three times, twice as captain, as well as winning his domestic league title four times. Muñoz was a Real Madrid hero to the core.

Perhaps it was within the sense of an eight-year detachment from the Bernabéu, combined with the abject failure of the national team since 1964, that Muñoz crept into the role under the radar somewhat. Throwing out improved results and a vague sense of style, he won unexpected friends and admirers.

In between leaving Real Madrid and taking on the onerous task of rejuvenating Spain's fortunes, Muñoz had taken charge of Granada, Las Palmas and Sevilla to varying outcomes. While he'd failed to save Granada from top-flight relegation, he had two inspiring years on Gran Canaria at Las Palmas, whom he led to the 1978 Copa del Rey Final, where they were beaten at the Bernabéu by the Barcelona of Michels and Cruyff, before taking the club to a creditable sixth-place finish in his second season.

These accomplishments brought Sevilla to the door of Muñoz in the summer of 1979, a club with a self-conscious image of where it should be in the great scheme of Spanish football. This wasn't a vintage Sevilla, however, and the top half of the table respectability that Muñoz delivered at the Ramón Sánchez-Pizjuán, along with a run to the semi-final of the 1981 Copa del Rey, was a respectable if unspectacular return. When the 1981/82 season began in erratic fashion, he was gone by early December, after a 1-0 home reversal at the hands of Hércules.

Largely seen as yesterday's man, Muñoz watched from afar as his nation systematically unravelled as the host of the 1982 World Cup. When José Santamaría was ushered aside as part of the post-tournament recriminations, Muñoz found himself centre stage once more, classed as a wise elder. The role of head coach to the Spanish national team was perfect for Muñoz, the job suiting him just as much as he suited the job. By now 60 years old, he was the ideal candidate for what was basically a part-time role. With little in the way of expectation and seen as a safe pair of hands, he set about revolutionising the team he inherited.

In eternally questioned circumstances, Spain qualified for the 1984 European Championship. Needing to beat Malta by an 11-goal margin on the final night of qualifying, at the Estadio Benito Villamarín Spain ran out 12-1 winners.

Whether the suspicious glances and innuendoes over how they reached the finals were deserved or not, Muñoz and his team excelled in France. Only seven members of Spain's squad for the 1982 World Cup were in the collective that Muñoz selected to take to the Euros.

While the pressure wasn't necessarily off Spain going into the 1984 European Championship, it was perhaps from a perspective that they couldn't possibly disappoint more than they had in 1982 that they took the short trip to France in such an emboldened manner.

All the way up to the last minute of the group stages Spain looked set to fall by the wayside again, when with a goalless scoreline against West Germany about to end their campaign, Antonio Maceda made a hero of himself by scoring the last-minute winner in Paris, a goal that not only sent them through to the semi-final but did so as group winners.

After overcoming the wonderfully talented Denmark in the last four on penalties, Spain eventually fell to the artistry of France in the final, Michel Platini answering the call of destiny in a match that didn't quite hit the sweet spot that the rest of the tournament had. A costly error from goalkeeper and captain, Luis Arconada, in the 57th minute took the match away from Spain, when he spilled an innocuous free kick over his goal line.

Muñoz's side had worked hard to reach the final of the 1984 European Championship. Holding their nerve when it was required, they threw out the occasional period of skill and penetration, like an experienced boxer beckoning forward a younger opponent to walk on to a devastating punch. Lulling their foes into a false sense of security, then hitting them with a fast, offensive flurry, which left them gasping for air on the floor. Pragmatic, compact, defensive at times and bludgeoning at others, Spain waited patiently for the right moment to strike. Over the course of the championship, they led the matches they played for no more than an accumulative 14 minutes, 13 of those minutes coming in their opening fixture against Romania, which had ended in a disappointing 1-1 draw.

Their campaign was built upon a resilience and ability to fight back that simply hadn't been in evidence at the 1982 World Cup under Santamaría. It was upon these footballing foundations, and within the company of such ghosts of relatively recent political history, that Spain prepared for the 1986 World Cup.

Successfully avoiding the heavyweight nations in the draw for the qualifiers, they were still handed a deceptively difficult task. Cocooned within UEFA Group 7 with the British duo of Wales and Scotland, plus the notoriously stubborn Iceland, Spain's new-found resilience was strenuously tested.

Comprehensively beaten in Glasgow and Wrexham, Spain played the percentages during the rest of their fixtures. Too strong for Wales at the Estadio Benito Villamarín in Seville, they had shown they had the stomach for a battle when edging out Scotland in the same city, except this time over at the Estadio Ramón Sánchez-Pizjuán. They then rounded out their qualification campaign with back-to-back 2-1 victories over Iceland, either side of the summer of 1985, when on both occasions they had conceded first.

Character first, skill second, having forced their way to the 1986 World Cup, Spain then embarked upon a five-match pre-World Cup tour of home, before setting off for Central America. Taking in matches in Zaragoza, Valencia, Las Palmas, Alicante and Cádiz, they emerged from that run unbeaten. The opposition had also been of a high calibre, and while Austria had only narrowly missed out on a play-off, Bulgaria, the Soviet Union, Belgium and Poland were all heading to Mexico too. It had been an impressive run of results, Spain conceding no goals whatsoever and failing to win only one of those five matches; the form of Míchel, Ramón Calderé and Julio Salinas had been particularly good.

Their pre-World Cup tour of Spain had almost been a lap of honour in reverence of Muñoz's seemingly successful regeneration of the national team after the nightmares of 1982. Passing through Gran Canaria, where Spain defeated the Soviet Union 2-0 at the Estadio Insular, the home of Las Palmas, where Muñoz had presided with style and purpose for two years, seemed a symbolic gesture. It also seemed symbolic that the goalscorers that day were part of the new wave of players who were now flooding through. Salinas scored on his international debut on Gran Canaria, while Eloy, the other player on target that day, was also a recent newcomer to the national team, having made his bow against Austria in Zaragoza, at La Romareda. Míchel was also another who had made his run to prominence a late one.

By the time of the 1986 World Cup finals, Spain had a new dynamic. Arconada, not only an iconic goalkeeper, but also captain of the national team, had been deemed badly culpable during the 3-0 defeat to Wales in Wrexham, and compounded this when sustaining a cruciate ligament injury at the beginning of World Cup season, thus missing the entirety of the domestic campaign. Injury or not, Muñoz had already taken the difficult decision to replace the Real Sociedad legend with his Athletic Club counterpart, Andoni Zubizarreta, who was upon the brink of a transfer to Barcelona in the summer of 1986.

Only six members of Spain's 1982 World Cup squad made the trip to Mexico four years later. Of those six, only four made an on-field contribution, and of those four Rafael Gordillo appeared only once, while Maceda, the hero in France, was restricted by injury and illness to playing the opening two matches only. Ricardo Gallego missed the opening two matches due to a stomach bug that swept the squad, and José Antonio Camacho, the new captain, was the only link to 1982 to play every match of Spain's campaign at the 1986 World Cup.

While there was no shortage of experience within Muñoz's squad, there was a distinct freshness to it, which succeeded in detaching them from the failures of 1982, via the feel-good factor generated by their unexpected run to the final of the 1984 European Championship. The main embodiment of this rise was *La Quinta del Buitre*, the collective of young talent that emerged at the Bernabéu and succeeded in ending the barren early 1980s for Real Madrid. Led by the predatory instincts of Emilio Butragueño and the intelligent promptings of Míchel, they were aided and abetted by the defensive mastery of Manolo Sanchís, the multiskilled midfield majesty of Rafael Martín Vázquez and, fleetingly, the attacking vision of Miguel Pardeza.

Between winning the 1979/80 LaLiga title and victory in the 1985 UEFA Cup Final, Real Madrid had suffered an uncharacteristic dry spell when it came to honours, collecting only the Copa del Rey in 1982 and the short-lived Spanish League Cup in 1985. It was an era peppered by near-misses on the biggest prizes at the Bernabéu. With a point short here and an inferior head-to-head record there, a succession of league titles slipped through their fingers, while the 1981 European Cup Final and the 1983 Cup Winners' Cup Final also went against them.

When it came to *La Quinta del Buitre*, in the cases of Vázquez and Pardeza, their international careers were further down the line, and the latter would have to depart the Spanish capital for Real Zaragoza to progress his career after Real Madrid signed Hugo Sánchez from their bitter cross-city rivals Atlético Madrid. Meanwhile, both

Butragueño and Míchel made Muñoz's squad for Mexico, while the uncapped Sanchís missed out, only through injury, on joining his team-mates in Mexico, having been heavily expected to be called up.

This was all within a perfect storm for Muñoz; the emergence of the finest crop of youngsters Real Madrid have arguably ever produced, all overseen by the watchful and ageing eyes of Santillana and Juanito, who still made cameo appearances for Real Madrid from the bench. A club that had just risen from a half-decade-long slumber by their impeccably high standards, Butragueño and Míchel were just two of seven Real Madrid players to make the squad for Mexico. Butragueño's ascent to stardom had been so spectacular that he made the Spanish squad for the 1984 European Championship finals, despite only making his senior debut for Real Madrid in the February of that year.

Combined with this, Muñoz was blessed by the mid-1980s rise of Barcelona under the leadership of Terry Venables, and the barbed wire-coated assaults on success of Athletic Club. Barcelona had won LaLiga in 1984/85 and reached the 1986 European Cup Final, while Athletic Club had won back-to-back LaLiga titles in 1982/83 and 1983/84, the second of those glories coming as part of a league and cup double. In a bid not to be outdone, Atlético Madrid had made a run to the final of the European Cup Winners' Cup. This meant that all three European finals in 1986 had a Spanish participant as, along with claiming their first LaLiga title in six years, Real Madrid also retained the UEFA Cup.

Barcelona provided Muñoz with Victor, Calderé, Julio Alberto, Carrasco and back-up goalkeeper Urruti, who intriguingly went to this World Cup six years beyond what would prove to be his last appearance for the national team, and within the shadow of his planned replacement at club level. In turn, Zubizarreta was joined in the squad from the San Mamés by Salinas and 'The Butcher of Bilbao' himself, Andoni Goikoetxea. Not only would Zubizarreta end up in Barcelona colours, but via a two-year hiatus at Atlético Madrid, Salinas was also at the Camp Nou by 1988.

Spain headed to Mexico in rude health but it wasn't long before the squad's general health was put to the test. A potent stomach bug meant that Gordillo was restricted to a place on the bench for their opening match against Brazil in Guadalajara at the Estadio Jalisco. He was joined on the sick list by Gallego, Hipólito Rincón and Calderé, who was so ill he had to be hospitalised.

Despite being severely depleted, Spain gave Brazil a substantial fright. After a tentative first half, where both sides probed for gaps and weaknesses without summoning up the bravery to land a killer blow, the game pivoted on a controversial incident when early in the second half a wonderful piece of skill from Míchel on the outside of the box resulted in a powerful effort striking the underside of the Brazil crossbar, from where it unmistakably bounced over the line. Not for the last time during the 1986 World Cup, a referee looked towards his linesman and a collaboratively wrong call was made. No goal was given and the pre-tournament fears of many observers, players and coaches came to pass.

There had been a very vocal protest over referees from the perceived lesser footballing nations taking charge of matches involving the biggest footballing nations. On only the second day of the tournament these fears had come home to roost, when the Australian referee, Chris Bambridge, along with his American linesman, failed to spot a perfectly legitimate Spanish goal.

Within ten minutes of the incident, the legendary Sócrates had headed home the only goal of the match, via a flurry of activity that had brought the encounter to vivid and scintillating life. Edinho handled the ball into Zubizarreta's goal, only for it to be thankfully disallowed, a tense moment that was followed by a costly miss at the other end by Butragueño, before Sócrates punished Muñoz's unfortunate team. It ended 1-0 to Brazil, and it was to be the only time that Bambridge would take charge of a match in Mexico.

Muñoz took the positives from their opening fixture and prepared his team to face one of the biggest ghosts of 1982, Northern Ireland. The six-day gap between their opening two matches gave Spain's missing players the time to recover from their various ailments, and they were generally the better team in a 2-1 victory, having gifted their opponents an entirely avoidable invitation back into the match via a combination of errors that had been started by Zubizarreta.

Five days later, at the Estadio Tecnológico in Monterrey, brain overcame brawn as Spain ran out 3-0 winners against an Algerian team that opted to try to kick their way into the knockout stages. The perfect situation for Goikoetxea, it was stunning that on an afternoon where, in retaliation of Algeria's heavy-handed approach, he caused the injury that would end Nacerdine Drid's day after only 20 minutes but he didn't earn himself a yellow card until the 89th minute.

Before Drid's exit, Calderé had opened the scoring, laid on by a wonderful cut back by Salinas, and it surprisingly took until the 68th minute until the same goalscorer added a second, repelled as Spain were by a succession of fine saves from Drid's replacement, Larbi El Hadi. Within two minutes of Calderé's second goal, Eloy had made it three, the last goal of a match where Spain could have scored twice as many, but also one during which Zubizarreta had to make a couple of key saves with the score 1-0.

Spain had earned a last-16 clash with Denmark, but Sepp Piontek's team had been billed as the new tournament favourites after winning all three of their group matches. However, those 45 second-half minutes in Querétaro belonged entirely to Muñoz and his men. At 1-0 down, Spain had been in danger of befalling a similar fate to that of Uruguay. Distinctly second best all over the pitch, their opponents were painting beautiful, esoteric footballing pictures until Jesper Olsen's stunning mistake. Gift accepted, what then broke out was a totally different Spanish performance, as the perfection of Denmark's play had been wilfully punctured. Out went the pragmatism and in came freedom of movement and expression.

Undone by overconfidence, Preben Elkjær wasted two fine opportunities to put Denmark back in front, before the avalanche of Spanish goals came. A 32-minute span where they scored four times, Butragueño netting three of them, turned the tournament on its head from the perspective of the likely European threat to lift the trophy.

Vulnerable at set pieces, increasingly making needless mistakes, Denmark's own actions emboldened Spain's approach. Butragueño headed his team in front in the 56th minute, and 12 minutes later Goikoetxea powered home from the penalty spot, as Piontek's team hit the self-destruct button.

Still, Denmark believed they could save themselves. On came Jan Mølby, who tested the reflexes of Zubizarreta, but Spanish confidence was beginning to soar, and as the Danes' efforts earned only increasing frustration, the punishment handed out by Butragueño was devastating, as he scored twice more in the last ten minutes. Míchel and the substitute Eloy combined to set up his hat-trick goal, before another penalty completed the scoring, the Real Madrid striker having earned his own spot kick.

Denmark had paid a heavy price for the suspension of Frank Arnesen, and Spain would count the cost of their own loss of Goikoetxea for the quarter-final against Belgium, having picked up his second yellow card of the tournament, against Denmark. Already without the injured Maceda, it meant that Muñoz would be without both of his two first-choice central defenders.

Billed as a clash of the party poopers, it was a disingenuous moniker to hand to a fixture that took place in Puebla, especially as Spain were fresh off the back of scoring ten goals in their last three matches. A team very much in form, Spain's encounter with Belgium was the last of the four quarter-finals and it was already known that Diego Maradona and Argentina would be waiting in the semi-final at the Estadio Azteca.

In came Chendo to replace Goikoetxea, the only switch Muñoz made, when he could have made another, as there were injury doubts hanging over Salinas. Given the stakes, Belgium were undoubtedly opponents to take as seriously as Denmark, but they weren't as talented as Piontek's team, so this was a match where Spain needed to conquer the hurdles of the mind as much as those on the pitch, considering they were now within the potentially uncomfortable role of being the favourites.

A recurring theme was now unfolding, and the 1986 World Cup continued to goad the best teams that Europe had to offer the tournament, as Spain fell to Belgium on penalties after a conscientiously chiselled outcome from Thys's men. During the initial 90 minutes of football, Belgium's stubbornness outrageously brought them to within five minutes of winning without the need for extra time and spot kicks, on an afternoon where Spain had thrown everything they could at the inspired Jean-Marie Pfaff.

Distinctly second best during much of the first half, Belgium refused to panic and were comfortable on the ball whenever they could gain possession of it. Using their fine technical abilities and intelligent use of space to draw breath, they even managed to occasionally counterpunch, testing the balance and durability of Spain's makeshift central defence.

It was on one such exploration forward that Belgium took the lead with ten minutes of the first half remaining, as Jan Ceulemans was gifted a ludicrous amount of space on the edge of the Spanish six-yard box, from where he planted in a wonderfully directed header, after a tempting cross from Franky Vercauteren.

No further first-half goals, it set up a fascinating second half, as Spain lay siege to the Belgian penalty area, only to be met by some outstandingly belligerent defending and fine goalkeeping, from which Thys's team would spring forth on the counter-attack, often carving themselves the better chances. One such opportunity fell to Daniel Veyt, who forced an excellent save from Zubizerreta. Ceulemans, who had skilfully laid the ball off to Veyt, was already celebrating a goal, before dropping to his knees in despair, yet he remained pivotal to every moment of Belgian positivity, his brilliance matched only by Pfaff at the other end, who pulled off magnificent saves from Míchel and Calderé.

More and more frantic the game became, as Stéphane Demol almost diverted the ball into his own net, only to later be the hero when clearing desperately from Butragueño, after Pfaff had uncharacteristically missed it. Regaining his composure, the Belgian goalkeeper then denied Míchel once more.

Peculiar in nature, as the second half wore on, while Spain deserved every sympathy in their bid to level the scoreline, it was also difficult not to will Belgium on towards the clean sheet their efforts warranted too. However, eventually, Spain did get their equaliser, from a clever set-piece routine after a free kick near the right-hand corner flag taken by Míchel. Real Zaragoza's Juan Antonio Señor powered the ball past Pfaff from just outside the D on the edge of the penalty area. It was a glorious goal, and it came with only five minutes remaining.

Instead of utilising their clear momentum, however, Spain then seemed to settle for extra time, and it was Belgium who had the best two chances to claim a late winner, which fell on both occasions to Nico Claesen, only to be denied by Zubizarreta.

Into an extra 30 minutes and still the chances came, as with signs of fatigue taking hold, Calderé snatched at an opportunity when in clear sight of goal, while Míchel and Butragueño also threatened. At the other end, Ceulemans, with socks around his ankles, played in Georges Grün, only for his shot to be blocked by Zubizarreta.

So, the match lurched into a penalty shoot-out, the third of the four quarter-finals to do so, and with nine out of ten penalties finding the back of the net, it was Eloy who proved to be fallible for Spain from ten yards, and Leo Van der Elst the hero with the decisive kick for Belgium. Luck deserted Spain in the most agonising of manners, and three times Zubizarreta would have been able to make the save if he'd simply remained upright for the penalty kicks, as three times Belgium's players opted to shoot straight down the middle.

With this outcome, another 1986 World Cup sliding door closed, as the mirage of a Spain vs Argentina semi-final evaporated, a match that would have given the watching global audience a rematch between Diego Maradona and his nemesis Goikoetxea, the best player on the face of the planet up against the man who once broke his ankle, and reputedly put the football boot he did it with on display in a glass case at his home.

Just how Spain might have fared in the semi-final against Argentina will never be known, but if anyone was going to have the power to unsettle Maradona in Mexico during the summer of 1986, then it could only have been 'The Butcher of Bilbao'. It makes for one of the most tantalising hypotheticals of the 1986 World Cup.

Chapter Fourteen

One Last Tango

BRAZIL WERE without cohesion, or a head coach, when the draw for the 1986 World Cup finals was made, in December 1985. Since Telê Santana had stepped down in the wake of the their exit to Italy at the 1982 World Cup, the three-times world champions had had four different head coaches, one of those being Santana once again, who took the reins on a temporary basis to guide them through the qualifiers and claim their place in Mexico.

Carlos Alberto Parreira had been the immediate successor to Santana beyond the 1982 World Cup, and the man in charge when Brazil lost out to Uruguay in the 1983 Copa América Final. When he paid the price for that failure, Zico's brother, Edu, was brought in, only to be moved aside too, not long after England beat them at the Maracanã, in the summer of 1984.

Next up, Evaristo was brought in with the 1986 World Cup qualifiers in mind, only to be jettisoned before the campaign had begun. He would still be a presence in Mexico at the helm of Iraq. In a blind panic the Confederação Brasileira de Futebol (CBF) turned to Santana, who was at that point within the employment of the Saudi Arabian club, Al-Ahli. An agreement was reached that Santana would be allowed to lead Brazil for their World Cup qualifying fixtures, which would be condensed within a four-week span across June 1985, before returning to the Middle East to resume his duties with Al-Ahli, with whom his contract wasn't to expire until December. This was the second time the CBF had attempted to re-employ Santana since his 1982 departure, but Al-Ahli had been unwilling to countenance the idea of relinquishing him in November 1984 when they had come calling.

Even after World Cup qualification had been secured, indecision continued. Despite Santana having unpicked himself from Al-Ahli by December, there was a split in opinion at the CBF, with some committee members favouring the appointment of Rubens Minelli, a head coach with an impressive back catalogue of his own, inclusive of winning a hat-trick of national titles between 1975 and 1977 with Internacional and São Paulo.

It wasn't until the January of World Cup year that Santana was finally handed the job of leading Brazil to Mexico. Swiftly into action, however, by February he'd named a provisional squad of 29 players, and for the best part of three and a half months he had a clear run with his preparations for the tournament, shorn only of regular sightings of his European-based players.

Far from plain sailing for Santana, there were a cluster of flashpoints and curveballs for him to deal with between setting off on a mini tour of Europe in March and arriving in Mexico, via a tour of Brazil for five pre-tournament friendlies that took in visits to São Luís, Goiânia, Brasília, Recife and São Paulo. Significant-looking losses were sustained within four days of one another with semi-scratch line-ups in Frankfurt and Budapest against West Germany and Hungary, respectively, at a combined deficit of 5-0, before performances and results took an upturn upon Brazil's return home. Impressive victories were collected against

Peru, East Germany, Finland and Yugoslavia, with 14 goals scored along the way, before being held to a 1-1 draw by Chile as way of a farewell for Mexico.

Travails of Europe forgotten, Brazil were now shaping up nicely. While it was the only match of the five on home soil that they conceded in, the Yugoslavia fixture had been pivotal to Santana's preparations. A 4-2 win in Recife, it was the match where Zico had seemingly proved his fitness for the finals, scoring a hat-trick to complete a stunning fightback from a standing start of having ruled himself out of the World Cup a few months earlier.

Others were less fortunate. Dirceu, a wonderful attacking threat and a veteran of Brazil's squads in 1974, 1978 and 1982, was denied a trip to a fourth World Cup when suffering an injury during a training pitch collision with back-up goalkeeper, Paulo Vítor. He was replaced by the Atlético Mineiro striker, Edivaldo, ahead of the popular claims of Bangu's Marinho Emiliano. Direcu was almost 34 but had just enjoyed one of the best seasons of his career, defying individual and collective gravity with Como in Serie A, where he helped them to mid-table respectability, finishing ahead of the reigning champions, Hellas Verona, as well as the fast-emerging Sampdoria. Given Zico's problems to come, Dirceu would have been a valuable member of Santana's squad, while his replacement, Edivaldo, went on to play no active role in Mexico.

Not the only blow, Santana was also without the defensive midfield qualities of Toninho Cerezo, with the AS Roma star missing through a persistent hamstring problem. This issue was exacerbated by a pre-tournament injury that ruled out Carlos Mozer, the man initially projected to fill the void left by Cerezo.

Santana was left with a tricky conundrum, as he'd formulated a plan for the World Cup that would essentially mean him deploying two defensive midfielders, one to sit in front of the defensive line, the other to have a deep-lying but more mobile and ball-playing remit, something that would compensate for the older legs of Sócrates, Júnior and, earlier in the tournament in cameo appearances from the substitutes' bench, Falcão.

Elzo, having been called up to step in for Cerezo, would play 11 times for Brazil, all those appearances landing between March and June 1986. The loss of Mozer then brought Alemão into play, the Botafogo man having been an intermittent presence for Brazil since 1983.

Constantly having to reconfigure his plans, Santana had also lost the rampaging full-back Leandro, who was true to his threat of refusing to go to the World Cup should his good friend Renato Gaúcho not make the squad. Leandro and Renato had broken curfew one night during the exhaustive preparations for Mexico, and suffered the repercussions. Whereas Renato's inclusion in the final 22 was touch and go, thus he was easy to make an example of, Leandro was of huge importance to Santana, having been the partner in attacking full-back crime to Júnior four years earlier in Spain. With Júnior now having stepped into midfield, it meant that Leandro had become the main threat from full-back.

In the self-imposed absence of Leandro, a set of events unfolded that meant that Santana was forced to switch to Édson at right-back, only to be dispossessed of his services by an injury picked up in Brazil's second group match against Algeria. It was this domino effect that would eventually bring the uncapped Josimar into play, who proved to be such an explosive element as the tournament progressed.

This was also a situation that brought an inadvertent end to Falcão's entire career, as when Édson's World Cup came to an end in the tenth minute against Algeria, it was Falcão who was summoned from the substitutes' bench, slotting into midfield, with Júnior dropping back to cover. Falcão had played very little club football across the two previous seasons, and until being recalled to the national squad at the beginning of World Cup year, he hadn't appeared in a Brazil team since 1982.

Of all the risks that were taken by Santana on calling on the legends of the previous World Cup, the most questionable one centred on Falcão, especially as Éder had already been jettisoned due to a combination of a loss of form, a lack of fitness and the red mist descending against Peru, when he was sent off within 30 minutes for throwing and connecting with punches.

Against Algeria it was clear that the match was passing Falcão by, if not to the naked eye of the spectator, then certainly to the player himself, who would play no further part in the tournament, and then subsequently announce his retirement from football once Brazil's campaign had ended. It won't have been something that was lost on Santana either. When cast alongside the eminently casual yet visionary nature of Sócrates, Falcão took on the image of a luxury too far, and the Brazilian head coach acted accordingly.

Another issue had been the loss of form of Oscar, the central defender with thunder in his boots who had made such an impression in Spain and was the man who had captained Brazil all the way through Santana's warm-up fixtures, prior to the World Cup. In Mexico, he would be usurped by Júlio César as the partner of the new captain, Edinho, and spend the entire tournament as an unused substitute.

Thankfully, despite all the problems Santana had faced with regards to the form, fitness and discipline of the players he wanted to take to Mexico, at least Careca hadn't given him a single moment of anxiety as the World Cup loomed.

Careca had missed the party in 1982, when suffering significant injury on the eve of the tournament, and this time around he was eager to make up for the missed opportunity of four years earlier. The eyes of Europe's biggest clubs were also trained on him.

The big question was who to field alongside Careca. While the bludgeoning Wálter Casagrande had been in fine form in the warm-up matches, in terms of style of play he was ill-fitting when it came to *O Jogo Bonito*, Santana's embraced method of football. Casagrande was a regular on the scoresheet, but he was almost cut from the same cloth as a traditional English centre-forward. Big, strong, direct, and punishing in the air, yet blessed with an awkward, if effective style with the ball at his feet, he would be the prototype of Diego Costa in many respects. Yet for a nation and wider world that was desperate to see Zico in action, he was an unwelcome sight in the Brazil line-up for their first two matches.

In the middle of this tug of war for the place alongside Careca was the precocious and skilled 20-year-old Müller, a São Paulo legend in the making, and future Serie A star, whose case was only further enhanced after an electric 24 minutes in Brazil's opening match against Spain. He appeared as a substitute, replacing Casagrande, being introduced just two minutes after Sócrates had scored what was to be the only goal. So scintillating had Müller been in his brief cameo, almost scoring with his very first touch of the ball, that when the Algeria match drew into their line of vision less was made of Zico's continued presence among the substitutes and more was made of Müller's.

Müller had by no means been the only major talking point during Brazil's opening match, as they escaped a perfectly legitimate Spanish goal from Míchel, during what was a generally excellent encounter, one that genuinely felt as if it had brought the 1986 World Cup to life. A fascinating 90 minutes of football, to compound the Spanish sense of injustice Edinho had the ball in the back of Andoni Zubizarreta's net via use of his hand, an infringement that was mercifully picked up by the officials. When the goal did come there were question marks over whether Sócrates was onside or not, after he was the first player to the ball when it rebounded from the underside of the crossbar, Careca having caught his shot beautifully when played in by Júnior.

Careca was the next to come close, as Brazil began to tighten their grip on the match, but without that second goal there was still a sense of jeopardy for Santana's team that was never more evident than when Míchel again launched an effort from distance, this time saved by Carlos. This was followed by Müller dragging a shot wide, and José Antonio Camacho, Spain's captain and a future national team manager, testing Carlos with a header, as the match played its way towards its conclusion.

Toughest group game on paper won, Brazil were restricted to another 1-0 win in their next match, against Algeria, although it could easily have been more. Júnior was in excellent form, constantly joining the attack, even when dropping into defence to cover the injured Édson, and he had what seemed a perfectly good goal disallowed.

Another enthralling match, as Brazil were being constantly frustrated by a wonderful Algerian rearguard action Carlos was called upon to pull off an important save at 0-0, prompting Santana to make his change, removing Casagrande once more and bringing on Müller, who within seven minutes of his arrival had set up the winner for Careca, pouncing on a rare instance where Algeria's defence switched off.

Brazilian shoulders loosening after the goal, Careca again came close with a shot that whistled just wide of the post. There was also a peculiar incident where a Sócrates shot was saved low down by the Algerian goalkeeper, Nacerdine Drid, only for the ball to loop up and come agonisingly close to dropping in beneath the crossbar, only to be cleared off the line. This was then followed by an excellent run and shot from the unlikely figure of Elzo, and Careca provoking another save from Drid. It was chance upon chance, and as matches go, it should never have finished 1-0, and nor should Brazil have kept a clean sheet.

Two 1-0 victories but with supreme entertainment having been provided, Brazil then made up for lost goalscoring opportunities by putting three past Northern Ireland, against another team that had put up admirably strong resistance. Two goals from Careca, either side of Josimar's incredible debut strike, this was Brazil finding their range, finding themselves, in a match where Zico was afforded a 22-minute run as a substitute. The only setback was that having finally handed a start to Müller he had to be withdrawn with an injury after just 27 minutes, which brought Casagrande back into play.

Three wins out of three in the group stages, after scoring just twice in their first two matches, Brazil's second two games yielded seven goals, as Santana's team continued to grow accustomed to their Estadio Jalisco surroundings in Guadalajara, the stadium in which they would play all five of their fixtures and had also played every match at the 1970 World Cup until the final itself.

Against Poland in the last 16, Santana had the benefit of selecting an unchanged line-up, as Müller recovered from the injury that had ended his afternoon early against Northern Ireland. Brazil were boosted by a 3-0 victory in their final group fixture, but their opponents were in the reverse situation, having been beaten 3-0 and with confidence severely punctured.

That was the theory at least, until Poland tore into Brazil from the off, Włodzimierz Smolarek hitting the post, and Jan Karaś shuddering Carlos's crossbar from distance. It was like walking up to a sleeping bear and pulling its tail. Santana's team roused themselves, and both Müller and Branco came close, before Careca was carelessly brought down inside the Polish penalty area on the half hour. Sócrates, calm as you like, took a two-step stroll up, sending Józef Młynarczyk the wrong way and putting the ball into the top left-hand corner.

Poland hung in there until the 55th minute, when Josimar produced his next masterpiece of a goal, picking up the ball on the right after a botched Brazilian free kick, before slaloming his way into the penalty area and letting loose with an unstoppable shot from a seemingly impossible angle. It was another moment of shock and awe from a nominal right-back who now had two goals from two international appearances to his name.

Continuing to chance their arm on the attack, Poland were leaving gaps at the back that Brazil were stylishly exploiting. Júnior came close to breaking through, and Careca almost scored. It was 11 minutes from time that the third goal came, via a move that began with Edinho unceremoniously putting his foot through the ball in defence, only to set off in pursuit of it, as if aghast at the agricultural clearance he'd felt had been necessary. A moment or two of Careca magic later and the ball had been rolled back to Edinho, who produced a truly beautiful body swerve before finishing emphatically.

Four minutes later, Careca was making it 4-0 from the penalty spot, after Zico was brought down just inside the Polish penalty area, having been handed another cameo from the bench for the last 21 minutes. An impressive scoreline that they had been made to work for, Brazil now advanced into the quarter-finals, where they would go up against the reigning European champions.

While European glory had been a wonderful compensation for France in 1984, as the 1986 World Cup came into view *Les Bleus* still had the ghosts of the 1982 World Cup to deal with, and West Germany would again loom large in the latter stages of the tournament.

Within the slipstream of glory at the 1984 European Championship finals, France had had to absorb some significant losses of personnel. Their inspirational head coach, Michel Hidalgo, had stepped down from a role he'd occupied since March 1976, having succeeded the free-thinking former Ajax head coach, Ștefan Kovács, to whom he'd acted as assistant before taking on the top job himself. Added to this, in a playing capacity, both Didier Six and Bernard Lacombe had opted to go into international retirement while they arguably still had plenty to offer the national team.

With a wealth of talent at their disposal, France were more than armed with the tools to adapt, and the Fédération Française de Football (FFF) turned to Henri Michel as the replacement for Hidalgo, the man who was in the process of leading the French Olympic football team to the gold medal in Pasadena, defeating Brazil in the decisive match in front of over 100,000 spectators.

Michel seemed to be the perfect fit in many respects, a man whose own playing career had only ended in 1982, a midfielder who had been named in Hidalgo's squad for the 1978 World Cup finals, alongside four of the players he would take to Mexico eight years later as head coach. Within this, Michel was perhaps not yet disassociated enough to a squad of players of whom some will have viewed him not only as an equal but as a rival too, with Alain Giresse having missed out on France's squad for

Argentina when his new national head coach took up one of the midfield berths.

Some of this potential for discord was evident during the qualifiers, when difficulties in defending the aerial ball was a clear issue during defeats away to both Bulgaria and East Germany. In their positions as senior members of the team it had been up to Giresse and Michel Platini to talk frankly with Michel over the suitability of the approach being taken.

France had made an impressive start to qualifying, dropping only one point across the span of their first four matches, inclusive of victories at home to Bulgaria and East Germany, plus gaining a valuable point in Sarajevo against Yugoslavia. Within these first four fixtures, four clean sheets had been kept, but their defeats in Sofia and Leipzig had thrown the group wide open once again. By the time Michel's side went into their final qualifier at the Parc des Princes against Yugoslavia, only a win would offer them a guarantee of going to Mexico.

An early goal from a beautifully taken Platini free kick eased nerves, clipping the ball towards the top left-hand corner and leaving the Yugoslav goalkeeper, Ranko Stojić, rooted to his spot. When Platini scored again with a low left-footed effort with 19 minutes remaining, a captain's job had been done.

Throughout qualifying, Michel had struggled to settle on a favoured line-up, with only Joël Bats, Luis Fernández and Platini himself appearing in all eight matches. Missing a handful of fixtures between them, Manuel Amoros, Maxime Bossis, Jean Tigana and Giresse were the next set of regulars, but beyond that core of talent the new head coach was drawn into a world of rotation and indecision that included the dropping and eventual recalls of both Dominique Rocheteau and Patrick Battiston, plus the marginalising of Bernard Genghini and what appeared to be a total lack of interest in the unlikely European Championship semi-final hero Jean-François Domergue.

Michel used 23 different players throughout qualifying, of which 17 went to Mexico for the finals, and he attempted to fuse the best of the European Championship-winning squad with his favoured elements from the party he took to Los Angeles for the 1984 Summer Olympics. Four of the 17 players that went to those Olympics went to Mexico two years later, and had it not been for injury there would have been a fifth. Added to this, another three had missed out, having either taken an active part in the qualifiers or the warm-up friendlies prior to the tournament. Michel might have inherited the reigning European champions, but he was under no illusion that new blood would be needed before long; however, some instances seemed to be change for the sake of change.

Of this new generation, the Nantes midfielder José Touré was earmarked for a crucial role within the team, until being ruled out of the tournament after picking up a serious knee injury during a UEFA Cup encounter with Internazionale. It was a turn of events that opened the door to the late-developing yet prolific striker Jean-Pierre Papin, fresh off the back of a productive season with Club Brugge.

Of the other players to emerge from the Olympics, William Ayache was the one to make the biggest impression in Mexico, playing at left-back in four of France's matches, while the Lens striker Daniel Xuereb was so trusted by Michel that it was to him he would turn when looking for a way back into the semi-final against West Germany. It made for a varied landscape of the old and the new in France's squad for the finals, with only eight players transferrable from Hidalgo's squad of 1982. Within this, there was overlap between the icons that had served France so well under Hidalgo and the players who would go on to fail in their efforts to qualify for both the 1988 European Championship finals, and the 1990 World Cup.

Even in Mexico it was clear that the successors to the likes of Six, Lacombe, Christian Lopez, Marius Trésor and Gérard Janvion were of a lesser grade, and this would be a theme that would continue beyond the 1986 World Cup, when the voids left behind by Giresse, Rocheteau and eventually Platini, Tigana and Battiston over the following few years proved impossible to fill, until the generation that would sweep to World Cup success in 1998 came ploughing through.

France's build-up to the World Cup was quite an austere one compared to other nations, with them taking on only two official friendlies between qualification and the finals. These were a shock goalless draw against Northern Ireland and an impressive 2-0 victory over a strong Argentina line-up, with both matches having taken place in Paris. This was in stark contrast to Hidalgo's approach to the previous two World Cups, during which he took in five friendlies, something that might have been viewed as overkill within the corridors of power at the FFF, considering that France had started the finals of both tournaments with a loss.

Michel's reward for a more relaxed approach to Mexico did result in an opening win, but it was by no means a convincing one, as they edged past Canada 1-0 in León. They were made to wait until the 78th minute for their goal, which was bundled in by Papin after having missed an array of opportunities.

Blushes spared, France then did well not to be picked apart by the Soviet Union, so overpowered were they for much of the first hour. Vasyl Rats's wondrous opening goal was cancelled out by a well-worked equaliser that Fernández got on the end of, and it was a result that all but sent both teams through to the knockout stages.

Finishing up the group stages against a demoralised Hungary, it was here that France began to look like they were enjoying themselves, collecting a 3-0 victory in which the speed of thought and movement of Michel's side was far too much for their opponents to cope with. Yannick Stopyra thundered in a fine header, Tigana slotted home with all the assured nonchalance of a 15-goals-a-season midfielder, although this would prove to be his first and last goal for his national team, and Rocheteau got his tournament back on track when climbing from the bench to guide in France's third goal of the afternoon.

Although matching the Soviet Union for points, it was their rivals' 6-0 drubbing of Hungary that meant France were to advance as the runners-up of Group C, where they would face the holders, Italy, at the Estadio Olímpico Universitario in Mexico City. Not the task that it would have appeared to be on paper, Italy were surprisingly flat and lacking the usual technical abilities we know them to possess. Nor were they able to utilise the darker footballing arts that they're generationally capable of whenever caught in a tight spot.

As soon as Platini opened the scoring in the 15th minute it felt as if the match was already beyond the reach of Enzo Bearzot's team, despite Italy's brilliant historical record over France. When Stopyra chipped in with the second goal before an hour of play, there seemed to be a truce in operation, which suggested that Italy wouldn't attempt anything foolish just as long as France agreed not to humiliate them.

It was four days later that France headed to Guadalajara and the Estadio Jalisco, into the bearpit that was Brazil's enduring home from home. Before a ball had been kicked, mourning was already underway, as everybody knew that one of these two wonderful teams, which were simultaneously lifting their performances match by match, would soon be out of the tournament. No day to be a neutral, though. While those who could enjoy the occasion from a detached perspective wouldn't begrudge either side progression into the semi-final, most had a defined preference as to which one they wanted it to be. If you were kicking a ball around outside before kick-off, you were either Platini or Zico.

Both teams having been bundled out four years earlier by perceived pantomime villains, for one there was going to be the potential for some partial closure on the 1982 World Cup, but for the other there would only be yet another dose of pain.

For Brazil it was an unchanged line-up, but for France there was to be one enforced alteration, as the returning Thierry Tusseau replaced the suspended Ayache, with Amoros switching from left-back to right-back to accommodate the change required.

Pre-match psychology was difficult to gauge. While Santana was openly candid about the dangers posed by Platini, he still wasn't willing to consider any special plans to contain him, happy instead to contend that France should be worrying about how to deal with Sócrates and Júnior. On the other hand, in a training pitch match of first XI vs the rest of the squad, it was Brazil's second string that had won the bragging rights, 4-2.

Yet, even this betrayed no real clues as to the mental state of the Brazil team. João Saldanha, journalist, broadcaster and former Brazilian national coach, was certainly in no doubts as to the condition and talents of Santana and his players, stating on the eve of the match that this vintage was better than four years earlier, blessed as it was with a stronger defence and greater balance. He was also effusive about the contribution of Elzo, whom he considered to be the man who carried the piano.

At the Estadio Jalisco, kicking off at midday, 120 minutes of magnificent football and a dramatic penalty shoot-out erupted, amid temperatures of 120°F. This was peak 1986 World Cup lunacy, as the two teams defied the furnace-like heat and logic during an afternoon that arguably cost both nations their shot at glory, as while Brazil would falter, France were left to carry their weary minds and bodies into the semi-finals.

End to end at an obscene rate, this was undeniably the best match of the tournament with 31 efforts on goal, Brazil shading France on this count by 16 to 15. It amounted to a footballing version of Sugar Ray Leonard vs Thomas 'The Hit Man' Hearns, except without the definitive knockout blow being landed during regulation play.

Brazil, the better team throughout most of the first half, had the lead within 17 minutes, a deserved prize for their boldness and desire for possession of the ball. It of course fell to Careca, who found himself on the end of a majestic move that began when Júlio César dealt with a long kick downfield by Bats with a beautifully cushioned header to Josimar. He collected it on his chest, turned and chipped it on to Sócrates, who was loitering around the halfway line with his back to goal. Turning and bringing the ball forward, he laid it inside to Alemão, who then played it towards the right-hand touchline where Josimar was reunited with it. From here, the ball was in the back of the French net within eight seconds.

A forward ball played inside and diagonally, it arrived at the feet of Müller, who, when converged upon by three opposition players, twisted and turned himself into space. He evaded the lunge of a fourth assailant, managing to offload the ball to Júnior, just to his right, combining to open up what remained of Michel's defence, and there was Careca, in as much space as he could possibly want, to sweep the ball past the exposed Bats, just 26 seconds after the French goalkeeper had launched the ball into the Brazil half. As ruthless as it was beautiful, and an utter joy to watch, this was *O Jogo Bonito* at its very zenith and, as sacrilegious as it may sound to some, it was as good, if not better than anything that the legendary 1982 vintage had produced.

Unknown to any spectator or viewer, away from the eventual penalty shoot-out, this was the last Brazilian goal of the 1986 World Cup, at a point of the tournament when they had yet to concede any.

France had actually been fast out of the blocks, aiming to unbalance Brazil before Santana's team took control, dominating a first half where Sócrates should have opened the scoring just moments before Careca eventually did, when forcing Bats into an important save. However, apart from a short spell after Brazil's goal, France hardly laid a glove on their opponents during the first 40 minutes, Rocheteau coming the closest at the near post after a low cross from the right by Amoros. This was in riposte to the wave upon wave of Brazil attacks, the best of which was when Müller struck Bats's left-hand post after some wonderful work by Careca when getting on the end of a delightful long pass from Sócrates. He'd again slipped the attentions of Bossis to whip the ball across the French six-yard box.

France, unable to get a foothold in the match, were forced to switch the roles of Bossis and Battiston, the sweeper and man-marker, respectively, due to the hard time Careca was giving Battiston. Within this, Platini was also struggling to work his own brand of magic, so marginalised had he been by Elzo and Alemão. Still, despite Brazil's clear superiority at this stage, they hadn't been able to extend their slender lead, and the price was paid when out of nowhere France struck their largely undeserved, but excellently crafted, equaliser.

From Tigana to Giresse to Amoros and back to Giresse, the ball moved effortlessly in an exploratory pattern before finding Rocheteau in space on the right of the Brazil penalty area. He elected to cross it as swiftly as possible and it took a deflection off Edinho along the way. Stopyra stooped just inside the six-yard box in an attempt to get his head to the ball, confusing Carlos as he did, who made a desperate dive to try to intercept the ball, only for both to miss it completely. This allowed it to run to the unmarked Platini, who was able to steal in to guide it into the now unguarded Brazil net.

On his 31st birthday, it was the perfect gift for Platini, and it took the match in an entirely different direction to the one it had been threatening to travel. Vision, coupled with great fortune, France had taken their first step towards the semi-finals.

On the second half rolled, French confidence steadily rising, Brazil probing for openings and mistakes, chances falling to both teams, but fatigue beginning to kick in, during what was a match played out with a fabulous mutual respect. Punch and counterpunch, Tigana had the next big opportunity, but his effort was well-saved by Carlos, while within seconds Júnior was forcing Bats into an unorthodox block. This was soon followed by Careca heading against the French crossbar.

And then, in the 71st minute, Zico entered the fray to replace Müller, and within four minutes he was faced with the golden opportunity to restore Brazil's lead. In many respects it was a peculiar substitution to be making, as Brazil had begun to gain the initiative once again. Just five minutes or so earlier, when Zico had started warming up, Santana's team did look in need of inspiration and fresh ideas, but the run of play had started to alter again by the time he did enter proceedings in place of Müller.

With 17 minutes remaining, Branco came into possession of the ball, intercepting an attempted pass from Fernández to Rocheteau and running it into the France half before squaring it to Zico. He played a beautifully weighted through ball for the still rampaging Branco to latch on to. Into the penalty area he went, and out rushed Bats, who needlessly caught the Brazilian player. Over he went for a clear penalty. Given the angle that Branco was running and how the ball wasn't quite within comfortable reach to take a shot on goal, Bats's aberration was a stark one.

While both Sócrates and Careca had successfully converted penalties in this World Cup and both were still on the pitch, it seemed peculiar that Zico was allowed to grab the ball. He placed it on the spot and took his run-up, only to see his kick easily saved by Bats and cleared from immediate danger. It was a shocking moment and one that Brazil didn't really recover from, as doubts began to creep into their play, while France were emboldened.

However, this still didn't stop Santana's players from trying to snatch the winner, Careca failing to make the most of a brilliant opening, and Bats clawing away a close-range Zico header after a lovely cross from the tireless Josimar.

Into extra time it went, Brazil having marginally been the better team. By way of adding fresh legs, Santana withdrew Júnior, replaced by Silas, a player who was 11 years his junior.

Understandably, the pace of the play dipped in the first half of extra time, although compelling chances still fell to Rocheteau and Stopyra for France, and Elzo, Silas and Sócrates for Brazil. The biggest issue for France was that Platini was visibly wilting, almost to the point of being a passenger for his team-mates, yet Michel wouldn't remove him from the pitch. When Bruno Bellone came on, it was instead to replace Rocheteau, Giresse already having departed the pitch, switched for Jean-Marc Ferreri.

With only 15 minutes standing between Brazil, France and a penalty shoot-out, this is where cramp began to make its presence felt, as down went Tusseau, who wasn't the only player to spend time on the turf receiving treatment.

Then came the big contentious moment in extra time, as with five minutes remaining Bellone was sent through on goal from deep by a wondrous ball by Platini, brilliantly springing the offside trap for a one-on-one with Carlos. He stormed from his penalty area to meet the Frenchman head-on, where with shades of Schumacher four years earlier, he caught Bellone on his shoulder after the ball had been knocked beyond him. Admirably keeping his feet, the chance was soon gone for Bellone, as by the time he'd regained his balance the ball had been spirited away and was off down the other end, where Sócrates missed a wonderful opportunity to win it for Brazil.

A shocking moment. Not even a free kick had been awarded to France and suddenly Brazil were the villains, just as France had been when scoring against the run of play. It all made for a disorientating adventure.

Extra time ended and the match went into a penalty shoot-out, at this point only the second time the World Cup had ever needed one, the first having been at the end of that iconic 1982 semi-final between France and West Germany.

Incredibly, up stepped Sócrates first for Brazil, only to see his kick saved brilliantly by Bats. This was then followed by six successful efforts from Stopyra, Alemão, Amoros, Zico, Bellone and Branco. Zico lashed his in almost in frustration, while Bellone's took the peculiar route of hitting the post, then the back of Carlos, before finding the back of the net, as football extracted a heavy slice of karma on Brazil's goalkeeper for his unpunished assault on Bellone. Despite protests from Edinho that the penalty shouldn't stand, he was given short shrift from the referee, Romania's Ioan Igna.

After Branco converted his, next came Platini, who should have come with a guarantee of scoring, yet he shockingly ballooned the ball over the crossbar. Immense drama, it meant that the impressive Júlio César now had the chance to give Brazil the lead in the shoot-out and to ladle copious amounts of pressure on France's last penalty taker. Stunningly, the post was hit instead, handing France the opportunity to win.

Such pressure, amazingly Careca hadn't stepped up, and now here came Fernández, who coolly slotted his penalty past Carlos to send France into the semi-finals and Brazil home, ending the Santana era and the concept of *O Jogo Bonito* for good.

Such a lucky stadium for Brazil for so long, now the Estadio Jalisco was unforgiving, as the favourites again went out of a second successive World Cup after five incredible matches of football. For France it was redemption for four years earlier, and the role of the new favourites to lift the World Cup was theirs.

What could possibly go wrong?

Chapter Fifteen

Totally Mexico

IT WAS their party, but it kind of wasn't their party.

Hosting two World Cups within 16 years of one another is gluttonous. Yes, FIFA needed a reliable pair of hands to carry the 1986 World Cup once Colombia had bailed out, but the whys and wherefores of how it came to be Mexico are myriad and the seemingly preordained nature of the decision set a permanent air of suspicion on all future bidding processes. The World Cup had been a political beast from its very birth, but now it had no shame.

None of this was the fault of Mexico's players, nor was it the fault of their passionate supporters, both entities of which helped to paper over the cracks of a tournament where the wider infrastructure creaked constantly.

Not all that far off an aggregate of half a million spectators clicked through the turnstiles to watch Mexico's five matches at the 1986 World Cup finals, with all but their quarter-final in Monterrey clocking up individual attendances that stretched into six figures, thanks to the other four taking place in the Estadio Azteca.

It might not have felt right that Mexico was hosting a second World Cup so soon after 1970, in political terms, but it did feel very right in terms of helping an earthquake-devastated city get back on its feet.

Since the 1970 World Cup, Mexico had laboured on the international football scene, qualifying for the finals of the tournament on only one further occasion, in Argentina in 1978, where they had struggled badly, losing all three matches and conceding 12 goals in the process. In 1982, they had once again failed to qualify, instead watching on as Honduras and El Salvador went as CONCACAF's representatives.

For the next four and a half years they undertook an exhaustive run of friendlies and hastily arranged mini tournaments that stretched to an incredible 62 recognised internationals. On top of this there were no shortage of unofficial and practice matches. This all started at a reasonably sedate pace, with nine fixtures during the span of the traditional European season of 1982/83, dropping to just six during 1983/84, before they played a truly ludicrous 47 friendlies between July 1984 and kickstarting their 1986 World Cup campaign against Belgium.

Casting around for somebody to bring greater focus to the Mexican national team, the prolific Bora Milutinović was brought on board, with the 1986 World Cup acting as the first of an incredible five successive tournaments that he undertook at the helm of five different nations. No stranger to Mexican football, as a midfielder of purpose he'd signed for the Mexico City-based UNAM in 1972, with whom he would spend the last four years of his playing career, eventually beginning his coaching career with them in 1977, remaining in charge until Mexico came calling.

Much travelled and with a sense of adventure, Milutinović had left his native Yugoslavia shortly before his 22nd birthday, going on to play his club football in Switzerland and France, before the offer of a contract with UNAM was presented to him. All in all, he would spend the next 15 years in Mexico, before his footballing odyssey really escalated, a meandering path that took him to South America, North America, the Caribbean, Europe, Africa, Asia and the Arab world, all punctuated with occasional returns to Mexico to coach at both club and national level once again.

Fluent in five languages, Milutinović continues to strike the image of the international footballing man of mystery, and he was the perfect man for the Mexico job when he took it in 1983. Sifting through every Mexican player of talent, apart from one very special exception, his squad for the 1986 World Cup would be exclusively drawn from the Liga MX.

Milutinović swiftly had Mexico moving in the right direction, winning eight and drawing one of his first nine matches in charge, until being handed a reality check by Italy when beaten 5-0 at the Stadio Olimpico, in Rome.

Stretching Mexico's boundaries, this wouldn't be Milutinović's last foray into Europe with his team. They were back later that summer for a more extensive programme of fixtures, which took in visits to Dublin, East Berlin, Helsinki, Leningrad, Malmö and Budapest, where wins would be picked up against Finland and Hungary, while the only defeat came against the Soviet Union.

Milutinović and Mexico were making up impressive ground. Of the squad he took to Europe, many components of the team that he would field at the World Cup were coming to the fore, with Pablo Larios now the undisputed first-choice goalkeeper, plus Rafael Amador appearing in defence alongside the dependable Fernando Quirarte and Mario Trejo, a crucial development given that Mexico would be without their captain, Alfredo Tena, for the World Cup.

Added to this, the influential Miguel España was now present in midfield, as was the excellent Javier Aguirre, the stubborn Carlos de los Cobos and Mexico's own wonderful *fantasista*, Tomás Boy. He would take the armband at the

World Cup when the magnificent Tena was denied it due to the strictest of clauses within his personal sportswear contract, which meant he couldn't wear his nation's Adidas supplied kits.

Up front, Milutinović was also spoilt for choice, as Luis Flores and Manuel Negrete had hugely enjoyed taking on European defences, while coiled and ready to pounce, whenever his LaLiga club commitments would permit, was Hugo Sánchez. Post-European tour, other options would fall into place, as Félix Cruz came back into the defensive picture and Raúl Servín would rise to prominence. Midfield was also boosted by the return to form of Carlos Muñoz.

Everything was coming together for Milutinović, and in their first match back on Mexican soil after their European endeavours, their efforts bore the fruit of a well-deserved draw against a strong Argentina line-up in Monterrey. Before 1984 had come to an end, they had drawn with Argentina again, this time in Buenos Aires, a fine result that they were able to add to victories against Colombia, El Salvador, Trinidad and Tobago, Ecuador and the USA. They had also obtained a highly creditable draw in Montevideo against Uruguay, and suffered only a narrow defeat three days earlier against Chile in Santiago.

Wanting to test his team against the best opponents available, in February 1985 Milutinović saw his players demolish Poland 5-0 in Querétaro, only just being edged out by Switzerland in another friendly, 24 hours later, having split his squad in half for the back-to-back fixtures.

Then came June 1985, and a four-nation mini-tournament that was to be the biggest test possible this side of the World Cup finals, yet it would also act as acclimatisation missions for Mexico's opponents. Italy, England and West Germany pulled no punches and fielded strong line-ups in each match. All three fixtures took place at the Estadio Azteca, where

Mexico drew 1-1 against Enzo Bearzot's reigning world champions, before defeating both Bobby Robson and Franz Beckenbauer's former World Cup winners. All this while still without the goalscoring services of Sánchez.

Due to the devastating earthquake in September 1985, Mexico wouldn't return to the Estadio Azteca until February 1986, a span of time during which they played 15 times, and understandably the results were lacking previous consistency. Between late September and the start of November, they played eight times, winning only twice and losing on trips to face Libya and Egypt, preparatory games with Iraq very much in mind. These adverse results caused some rumbles of discontent at the Federación Mexicana de Fútbol Asociación, A.C.

Prior to the horrors of the earthquake, Milutinović had been able to field Sánchez against Chile and Bulgaria in Los Angeles towards the end of August, before he headed back to Spain to join up with his new team-mates at Real Madrid, having just made the contentious switch from Atlético. He scored in the 2-1 victory over Chile.

In mid-November Mexico then faced Argentina again, twice within four days, firstly back in Los Angeles and then in Puebla, as Mexico finally returned to play on home soil. Diego Maradona was available for both matches, yet Milutinović mastered two 1-1 draws. He and his team were back on track, and they embraced December with four successive wins, twice against South Korea and once each against Algeria and Hungary, in matches played in Los Angeles, Irapuato, Guadalajara and Toluca.

It must have been a draining schedule, but fitness levels will have been through the roof, while squad bonding shouldn't have been a problem for Milutinović, as team-mates would arguably have been more familiar with one another than they were with members of their own families.

Into World Cup year Mexico finally went, Milutinović affording his players a two-month break from international football before reconvening in mid-February for the first of eight warm-up fixtures leading up to the tournament. Embracing the new year with a 2-1 loss to East Germany in California, four days later it was a better outcome against a reasonably strong Soviet Union, as Mexico at last made their return to the Estadio Azteca. Aguirre scored the only goal, in front of a tentative 40,000 spectators.

March was almost sedate, with Mexico playing only twice, both against Danish representative teams, both on the same day in the same Los Angeles stadium. Milutinović again split his squad in half to take on a Denmark under-21 team and a Danish XI, neither of which were without liberal helpings of talent. Two 1-1 draws were played out.

Squad settled, but Sánchez still to join up, Milutinović led Mexico into one last grind of friendlies before easing off the accelerator a fortnight before the big kick-off. Uruguay, Chile, Canada and England offered the opposition, with the first and last of those fixtures taking place in Los Angeles, the middle two in Mexico City. Narrow 1-0 victories were chiselled from Uruguay and Chile, plus a 3-0 win and a 3-0 defeat in their encounters with Canada and England, respectively.

The loss to England was Mexico's joint heaviest since that 5-0 reversal at the hands of Italy in Rome early in Milutinović's reign, a match that now sat well over two years past. It wasn't the ideal way to end their official warm-up fixtures but there was enough positivity surrounding Mexico to take them into the tournament, even if they weren't hitting the type of heights they were 12 months earlier.

At the Estadio Azteca, Mexico got off to a winning start, shooting into a 2-0 lead against Belgium thanks to headed goals from Quirarte and Sánchez, only to concede shortly before half-time. From there they experienced a far tougher second half than was strictly required. But, while Guy Thys's team might have dominated the second half, they failed to create enough compelling opportunities to level the scores.

Mexico had cause for celebration but also to breathe a significant sigh of relief, after a match that swung from comfort and joy to abject nervousness, one in which Sánchez picked up a needless yellow card when kicking the ball in celebration into the crowd after the opening goal. Despite having to wait so long to see him in a Mexico shirt, Sánchez was already an icon to the football lovers of his nation, his LaLiga exploits long having been broadcast to proud viewers. When he popped up at the back post to nod the ball into the Belgian net via a Boy corner kick that had been flicked on by Flores, the noise within the Estadio Azteca was deafening.

One of the main talking points prior to the match had been which striker would make way for Sánchez. Would it be Negrete or would it be Flores? As it was, it was neither, as Milutinović opted for what amounted to a 4-3-3 formation, which when Mexico were on the front foot had vaguely resembled a classic 2-3-5 from yesteryear. Conversely, with the scoreline at 2-1, the playmaking exuberance of Boy was removed, with the more disciplined España entering the fray, as Mexico collectively fell back into a 5-4-1, in a successful bid to protect their lead.

One of the main concerns for Milutinović was that when Belgium got their goal back it was due to an entirely avoidable error from his goalkeeper, Larios. If Mexico were to go far into their own World Cup, then they would have to stop presenting gifts to their opponents.

Easier said than done, though, as four days later, again at the Estadio Azteca, Mexico conceded an equaliser against Paraguay with only five minutes remaining, having led since as early as the third minute, Flores turning from assister of goals to scorer.

With Sánchez picking up a second yellow card of the tournament, to go alongside him missing a penalty, he would be suspended for the final group match against Iraq. Already through, Milutinović's team were playing for the top of the group and once again it was Quirarte who cut through the frustration, scoring nine minutes into the second half.

It was a match that Mexico could have run away with, but because they didn't do that, the narrow lead meant that Iraq were very much still in the mix until the very end, and the change in formation to compensate for the loss of Sánchez didn't really do Mexico the favours that it possibly could have done. Without Sánchez for most of their build-up to the World Cup, his availability for the finals brought with it the conundrum of how to fit him into the team, but with him being unavailable to face Iraq, Mexico were able to revert to what they had built without their superstar.

When Flores picked up an injury that would rule him out of the remainder of Mexico's matches, it meant that Milutinović no longer needed to make a difficult decision, and Sánchez would be paired up with Negrete, which paved the way for a very special goal in the last 16 against Bulgaria.

Remaining at the Estadio Azteca, momentum was now on Mexico's side. Against Bulgaria, Milutinović's team put in their best performance yet, and Negrete's moment of magic came in the 34th minute. Collecting the ball, he advanced towards the Bulgaria penalty area before exchanging passes with Aguirre and letting loose with a majestic scissor-kick, sending the ball beyond the helpless Borislav Mihaylov. A work of art, and the defining image of the hosts' contribution to the 1986 World Cup, Negrete's notoriety would gain him a short-lived year in Europe, divided between Sporting CP in Portugal and Sporting Gijón in Spain, before swiftly returning to Mexico.

The lesser-remembered goal that Mexico scored that day fell the way of Servín, set up as he was by a Negrete corner, heading home from very nearly the goal line itself. It made for a popular victory, not only with the Mexican supporters, but with football lovers across the board, given Bulgaria's unabashed pragmatism, even if it did come with no shortage of excellent technique, which still entailed not much more than long percentage-playing balls into the channels that were rarely retrievable, and pot-shots from distance.

Victims of their own success, Mexico's progression as Group B winners sent them to Monterrey for their quarter-final against West Germany, when intriguingly, had they finished second in the group stages, they would have remained at the Estadio Azteca all the way through their campaign, no matter how long it were to stretch.

Only the 1986 World Cup organising committee could tell you for certain what the thinking was in this respect, and whether they had expected Mexico to go forth as group winners or not. Regardless, it was off to the Estadio Universitario that the host nation now went. Considerably smaller and nowhere near as intimidating as the Estadio Azteca, although the Monterrey locals did their best, Mexico had cashed in their very vociferous 12th man. Most of the invective feel to this match came from those on the pitch, as the two teams shared nine yellow cards and two red, yet little in the way of entertaining football.

For the last 25 of the initial 90 minutes, and for the first ten minutes of extra time, Mexico held a one-man advantage, when in an ill-tempered affair Thomas Berthold was flashed a red card when taking a frustrated swing at Quirarte. Aguirre then carelessly gave away this advantage in the 100th minute when he lunged in to bodycheck the advancing Lothar Matthäus. Contact undeniably having been made, the Bayern Munich midfielder literally rolled with the invitation to go to ground, this now being the second time he'd assisted in an opposing player being shown a red card at the 1986 World Cup. It was an incident that didn't need to happen, and the sight of Harald Schumacher being the voice of reason, consoling Aguirre as he forlornly exited the pitch, was nothing short of surreal.

Both teams down to ten, match-winning inspiration couldn't be found by either. When the match drifted to a penalty shoot-out it seemed inevitable that West Germany would prevail, which of course they did, as Schumacher saved the spot kicks of Quirarte and Servín.

A sadly meek end to Mexico's World Cup campaign; just when a little bit of composure was required it totally deserted them, and through went West Germany instead. A lost opportunity, Mexico haven't travelled as far into a World Cup since. They had equalled their best run, which also came on home soil as hosts in 1970.

Mexico had got progressively better with each match they played but changed their approach when faced with not only the imposing spectre of West Germany, but also a switch of venue. It all seemed to be a little too much for them, nursing as they were the scars of facing the same opposition as they had at the 1978 World Cup, when beaten 6-0.

Psychologically, West Germany quite possibly beat Mexico long before they set foot on the pitch.

Chapter Sixteen

The Ambassador is Spoiling Us

JAN CEULEMANS was the type of player who really should have had a nickname, one that spoke with gravitas on his status and importance. Something like 'The Ambassador' would have sat perfectly. A magical player of skill and vision, he once agreed in principle to a transfer to AC Milan, going as far as posing for publicity photos with delighted board members, only to change his mind, opting to remain with Club Brugge for the rest of his career.

Completely underappreciated, Belgium were bracketed among the pragmatic spoilers of the 1986 World Cup, never truly forgiven for barring the way to the tournament of the Netherlands, whom they dramatically denied with only five minutes remaining of the second leg of their play-off encounter.

This wasn't the only blemish on their crime sheet either. Six years earlier, at the 1980 European Championship, Belgium had gone all the way to the final itself when playing the percentages during draws against England and Italy, and narrowly beating Spain. In a tournament where the two group winners went directly through to the final, Belgium had won just one of their three group matches, scoring only three goals. Across the breadth of 270 minutes of football they had found themselves in the lead for no more than 44 minutes, all of which came during two separate spells in each half of their encounter with Spain. Even in the final against West Germany, Belgium came to within two minutes of taking the match into extra time, despite never having been in front.

It had been their first major tournament for eight years and cast against the landscape of the international variant of the game it came totally out of the blue. Two years later they qualified for their first World Cup since 1970, where they again progressed as group winners, with a grand total of three goals scored. They caught a distracted Argentina cold in the opening match, only managed to beat El Salvador 1-0 four days after the CONCACAF representatives had conceded ten goals, and then came within 14 minutes of being knocked out by Hungary. Belgium were almost apologetic Group 3 winners.

Limitations laid bare in the second round of group matches at the 1982 World Cup, Belgium were picked apart by Poland and defeated once more by the Soviet Union, where they at least put up greater resistance in the second of their two Group A fixtures.

Belgium played five matches in Spain, each offering an austere visage of their capabilities. Their greatest contribution to the 1982 World Cup was the part they played in that iconic image of Diego Maradona, when with an Adidas Tango at his left foot, he's confronted on a litter-strewn Camp Nou pitch by six red-shirted Belgian players.

Of course, there's more than meets the eye when it comes to that image of Maradona, which for years was deemed to be one of the Argentine genii trying to take on over half the Belgium team on his own, only to be later unmasked to be one in which a free kick has been squared to him and the line of Belgian players is simply the defensive wall in the act of hastily fragmenting.

There's no better image to sum up that early to mid-1980s Belgium. On the back foot, organised, yet vulnerable, although not everything that meets the eye is as it seems. The part they play is generally unconsidered and unappreciated, yet is of huge value.

At the 1984 European Championship finals, Belgium weren't quite themselves. They flew out of the blocks, 2-0 up against Yugoslavia by half-time in Lens during their opening match, before spectacularly capitulating to France, Michel Platini and a peak *Le Carre Magique* in Nantes, conceding five without reply. They then ended their campaign against Denmark in Strasbourg, when in a match they needed to win to progress to the semi-finals, Guy Thys's team threw away a 2-0 lead to lose 3-2, blown away in what was one of the finest moments of the 'Danish Dynamite' movement.

It had seemed that, even for Belgium, it had been impossible not to get carried away by the *joie de vivre* that 1984 European Championship Group 1 had created, caught as they were in the eye of a footballing storm that saw 23 goals scored across the span of just six matches, a cluster of fixtures in which Belgium weren't even the lowest-scoring nation.

You might have had to cock your head a little bit, but there was something about Belgium, which was embossed by the style and substance of Ceulemans and accentuated by the wondrous nature of their kits. Pragmatic, stubborn, talented and skilled. Belgium were damned for so many reasons, both in terms of football and politics. With 'Brussels bureaucracy' being constantly lambasted by UK newspapers, when it came to football and their role as the Low Countries sibling of the Netherlands, they were forever unfavourably compared to their enigmatic neighbour.

In terms of club football, however, Anderlecht, Club Brugge and Standard Liège had all contested major European finals across the span of the previous decade, springing from a league that was one of the most compellingly competitive and attractive on the Continent, where their finest domestic players were joined by some of the best that the Netherlands and Denmark had to offer. On the down-low, the Belgian First Division was quite the hipster's paradise.

Moving away from the shock and awe that was the 1984 European Championship finals, Belgium withdrew into their protective shell and went for a safety-first approach to the World Cup qualifiers. Drawn into one of the three four-nation groups that would provide only one automatic qualifier, from Group 1 the runners-up would face a UEFA play-off with the second-placed team from Group 5.

Still licking their wounds from the events of the summer of 1984, Belgium limped to a 2-0 defeat to a threadbare Argentina team, without the services of Maradona, in Brussels six weeks prior to the World Cup qualifiers beginning. Before the year was out, Belgium's hopes of automatic qualification were looking grim. One win, one draw and one defeat meant that by the new year they had already played half their fixtures and worryingly found themselves marooned in third place, despite only having played the two weakest teams in the group. A 3-1 victory over Albania in Brussels in October had been an adequate start, but taking only one point from their trips to Athens and Tirana in December against Greece and Albania had been utterly careless.

Held to a goalless draw in the Greek capital, this hadn't been as bad an outcome as the result suggested, as while Greece could offer easy pickings at times, whenever the will to be stubborn made itself known, they could also be a nightmare to face. During the qualifiers for the 1984

European Championship, Greece had made heavy weather of taking two narrow wins against Luxembourg, and meekly handed over the points at home to both England and Denmark, yet they had made Sepp Piontek's men earn their win in Copenhagen and held Bobby Robson's team to a damaging goalless draw at Wembley. On top of this, Greece had taken three of the four points available against Hungary, even winning in Budapest.

With Greece, you could never be entirely certain which version would be on display, and by the time Belgium went to face them in Athens it was already the seventh time their opponents had taken to the pitch since the beginning of the 1984/85 season, the last of those previous six times being a morale-boosting win in a friendly against Romania. Thys would have been well within his rights to consider the point his team took against Greece to be one gained rather than one dropped, but the loss in Albania three days later, just three days prior to Christmas, was another matter entirely. It was a result that saw the two opponents swap places in the group standings.

The logistics and theory of pairing up the two away fixtures in Athens and Tirana was sound enough, but the execution of the practicalities had gone badly awry, as Belgium failed to even emerge from these matches with so much as a goal scored.

With three matches remaining, and two of those being against Poland, it made for sleepless nights in the Belgian camp. The biggest concern was that while Thys's team had won in Brussels without the services of Ceulemans, he'd been on the pitch in both Athens and Tirana as one of five changes to the line-up that had kicked off the qualifying campaign with a win. The Belgian head coach had much to ponder, and not many matches left to put things right.

Opting against arranging any friendlies between their travails in Greece and Albania and the return visit of Greece to Brussels towards the end of March 1985, a busy club schedule had made the prospect of working things out on the pitch one that was out of Thys's reach. It might have done him some favours though.

When Greece defeated Albania in Athens a month before travelling to Brussels, it was enough to lift Belgium back into second position on goal difference without them kicking a ball. Avoiding a loss would have put Albania top of the group as opposed to sinking to the bottom on the back of the defeat.

Greece's win also seemed to satisfy their appetite for some form of tangible success, and they were far blunter than might have been the case by the time they arrived in the Belgian capital. Added to by the return to Thys's team of Michel De Wolf, René Vandereycken and Erwin Vandenbergh, especially with the recall of the latter, it made for a much more balanced line-up, as Ceulemans could drop deeper, freed from the need to be a focal-point attacker.

Now Ceulemans had the run of the pitch, and it was no coincidence that Belgium were a more potent force after the return of Vandenbergh, with Nico Claesen dropping out. It still didn't stop Greece from frustrating Belgium until the 69th minute, however. A Franky Vercauteren free kick broke the deadlock, and it was only in the final minute that Ceulemans sent Enzo Scifo through to settle Belgian nerves with another goal.

Those last 21 minutes against Greece changed the whole complexion of Belgium's qualifying campaign, as not only did it put them top of the group, albeit having played one match more, but five weeks later they were to prove too strong for Poland in Brussels. An identical scoreline to the one procured against Greece, but via a very different performance, Belgium dominated and should have had the lead long before Vandenbergh secured it for them, denied until then as they were by the excellent goalkeeping of Jacek Kazimierski, along with the frame of the goal. A wonderful finish from an acute angle by Vercauteren eight minutes into the second half settled matters, giving Belgium a win that brought with it a four-point lead at the top of the group, although having played two matches more.

Poland fared better with their own double-header trips to Athens and Tirana, picking off two victories that took them back to the top of the group and set up a final decider in Chorzów. There the goalless draw that was played out sent Poland to Mexico automatically and propelled Belgium into their two-legged play-off with the Netherlands. Having clawed hope from the jaws of despondency, Belgium had now opted for disappointment, as their qualifying campaign lurched from one extreme to the other. Yes, there was still a chance, but the Netherlands had been such a regular tormentor in similar circumstances that it would be the natural Belgian reaction to fear the worst.

A narrow first-leg victory for Belgium didn't exactly ease the shoulders, although Vercauteren's winning goal was beautifully struck. Only 20 minutes had elapsed, and a stand-off unfolded where Belgium couldn't make a second breakthrough and the Netherlands failed to push for what would have been the all-important away goal.

Led by Leo Beenhakker, whose team boasted the presence of not only a ghost of World Cups past in the shape of Willy van de Kerkhof, but many elements of European Championship glory to come, such as Hans van Breukelen, Frank Rijkaard, Ruud Gullit, Wim Kieft and Marco van Basten, Belgium's success in overcoming their biggest traditional rivals also served to make them even more unpopular in the eyes of many professional football observers.

A ludicrous five weeks separated the two legs of the play-off, and when the saga recommenced in Rotterdam, Belgium kept their hosts at bay for an hour, until Peter Houtman grabbed the crucial first goal of the night, and the aggregate equaliser. By the time Rob de Wit put the Netherlands ahead with only 18 minutes left to play, it was Beenhakker's team that looked set for Mexico, but then came the twist to the tale, as the unlikely figure of Georges Grün powered home a header that stunned the Netherlands and took Belgium to the World Cup finals instead.

Grün, a defender by trade, had started all seven of Belgium's qualifying matches up until Rotterdam, only to be stood down to the bench. Thrown on at half-time at De Kuip in place of Leo Van der Elst, he'd clearly been on a mission to prove to Thys that his team selection had been the wrong one, but even he must have been surprised to have ended up being the match-winner.

With the world seemingly underwhelmed by their presence in Mexico, even Belgium's send-off from home had been short on inspiration, beaten in Brussels 3-1 by Yugoslavia on an evening when Thys's team had been 3-0 down inside 35 minutes, an evening when only 10,000 spectators had bothered to show up. Prior to this, there had been another numbing defeat against Spain, in Elche in February, which had at least been followed by a victory over Bulgaria.

As a way of acclimatisation preparation, Thys took his squad to the Swiss mountain village of Ovronnaz, where the temperature was 20 degrees lower than those they would experience in Mexico. A peculiar pre-tournament plan, it was just something else that made little, or partial, sense about Belgium's qualification and build-up, which included welcoming players back from bans they were serving for being embroiled in a Standard Liège bribery scandal from 1982.

Even once in Mexico the curveballs kept coming, as Thys stunningly lost the services of De Wolf, Vandenbergh and Vandereycken within the first two group matches, these not being the only players whose tournaments were curtailed but certainly the most prominent. As the World Cup rolled onward, Thys adapted his team, with Claesen, Grün, Stéphane Demol, Michel Renquin, Patrick Vervoort and Daniel Veyt all stepping up to cover impressively, the Belgian defence being the most injury ravaged.

Belgium drifted their way through the tournament without the suspicion of greatness ever arising, even when they found themselves in the semi-finals, as they forever seemed to be the supporting act in everybody else's adventures, be that their opening defeat to the host nation, being tested by Iraq, struggling to deal with Paraguay, being the party poopers against the Soviet Union, the assailants of Spain, or the patsies against Argentina and Maradona's magic.

In a similar manner to Bobby Robson and England, Thys and Belgium's best responses at the 1986 World Cup came when faced with the loss of important players and staring at presumed adversity. Ceulemans, Vercauteren, Claesen, Scifo, Demol and Pfaff all offered magnificent service. Defying gravity, there's no way that Belgium should have made it to the semi-finals of the tournament, given that their strength lay in the stubborn durability of a defence that had been decimated by injury. Yet they pulled themselves together in the most unexpected and incredible of ways, with Ceulemans the conductor and Scifo the generator, balance having been stumbled upon almost by accident.

By the time the semi-final had drawn into view it was obvious that it would be a bridge too far for Belgium, with

Maradona now in an unstoppable frame of mind and body, yet Thys's team could shoulder no shame whatsoever for falling to the new world champions elect. Belgium had proved their detractors wrong in Mexico, but still nobody seemed to sit up and take notice.

Chapter Seventeen

Revenge is a Dish
Best Served Uneaten

REMATCHES AREN'T meant to end this way. When France walked out to face West Germany at the Estadio Jalisco for the first of the 1986 World Cup semi-finals, it was supposed to be an occasion where *Die Mannschaft* were going to be on the receiving end of a comeuppance that had been four years in the making.

July 1982, in Seville, France had been in such a strong position that they could almost touch greatness, as the team that had come as close as humanly possible to a World Cup Final without going on to reach it. In the final embers of the 90 minutes, with the scoreline at 1-1, Amoros had struck the West German crossbar, and in extra time they had led 3-1, before being pegged back to 3-3. Yet all of this gave way to the abiding images of a prone Patrick Battiston, having been rendered unconscious and minus some teeth after being needlessly mown down by the outrushing Harald Schumacher.

A watching world was aghast at the challenge, and a state of anger escalated when the West German goalkeeper escaped sanction, as Battiston was carried away on a stretcher. Stunningly, a goal kick was awarded and the images of

Schumacher, hands on hips and with a facial expression set to complete and utter ambivalence, have haunted the rivalry between the two teams ever since.

By the time that France were losing out in the penalty shoot-out, with the added torture of having held the advantage with three spot kicks remaining, there was an evocative inevitability about the fate of Michel Hidalgo's team that was almost drawing them magnetically to the most painful of footballing defeats possible. France had the sympathies of a huge global audience, but West Germany had the spot in the 1982 World Cup Final, where they would be mercifully beaten by an Italian team that had been cast as pantomime villains themselves a week earlier when knocking Brazil out of the tournament.

I would imagine not even Spanish supporters truly begrudged France the compensation of glory at the 1984 European Championship finals two years later, in what was almost the perfect storm for Hidalgo and his talismanic genius of a captain, Michel Platini. Almost perfect, the only ingredients France could possibly have desired in the summer of 1984 that didn't come their way was an iconic final, rather than a functional one, and the chance to vanquish West Germany, ideally in the semi-final.

It meant that by the time Mexico came around, there were still some leftovers to be sorted out, and once France and West Germany were locked into the same side of the draw for the knockout stages the prospect of a rematch cast its shadow across the last 16 and the quarter-finals.

To get to this point, France had overcome Italy and Brazil in the previous two rounds, on top of having faced the Soviet Union in the group stages, while West Germany's route, at least on paper, seemed that little bit more serene, having been dealt knockout assignments against Morocco and Mexico, although having emerged from the group of death.

It took West Germany nine minutes to obtain the lead against France, and as soon as they did a sense of trepidation, which had kicked in with the committing of their first foul after just 20 seconds, had been fully verified. If ever a match needed the opposing team to score first at the 1986 World Cup, then this was that match.

Like France, Franz Beckenbauer's team had also been stretched to 90 minutes and penalties in their quarter-final, against Mexico, but it was a match that had never been in any danger of hitting the heights, making the demands or touching the soul in the same way that the one France and Brazil had shared. Stronger in the tackle, faster to the ball, swifter in anticipation and infinitely more intimidating than France, West Germany were impressively prepared, playing on all the base fears that Michel's team nursed. This was France vs the Bogeyman, with the Bogeyman winning.

So much had been hoped, rather than expected, of France going into this match, yet revenge wasn't to be sweet. It was instead too heavy a weight to carry, along with understandably tired legs. How anyone could have thought West Germany would roll over seemed so foolish, almost as soon as the match had begun. Sharper, more incisive, technically superior and better off-the-ball movement, while there was a stroke of fortune in West Germany's opening goal, scored by Andreas Brehme, it would only have been a matter of time before they made the breakthrough.

A free kick towards the right-hand angle of the French penalty area, a brush of the ball to the left and across Brehme from Felix Magath, and the ball was hit low and hard at Joël Bats's bottom left-hand corner. Powerful, but stoppable, the ball squirmed from Bats's arms and over the goal line. It had shades of the mistake that Luis Arconada had made against France in the 1984 European Championship Final. For a team that needed to be as strong of mind as much as of body this was a hammer blow that they never properly overcame.

France had already entered the match without the services of the injured Rocheteau, who had succumbed to a hamstring problem, his place taken by Bruno Bellone. This was to be a slow puncture of a defeat rather than the assault of four years earlier. Death by a thousand disappointments.

Chances did come France's way. Platini forced Schumacher into a smart save when teed up by Giresse from a clever free-kick routine, while Maxime Bossis put the resultant loose ball over the top of an open goal, although he was adjudged to be offside, a borderline decision that saved Bossis's blushes and a glut of potential sleepless nights for decades to come.

It was a match that predominantly flowed in the opposite direction, however. Bats given plenty of scope to redeem himself, saved from Karl-Heinz Rummenigge, Lothar Matthäus and, most impressively, from Klaus Allofs at the end of a beautiful passing movement that France would have been proud to call their own.

Michel's side were left to hit on the counter-attack, as West Germany surprisingly went in search of the second goal that would have left France with a mountain to climb. Tigana stung the hands of Schumacher, but it was more a case of the West German goalkeeper making heavier weather out of the save than any genuine danger that the shot posed.

The main cause for French concern revolved around their iconic midfield quartet being unable to get the upper hand in the crucial central zones of the pitch, despite having the backing of the vast majority of those in attendance, as chants of 'Francia' boomed around the Estadio Jalisco. This was a day where not even Giresse could work himself into a lasting contribution.

As the second half wore on, French desperation was offset by greater West German focus and precision. Wolfgang Rolff tested Bats from distance, with the goalkeeper pulling off a truly magnificent one-handed save. While West Germany seemed to operate within absolutes, for France it was all agonising what ifs. A rare piece of Giresse vision almost put Platini in on goal, but the French captain was a millimetre or two away from making contact, while Bellone was almost gifted a chance when the ball came to him towards the left of the West German goalmouth, yet the opportunity went unaccepted, when Rocheteau's replacement seemed to be shocked to see the ball arrive at his feet.

A fascinating duel, one of France's best chances was created for himself by Yannick Stopyra, when cutting in from the right he swerved past Ditmar Jakobs and powered into the West German penalty area. He shot low and hard at Schumacher, only for him to be frustratingly equal to the test. The stereotypical Bond villain of Seville was proving an unpassable obstacle.

As games of football go, it could never truly hope to match the drama and skill of four years earlier, but considering this one, by virtue of its outcome, was essentially buried in the garden in a *Blue Peter*-style time capsule and ignored for three and a half decades, it actually had a lot going for it.

With the minutes ticking by, West Germany dropped deeper and deeper, compressing their defence and midfield, asking almost the impossible of France to pick the lock. Platini did put the ball in the net but was marginally offside.

From the midway point of the second half, Bellone and Giresse were replaced by Daniel Xuereb and Philippe Vercruysse within a six-minute span of one another, changes that were indicative of what was to come across the remainder of the decade, as certainly in the case of Giresse, great footballers were being replaced by good ones. France would go onward to suffer the repercussions in spectacular fashion, as the 1986 World Cup would be the last one they would participate in for 12 years, a spell of absence that would have been unthinkable on that day in June 1986 when they defeated Brazil.

Now it was West Germany who were reliant upon the counter-attack. Once again Bats spilled a Brehme free kick that was taken from an almost identical position, except at the other end of the pitch, this time the French goalkeeper reclaiming the loose ball.

With only seconds remaining, the story of the entire match was played out within the macrocosm of the ball sweeping from one end of the pitch to the other, as within the slipstream of Battiston being played in on the left to press Schumacher into another save to deny France what would have been the most delicious slice of karma, and Bossis being repelled when not catching the ball as fulsomely as he would have wished, the action switched to the opposite end, where, via a wonderful pass from Magath, the substitute Rudi Völler lobbed the ball over the advancing Bats and rolled it into the empty net.

It was the last kick of the match and it cemented West Germany their progression to a second successive World Cup Final at the expense of France. The French symbolism and frustration on show in the West German penalty area in the minute or so prior to Völler scoring was stunning. Platini's physical response to Schumacher's final save was to draw his foot back and make an eventually withdrawn kicking motion towards either the West German goalkeeper's head or the ball itself, while the identity of the two players to whom the last two French chances fell couldn't have been more apt. Battiston had been the man who departed the pitch in Seville four years earlier on a stretcher at the behest of the reckless actions of Schumacher, while Bossis had been the player to miss France's last penalty in the shoot-out at that iconic 1982 semi-final.

Partial rancour met the final whistle, as the anger experienced by some French players spilled over into physical altercations with a few of the West German players. It was a bitter end to what was a far better match than many people give credit for, yet it was perhaps an understandable one.

Again, France had played their part in something special, but were left with only the dubious comfort of a third-place play-off, which, unlike four years earlier, they won, defeating Belgium. It was another 120-minute epic, this time in Puebla, on a day when Michel rang as many changes as possible, managing to gift a World Cup experience to every member of his squad, aside from his third-choice goalkeeper, Philippe Bergeroo.

Into international retirement went Giresse, as did Bossis and Rocheteau, and within a year Platini had followed. All impossible to replace, beyond Mexico Michel struggled to put together a cohesive French team, even though he still had a lot of talent at his disposal. The loss of key ingredients was too much to roll with and failures to reach the finals of either the 1988 European Championship or the 1990 World Cup were sobering.

By November 1988, Platini was back with the French squad, but this time as head coach, in succession to Michel, his former team-mate. An understated job was done and he took France to the 1992 European Championship finals, where they underachieved after being classed as one of the favourites to lift the trophy, with a squad that contained three survivors of the one that went to Mexico in 1986: Amoros, Fernández and Papin. Platini stepped aside, and via failure to qualify for the 1994 World Cup finals, France would finally become world champions on home soil in 1998, with a pragmatic approach that was nowhere near as beloved as the teams that had lit up the 1986 World Cup and the two major international tournaments directly before that one.

For West Germany, the 1986 World Cup Final now loomed large. Unloved, uncongratulated and an unwanted visitor at the biggest game of football on the face of the planet, there were at least three other European nations that had been predicted and even willed on to reach this rarefied summit, yet here were Beckenbauer and his men. Wily campaigners, occasionally underhand, yet meticulously prepared and with no shortage of talent and belief, unlike in 1982, they had deserved to beat France this time around, and while they had impressed nobody up to reaching the semi-finals, they had timed their run to the final with a perfection of precision.

Given that Argentina and Diego Maradona were in the other corner of the ring, for many people watching on from England, it was the nightmare World Cup Final line-up.

Chapter Eighteen

And in the End

ON 12 September 1984 Franz Beckenbauer's West Germany played host to Carlos Bilardo's Argentina in a friendly at the Rheinstadion, in Düsseldorf. It was Beckenbauer's first match in charge of *Die Mannschaft*. West Germany's unusual failure to progress from the group stages of the 1984 European Championship had cost Jupp Derwall his job; the head coach had initially intended to see his contract through, taking his nation onward to Mexico, yet he was driven out of the position by a combination of a tabloid campaign and some worryingly aggressive encounters with the general public upon his return home from France.

Derwall had been associated with the West German national team since 1970, when he succeeded the legendary Udo Lattek as assistant to the head coach, Helmut Schön. While Lattek went on to lead both Bayern Munich and Borussia Mönchengladbach to silver-laden glories of both a domestic and European nature before enjoying a lucrative spell in charge of Barcelona, Derwall became a part of the national team's coaching furniture. By Schön's side he won the 1972 European Championship and the 1974 World Cup, coming to within a penalty shoot-out of winning a further European Championship in 1976.

Schön himself had been primed for the job, having served as assistant to the controversial yet revolutionary figure of Sepp Herberger. Herberger, a former member of the Nazi Party, had led West Germany to unexpected World Cup glory in 1954, eventually making way for his assistant in 1964. Schön had previously led the Saarland national team against Herberger's West Germany during the qualifiers for the 1954 World Cup, when for a short time they had their own national team while the coal-rich area was a post-Second World War protectorate of France.

Beyond the successes of the early to mid-1970s, the 1978 World Cup had been a bridge too far for Schön and his ageing team. With a defined dynastic blueprint, Derwall was the heir apparent, and he led West Germany to victory at the 1980 European Championship, then all the way to the 1982 World Cup Final in Spain two years later.

Seamlessly successful, it wasn't enough, however, to gain Derwall any leeway with a disgruntled nation after their early exit from the 1984 European Championship. West Germany had been just seconds away from a place in the semi-finals when they conceded a late winner to Spain in their final group match.

This simmering resentment towards Derwall wasn't simply down to the defeat against Spain in Paris. Its roots were planted firmly in the loss to Algeria at the 1982 World Cup, then egged on by defeats at home and away to Northern Ireland during the qualifiers for the European Championship. West Germany came to within ten minutes of not qualifying for the tournament when labouring in their final match of the campaign in Saarbrücken against Albania.

Defeat to Spain opened the floodgates, and his critics blew away any prospect that Derwall had earned himself the rights to correct the errors of the 1984 European Championship. After 14 years of involvement with *Die*

Mannschaft, there was a virulent public desire for something new, an appetite for a fresh start. In a break from the accepted protocol of the continuity in the baton passing from the head coach to his assistant, the call instead went out to Beckenbauer, a man who was an unmistakable legend on the pitch but had never worked in a coaching capacity for the Deutscher Fußball-Bund (DFB). In fact, he had no coaching experience at all.

At the Rheinstadion in Düsseldorf, Beckenbauer was given a rude awakening to the duties of the job he'd inherited from Derwall. Bilardo's Argentina ran out 3-1 winners, West Germany's goal a mere consolation garnered while 3-0 down. There was even a touch of foretelling when Jorge Burruchaga scored Argentina's third goal.

In retrospective it's a strange match to watch. Prior to kick-off Beckenbauer was sitting on the bench, almost blinded by the constant flashbulbs popping in front of him, as he was faced with a bank of photographers, all competing for the perfect shot of the projected saviour of the West German national team. He had an unfeasibly shiny forehead and was clearly startled when a man in a trench coat touched him on the shoulder, only to be a familiar face offering a handshake and pre-match words of encouragement.

The youthful-looking Beckenbauer had been away from the international arena for seven years, yet was still in his 30s when starting out as head coach. For West Germany, he played alongside two of his first starting line-up: Uli Stielike and Karl-Heinz Rummenigge.

Argentina were in their iconic light-blue and white stripes and black shorts, with West Germany in all green. Aesthetically, visually, we were 11 pairs of white West German shorts away from how the 1986 World Cup Final would look, if you could ignore the backdrop of the Rheinstadion and imagine it as the Estadio Azteca.

Before Burruchaga netted the third goal, José Daniel Ponce scored the first two for Argentina. Ponce was one of the four players Bilardo selected in Düsseldorf that wouldn't make the trip to Mexico. Five of Beckenbauer's line-up would befall the same fate. On an evening when Beckenbauer was the recipient of a valuable lesson, for Bilardo it was a rare occasion when his Argentina team looked like one that could potentially win the World Cup.

Beckenbauer and Bilardo would remain inextricably linked for the next six years, sharing two World Cup finals, one in Mexico City, one in Rome, and walking away from their respective jobs after the second of those finals.

When Bilardo took Argentina to World Cup glory, his nation was essentially left with no option but to apologise to him. As a player, Bilardo was the molten lump of iron in central midfield for the notoriously agricultural Estudiantes de La Plata, later coaching the club on four separate occasions, so when he ascended to the role of head coach of *La Albiceleste* he was painted as the anti-fútbol opposite of the more enigmatic and stylish Luis César Menotti, the on-pitch architect of Argentina's success in 1978. This wasn't only a battle of pragmatism vs expansion that had people picking aesthetic sides in the football stands of Buenos Aires, Córdoba, Rosario, Mendoza and Mar del Plata, it had people picking sides in the cafes, bars, taxis and workplaces of every major city and town across Argentina.

These were also battle lines drawn in press boxes, in radio and television studios, but beyond that the battle lines extended into the Argentinian squad that Bilardo inherited, a squad that was densely inhabited with players who heavily subscribed to Menotti's view of the game. Through the eyes of many, Bilardo was anathema. The World Cup was serious business and to hand the key to the door to him saw a rise in national footballing tension.

Not only was the Argentina captain, Daniel Passarella, defiantly Menotti's man, but Bilardo had to convince Maradona to return to the fold, which he didn't do until 1985, having not played for the national team since 1982. This within itself was a work of art by Bilardo. While the lure of the 1986 World Cup was always going to be irresistible to Maradona, getting him there in prime mental condition and focused on the collective rather than the personal objectives was what Argentina's hopes of glory hinged upon. Added to that, Bilardo didn't only have to get Maradona on his side, he had to guide him to a successful outcome in a power struggle with Passarella for the commitment of the squad.

In Bilardo's favour, Maradona was by no means a confirmed disciple of Menotti. The 17-year-old Maradona had been omitted from the Argentina squad for the 1978 World Cup finals. With a characteristically dramatic flourish, Maradona felt betrayed by Menotti and harboured a lifelong grudge, despite Bilardo's predecessor having been one of the biggest guiding lights of his early years in the game.

While the Maradona conundrum was still playing itself out, Bilardo wasn't helped in his attempts to assuage the fears and suspicions that surrounded him when Argentina made heavy weather of qualifying for Mexico. Having taken over in May 1983, most of the three-year build-up to the World Cup had been a bumpy ride for Bilardo. Winning only 13 of his first 34 matches in charge, while he was due a national apology on delivering World Cup glory, the rancour and worry surrounding him and his team was entirely understandable. It made that victory over Beckenbauer's West Germany in Düsseldorf, which was achieved without the services of Maradona, a perceived anomaly. In a more contemporary footballing setting, Bilardo would never have held on to his job until the World Cup.

The 1983 Copa América ended at the group stages for Argentina. On face value this would be viewed as a disastrous way for Bilardo to start his reign, yet in mitigation his team had been drawn into a three-team group that included Brazil. Yet to localise itself to a single host nation, the Copa América was played out on a pan-continental basis in 1983, unfolding between mid-August and early November. Argentina exited the tournament unbeaten, having defeated Brazil at the Estadio Monumental, and it was two draws against Ecuador that ultimately led to their downfall. Out of necessity due to the inflexibility of European clubs, Bilardo had gone into the tournament fielding only players from the Argentinian domestic club game.

In the qualifiers for the 1986 World Cup, Argentina were drawn into a four-nation group alongside Peru, Colombia and Venezuela. While Venezuela were expected to offer little in the way of resistance, Colombia were a compelling emerging threat, but the main challenge would come from Peru, qualifiers for three of the previous four World Cups, and South American champions just a decade earlier.

Maradona still had much to prove to the watching world in 1985. His two years at Barcelona had been unfulfilling ones, fresh off the back of an unsatisfactory and antagonistic end to his first World Cup in 1982. Joining the club with Lattek at the helm, Maradona was then thrown together with Menotti in March 1983. The combustible nature of their love-hate relationship played itself out amid a dressing room that was also inhabited by the wonderfully gifted yet stunningly volatile Bernd Schuster.

In the summer of 1984 Maradona was starting to resemble damaged goods and a move to Naples was something of a gamble for all involved. Napoli weren't one of the giants of Serie A at the time, they were a team that had flattered to deceive, and a club that had never been Serie

A champions. They were instead a club that had been ailing for the two seasons prior to the arrival of Maradona, ebbing away from serious contention, having flirted with greater successes during the 1970s; *Gli Azzurri* had narrowly missed out on the Serie A title to Juventus in 1974/75, compensating their supporters by winning the Coppa Italia a year later and narrowly missing out on the final of the 1977 European Cup Winners' Cup.

In the first half of the 1960s there had been multiple relegations from Serie A, offset by winning their first-ever Coppa Italia when languishing in Serie B during the 1961/62 season; it was in the second half of the decade that the club grew in stature. Finishing 12th in the 1983/84 season had been Napoli's lowest Serie A placing since their last relegation in 1962/63. Even in the summer of 1986, two years beyond the arrival of Maradona, Napoli were still only on the eve of greatness, and the great underachievers of the Italian game.

While Maradona had excelled personally, the club only finished eighth in his first season with them, even looking like relegation candidates until the turn of the year. The third-placed finish of 1985/86 was an indicator of what was to come during the following season, but when he walked into the 1986 World Cup, Maradona still had everything to prove to a watching global audience, half of which seemed to want him to succeed, while the other half willed him to wilt under the pressure once again.

In a personal visit, Bilardo offered Maradona the captaincy of his country, effectively being given the chance to swipe Passarella's seat from beneath his rival. The Argentina head coach had won the mind of Maradona and the ire of Passarella. Within the ensuing power struggle, Maradona and Passarella's relationship descended into a feud, during which rumours emerged that Maradona had been driven by the intensity of the levels of Passarella's invective campaign so much that he outed to the rest of the squad an affair that the former captain had been having with the wife of another player.

Any sympathies towards Passarella that remained in the squad were obliterated in one fell swoop. Unorthodox an approach as it was, Bilardo's position was strengthened yet again. Now he just needed to ensure that Argentina would attend the 1986 World Cup finals.

They actually came to within nine minutes of failing to qualify automatically for Mexico. It was Peru who denied Argentina a place at the 1970 World Cup finals in Mexico, and it was Peru who came perilously close to repeating a similar trick 16 years later. At the Estadio Monumental in Buenos Aires in their final qualifying match, Argentina entered the last ten minutes of the match 2-1 down, when a draw was the minimum requirement for World Cup qualification. A week earlier they had lost 1-0 to Peru in Lima, and here in the return Bilardo was staring at the unthinkable scenario.

It had all been going so well up until crossing swords with Peru. While it hadn't been entirely plain sailing, Argentina had won all four of their qualifying matches, against Venezuela and Colombia. Peru, meanwhile, had lost to Colombia in Bogotá and drawn with them in Lima. Peru needed what seemed to be an unlikely two victories against Argentina to qualify.

Bilardo's decision to remove the captaincy from Passarella and hand it to Maradona was validated within eight minutes of their opening qualifier, when the deposed captain gifted Venezuela an equaliser in San Cristóbal, just six minutes after the new captain had put Argentina ahead. Passarella made amends by edging Argentina in front again, but Maradona was the hero of the piece, scoring what proved to be the decisive goal in the Venezuelan capital, obtaining a nervous 3-2 win.

This was followed by a 3-1 victory in Bogotá against Colombia at the Estadio El Campín, a stadium that would have been central to the concept of the aborted Colombian World Cup. The scoreline was one that flattered Argentina to a degree, and the hint of something beginning to stir within the Colombian national team could be clearly seen in the way they performed, although it was another two years before greater consistency was found, under the leadership of Francisco Maturana.

A fortnight later, at the Estadio Monumental, Colombia made Argentina work hard for a narrow 1-0 win, with their two matches bookending a comfortable Argentina victory over Venezuela at the same venue.

It could be argued that Peru had nothing to lose going into their back-to-back matches against Argentina. Juan Carlos Oblitas scored the only goal of the first of the two encounters, amid an atmosphere that could have provided electricity for the Peruvian capital for days.

A week later, in Buenos Aires, that atmosphere was returned in triplicate. When Maradona spun and attacked down the left-hand touchline in the 12th minute, the roar of the Estadio Monumental crowd was terrifying. The ball was played towards the angle of the six-yard box, and Pedro Pasculli broke free from the attention of his markers. Upon collecting the cross with one touch, he'd created a clear shot at goal. He drilled his effort with power and accuracy just inside the far post of Eusebio Acasuzo's net. He turned in celebration the moment the ball departed his left foot, and bedlam ensued.

However, before half-time the match had been completely turned on its head. Slack defending from a free kick gifted Peru their equaliser, when José Velásquez forced the ball over the Argentina goal line. Then, with half-time approaching, a series of ricochets in the centre circle resulted in a Peru breakaway, with Gerónimo Barbadillo rounding Ulbaldo Fillol to make it 2-1 to the visitors. The Estadio Monumental was stunned into an eerie silence.

Argentina were made to wait until the 81st minute for their crucial equaliser, and when it came it was a scriptwriter's dream. The chance fell to Passarella, yet the ball hit the post and rolled along the goal line, with a race breaking out to be the first one to it. Ricardo Gareca was the first player to reach it, and prodded it into the net. Gareca had cast Peru into a World Cup wilderness that would last for 32 years, yet stunningly it was he, as their head coach, who would lead them to the 2018 finals.

In riposte to Gareca's equaliser, Peru mounted a desperate effort to regain the lead, squandering two very good late chances before the final whistle brought the match to an end. Holding out for the point they required, as dramatic a match as it was, Argentina looked far from the image of future World Cup winners.

Beckenbauer, meanwhile, had over a month beyond the loss to Argentina in Düsseldorf to prepare for the start of West Germany's qualifying campaign, taking on Sweden in Köln, at the Müngersdorfer Stadion. This was a Sweden caught between two defined eras. Beaten finalists, as hosts, at the 1958 World Cup, 20 years on from having reached the semi-finals in France, they had sporadically qualified until failure to reach the 1982 finals. The mid-1980s were something of a peculiarity for Swedish football, usurped as they were as Scandinavia's international nation of footballing purpose by the hypnotic rise of Denmark, yet on the club scene, the fearsome IFK Göteborg had won the UEFA Cup in 1982, and would do so again in 1987.

West Germany were 2-0 winners in Köln. A hard-earned victory, the breakthrough only came 15 minutes from time, thanks to the substitute, Uwe Rahn, with Karl-Heinz Rummenigge adding a second goal two minutes from time.

Before 1984 had come to an end West Germany went to Malta, where they laboured to a 3-2 victory. Two wins out of two in qualifying it might have been, but they had been gained without any genuine reassurance that the self-doubts that had crept in under Derwall were going to dissipate rapidly under Beckenbauer. These fears were further reinforced in January 1985, when beaten by Hungary in a Hamburg friendly.

This wasn't the most helpful preparation with trips to Lisbon and Prague looming upon the horizon to face Portugal and Czechoslovakia. Along with the return match in Sweden, these were undoubtedly going to be their most difficult fixtures of the qualifying campaign. Portugal had reached the semi-finals of the 1984 European Championship, while Czechoslovakia and 1976 European Championship Final torment was still relatively fresh in German minds.

These were to be huge tests of Beckenbauer and his vision but he and his team passed them with style. A 2-1 win in Lisbon in late February and a 5-1 victory at the end of April in Prague sandwiched a 6-0 stroll in Saarbrücken against Malta and a friendly hammering of Bulgaria in Augsburg.

Previous concerns suddenly feeling foolish, West Germany were well-positioned after five qualifiers, as their rivals insisted upon taking points off one another. Portugal beat Czechoslovakia and won in Sweden, only to lose to the return against the Swedes on home soil. Czechoslovakia even contrived to draw with Malta.

Yet 1985 was a year of contrasts for West Germany. The promise of the early months gave way to a less impressive summer and autumn. An acclimatisation trip to Mexico was taken, where they suffered defeats to their hosts and England. The new season then began with a loss in Moscow to the Soviet Union. Friendlies they might have been, but a degree of confidence was lost during those three successive defeats.

West Germany, with a comfortable points advantage, then failed to win any of their final three qualifying matches, as they threw away a 2-0 advantage in Solna, drawing 2-2 with Sweden in September, before a shock October loss in Stuttgart to Portugal, their first-ever World Cup qualification defeat. This was followed by a late face-saving draw gained against Czechoslovakia in November at a sparsely populated Olympiastadion in Munich.

Six matches without a win, West Germany had qualified comfortably, but many of the questions they may have felt they had answered throughout the spring of 1985 had reared once more during the second half of the year. In response, Beckenbauer and the DFB set up a series of high-profile friendlies from the beginning of 1986 to take them to the World Cup finals. Victories in Avellino against Italy and Frankfurt against Brazil blew away the cobwebs.

These positive results and performances were followed by a win, a draw and a win against Switzerland, Yugoslavia and the Netherlands, respectively, in Basel, Bochum and Dortmund. A convincing set of results and an environment in which Beckenbauer could fine-tune his squad. Five matches, four wins, one draw, nine goals for and three against. This is where Beckenbauer arguably began to grow into the role he'd inherited from Derwall.

Not all was perfect in the build-up to Mexico for West Germany, however. Beckenbauer obsessed over the composition of his team. The role of *libero* was a particular issue for him, having tried 16 different options in the position, a pivotal on-pitch responsibility in which he'd performed with such effortless grace himself. Beckenbauer hedged his bets by naming three candidates for the job: Matthias Herget, Klaus Augenthaler and Ditmar Jakobs. This oversubscription of *libero* meant that World Cup winner to be Guido Buchwald was omitted from the squad. Beckenbauer's indecision on the matter even rolled into the finals, as all three contenders were tried during the group stages, with Jakobs eventually keeping hold of the role during the knockout stages.

Another problem for Beckenbauer was that Rudi Völler had missed a large part of the season, and how capable he was of playing the entire tournament was open to conjecture. Added to this and with a heavy sense of déjà vu, Rummenigge was also carrying an injury into the tournament, just as he had four years earlier.

At the time, not considered as being anywhere close to previous West German vintages, this was still a squad that contained Rummenigge, Völler, Klaus Allofs, Harald Schumacher, Thomas Berthold, Andreas Brehme, Pierre Littbarski and Lothar Matthäus. Experience aplenty, apart from the back-up goalkeepers there were only two other players in the West German squad who hadn't played an active role during the qualifiers, those being the ageing wildcards of Norbert Eder and Dieter Hoeneß.

While Hoeneß would be restricted to a couple of cameo appearances as a substitute, one of which was in the final, Eder was to be a shock ever-present in the team. He represented West Germany only nine times, seven of which were at the 1986 World Cup finals.

For Bilardo there was much less continuity of personnel. Of the 19 players to appear in the qualifiers for Argentina, only ten made the squad for Mexico. Of those, only six would appear in the World Cup Final. Maradona, Jorge

Burruchaga, Jorge Valdano, Ricardo Giusti and Oscar Garré were the only players who translated from having played a significant role in the qualifiers to playing a substantial role in Mexico, with Garré not even appearing in the side beyond the last 16. This was a heavily reconstructed team, and it wasn't conducive to garnering Bilardo any faith from his compatriots back home. Many people in Argentina had campaigned for a change of head coach before the tournament.

The last links to the 1978 World Cup-winning squad to have been a part of the team that clinched qualification for Mexico were Filiol and Passarella. Both pillars of the Argentina team for over a decade, they played all six qualifiers but would take no part in the finals. While Passarella was named in the squad, he would find himself sidelined throughout the finals. Fillol, meanwhile, stepped aside completely and didn't travel to Mexico at all.

Another omission was Gareca, the man who scored the goal that saved Bilardo so late in the final qualifier against Peru. Bilardo showed no sentimentality towards his qualifying hero, and when he was found to be struggling for form and fitness, he was ruthlessly brushed aside. Gareca wasn't alone, as others suffered a similar fate. Enzo Trossero, Juan Barbas and Miguel Ángel Russo all went from being crucial members of Bilardo's team during qualifying to being discarded for the finals. While in some cases fitness concerns kept them out, for others it was purely on Bilardo's preference for other options.

When Argentina set off for the World Cup, they did so with only five members of the squad that Menotti had taken to Spain four years earlier. Maradona, Valdano, Nery Pumpido, Julio Olarticoechea and Passarella. With Passarella playing no part in Mexico, and neither Pumpido nor Olarticoechea having played an active role in 1982, a tournament in which Valdano was restricted to just 51 minutes of football, it meant that Maradona carried not just the hopes of his nation, but almost all of Argentina's World Cup experience on to the pitches of Mexico.

Bilardo had ridden his luck and now he'd created an air pocket in which he could build a team fit for World Cup purpose. A team where Maradona would be the puppet master, surrounded by a support system of players who were selected to service his needs. The Menotti collective was no more, and this was now the court of Maradona. Not a one-man team by any means, but a carefully constructed network of support designed to work at the behest of its pulsating engine.

The continuity that had been lacking within Bilardo's methods during the three years between him taking over from Menotti and rolling into the 1986 World Cup finals suddenly appeared out of nowhere in Mexico. Eight players started all seven matches Argentina played, while the tragic José Luis Cuciuffo came into the team for their second group match and kept his place for the remainder of the tournament. Added to this, Olarticoechea and Héctor Enrique, having made a string of cameo appearances from the bench during the first four matches, came into the team for the quarter-final and refused to let go of their places again. This was a level of cohesion that took everybody by surprise, possibly even themselves.

Rancour erupted upon Argentina's arrival in Mexico City, however, which just played to the preconceived notions of the watching gallery. Angry words had been exchanged between Argentine Football Association officials and reporters, as the media scramble was far in excess of that expected by the Mexican organisers. The tidal wave of interest that descended caused the planned press conference to be cancelled, with not enough press passes to go around.

It wasn't only the deluge of representatives from the media that caused the chaos. Besotted citizens of Mexico City had also assembled to catch a glimpse of Maradona and he was jostled by the growing crowd of onlookers, many of whom attempted to reach out and touch the world's greatest footballer elect. This provoked a heavy-handed reaction from police officers, who pushed the crowds back with excessive force, causing further anger to rise, prompting chants of 'Hugo, Hugo, Hugo' from the crowd, in honour of Mexico's own hero, Hugo Sánchez, perhaps feeling that Maradona himself was pushing the crowd back somehow.

Spirited away to their team hotel, matters only minimally improved as security was so lax that reporters simply broke through the cordon and approached players and coaches at will. It all added to the general concerns that Mexico just wasn't prepared for the World Cup. While Mexican media accused Argentina of displaying a lack of sportsmanship in cancelling their press conference, they did concede in an editorial in the newspaper *Ovaciones* that Mexico was an 'example of disorganisation' and that nobody had bothered to adequately organise the reception of the Argentina squad.

Written off by their own media, the sacking of the head coach demanded by the masses, almost failing to qualify, a rumbling discontent between Maradona and Passarella, no consistency in either performances or results in the build-up and now a far from perfect arrival into the country, where local hearts and minds had initially been lost, Argentina's climb to the summit of the 1986 World Cup started below sea level.

West Germany, however, weren't without their own issues. Their arrival in Mexico was marred by a rolling argument between Beckenbauer and his goalkeeper Schumacher, which stemmed from the fielding of Uli Stein, one of the back-up keepers, for the last official pre-tournament friendly against the Netherlands. When Schumacher aired his displeasure in the West German newspapers, Beckenbauer responded with a public rebuke of his own, which left genuine question marks over who the coach would opt for as his first-choice goalkeeper.

Stein's chances increased when a frustrated Schumacher left his team-mate, Matthias Herget, in a crumpled heap during a training match after a challenge that significantly impinged upon the borders of recklessness. With Schumacher's unpunished flattening of Battiston in the 1982 World Cup semi-final still reverberating four years on, the global audience pulled up its collective chair and reached for the popcorn.

Within days, Beckenbauer had upset the rest of his squad when he publicly aired his opinion that West Germany couldn't make the final. Whether designed to be a dose of reverse psychology or brutal honesty from Beckenbauer, the players caused enough of a protest that he would retract the comments at a later press conference. It all lent more credence to the theory that Beckenbauer was widely unpopular with a high percentage of his squad, as the stand-off between head coach and goalkeeper continued.

Given that Beckenbauer's captain, Rummenigge, was carefully nursing his knee injury, restricting him to a place on the bench as the World Cup began, it was possibly only the fact that Schumacher was the vice-captain that saved him from an ignominious exclusion from the starting line-up in their opening match against Uruguay.

Argentina stole a two-day march on West Germany, kicking off their campaign 48 hours before Beckenbauer's team. Bilardo selected a team that had only six of the line-up that had limped past Peru at the Estadio Monumental in the final decisive qualifier: Maradona, Garré, Burruchaga, Pasculli, Valdano and Giusti. Of those coming into the line-up, in the wake of the abdication of Fillol, Pumpido inherited the goalkeeping responsibilities, Néstor Clausen returned to the defence, José Luis Brown was drafted in to cover for Passarella when the former captain went down to a debilitating stomach bug, while the imposing figures of Oscar Ruggeri and Sergio Batista were brought into the defence and midfield, respectively, having previously only been on the periphery of the team.

Bilardo's fine-tuning of the team would continue into the early exchanges of the World Cup. Clausen would only appear in Argentina's opening match, while Pasculli would play just one further time beyond the opener. With both players having been integral components to the team that navigated a way through the qualifiers, their mutual dropping out of contention in Mexico would further distance Bilardo's new Argentina from Menotti's old one.

At the Estadio Universitario, South Korea's physical approach was dealt with via Argentina's brutality of the ball, obtaining the lead within six minutes and scoring their third less than 60 seconds after the restart. Bilardo's team coped better with South Korea than anybody else did in Group A, this when facing them in their opening match when enthusiasm would have been at its peak for a nation that's contested every World Cup since.

Valdano scoring twice and Ruggeri with one, it was the perfect start for Argentina. There was confidence to be built in getting off to a winning start, Maradona was imperious, there had been a brace of goals for Valdano, Ruggeri had repaid Bilardo's faith, and there were no problems in the absence of Passarella. It was a good performance and a good win. It was even a plus point that many would have dismissed it, simply due to the identity of Argentina's opponents. Bilardo's team were up and running, but they were still under the radar.

Over in Querétaro, West Germany launched their bid for a third World Cup against a Uruguay team that would be the only one to cross the path of both finalists. Beckenbauer was widely predictable in his team selection. Rummenigge was named among the substitutes as he continued to build up his fitness. He was joined by Littbarski, FC Köln's mercurial winger, whom Beckenbauer initially found difficult to harness to his plans but who would, in time, become a crucial component to eventually winning the 1990 World Cup, eight years after having played in the 1982 final against Italy.

Augenthaler's inclusion was symptomatic of Beckenbauer's indecision over who to deploy at sweeper, while Allofs's place in the starting line-up was due to Rummenigge's gradual conditioning programme. Both Augenthaler and Allofs had played only cameo roles during qualifying, but the core of the line-up was made up of what had become West Germany's cast of regulars. Only one of the 11 players Beckenbauer selected to face Uruguay hadn't made an appearance during their qualifying campaign.

The main curveball that Beckenbauer threw was the inclusion of Bayern Munich's Nobert Eder. Eder had been one of the brighter lights of a struggling FC Nürnberg team until he earned a transfer to the Olympiastadion, just a few short months before his 29th birthday. Very much a late riser to the top of his profession, an international debut was only gained at the age of 30, a mere 24 days before West Germany faced Uruguay at the Estadio La Corregidora.

Eder would play all but four minutes of West Germany's campaign at the 1986 World Cup, when he was replaced late in extra time during the quarter-final by Littbarski, with a penalty shoot-out in mind. The peculiarity was that after the tournament had ended, he never represented his nation again. His international career stretched for just 49 days, his first and last appearances separated by seven weeks, culminating in a World Cup Final.

Coming to within five minutes of defeat against Uruguay, the resultant 1-1 draw was a sweet-and-sour one. There was relief that something had been clawed from the match, but it was tempered by the fact that West Germany had been the better team without managing to obtain the victory. As starts go, it could have been both so much better and far, far worse.

Moving 206 miles south-east of Querétaro to Puebla, 24 hours later Argentina were walking into the Estadio Cuauhtémoc to face an audit of the true extent of their capabilities. Their opponents were Italy, the defending champions. Argentina were facing Italy at a fourth successive World Cup, a run that would stretch to a fifth successive World Cup in 1990. A 1-1 draw had been shared in 1974, while Italy had narrowly edged their encounters in 1978 and 1982. The 2-1 victory Italy had enjoyed, at the Estadi de Sarrià in Barcelona, had been a part of the iconic trilogy of matches that the two great footballing nations had shared with Brazil.

One of the greatest inter-continental international football rivalries of all time, while this wasn't the first heavyweight match of the tournament, it was the one that emboldened the 1986 World Cup. All 24 competing nations had now played their opening matches and Argentina vs Italy, along with the Soviet Union vs France, which kicked off simultaneously in León, began the cycle of the second set of group fixtures.

A 1-1 draw, claimed from having conceded from the penalty spot after only six minutes, spoke of a certain sense of character that was building within Bilardo's side. Yes, this was a poor Italy vintage, but neither they nor the watching world fully knew that yet. Maradona levelled the scores with his first goal of the tournament, and it was an often-forgotten goal of breathtaking beauty and simplicity.

When Giusti was played the ball midway inside the Italy half in the 34th minute, he was allowed the space and time to turn and pick his pass. Four years earlier, at the home of Español, he would have had Claudio Gentile bearing down on him, but not in 1986, not at the home of Club Puebla. Threading a pass to Valdano, it was met by the striker with one touch. Valdano sent a stunning lofted clip of a ball spinning high into the Italy penalty area, over the heads of the *Azzurri*'s static defence. A burst of acceleration from Maradona to the left of the goalmouth and he was in with a chance, albeit from an acute angle. Closed on by Gaetano Scirea, Maradona let the ball take one bounce, before connecting with the inside of his left foot, right on the angle of the six-yard box. It flashed past the outstretched hand of Giovanni Galli and into the far corner of his net.

Galli stood there, hands on hips, considering what he'd just seen, disbelieving what his eyes were telling him, like resigned parents looking at their infant offspring sitting before them with a bowl of food on its head and tomato sauce trickling down its face. Laughing.

Maradona, meanwhile, was off and away, leaping into the air with a punch, before clearing the advertising hoardings to celebrate in front of the longest Argentinian flag you're likely to see. In a tournament of iconic goals, it's one of those you see again and immediately wonder how you ever let it slip from your mind.

No further goals were added, as both teams seemed content to protect what they had, only chancing their arm if an opportunity seemed too good to ignore.

In the days that followed, Passarella was finally declared fit to play, not only by his own assessment, but also by that of the team doctor, Raul Madero. He'd spent ten days battling his stomach bug, lost almost half a stone in weight, but now he was ready to return.

Back in Querétaro three days later West Germany obtained a crucial victory against Scotland. The importance of this win has always been underplayed. After the draw against Uruguay and with the dangers of Denmark still to face, a stubborn Scotland, who would exit the tournament having given Denmark their toughest challenge of the group stages, were never going to be easy to face.

Andreas Brehme made way, as Beckenbauer brought in Littbarski, electing to fight a predictable British 4-4-2 formation with a 4-4-2 of his own. This thinking was undone, however, when Alex Ferguson deployed a 4-5-1 system. The extra man in midfield was at times a two-man advantage, due to the attacking intent of Littbarski.

A match with a wonderful openness unfolded, during which both teams enjoyed periods of dominance and Scotland took a surprise but deserved lead. Trailing only for five minutes, West Germany would turn the result around though, the win procured thanks to goals from Völler and Allofs. It was a positive step forward.

Once more Rummenigge had appeared as a substitute, replacing Littbarski with 15 minutes remaining. The captain helped ease the pressure as Scotland threw everything they possibly could at West Germany during the final few minutes.

Despite the win, Beckenbauer continued to publicly poke his squad with a stick, when he claimed his team didn't play as well in winning against Scotland as they had in drawing against Uruguay. Eder came under some of the heaviest criticism for the awkwardness with which he dealt with man-marking Gordon Strachan. But despite the complaints of Beckenbauer, it was a win that effectively put West Germany into the last 16. Thanks to Denmark's dismantling of Uruguay, and Scotland now being unable to surpass them, the lowest West Germany could finish was third and it would take a defeat to the Danes, plus a six-goal swing in goal difference, combined with Uruguay beating Scotland for even that to happen.

It all contrived to make for one of those major tournament peculiarities, when winning your group would offer a more arduous path to the final than the one gifted by finishing as runners-up. It was a scenario that gave Beckenbauer plenty to ponder.

Returning to the Estadio Olímpico Universitario two days later, Bilardo's Argentina needed a result against Bulgaria that matched Italy's against South Korea in Puebla. Top of the group was at play and, unlike West Germany's situation, topping their group had its attractions for Argentina. For a start, there was France to avoid and, beyond that, Argentina's eternal rivals, Brazil.

Bilardo opted for an unchanged team against Bulgaria. The Passarella question was answered when he pulled up in training with a strained leg muscle the day before the match. For Bilardo, who had publicly stated that Passarella would return once fit, this fresh problem was perhaps where he decided to stick rather than twist, when the former captain finally was fit to play. Brown had deputised well, and once the knockout stage had begun, any coach would have been ill at ease to alter a winning line-up. This theory still didn't stop Bilardo making changes, enforced or aesthetic, all the way up to the semi-finals. These changes just didn't involve Passarella and it simply massages the ego of the fable that the former captain was cast aside when eventually available.

An early goal from Valdano and another by Burruchaga gave Argentina a comfortable win on an afternoon when Bulgaria were reluctant to take risks. Again, it meant that Argentina had been seen to do just enough. They were yet to be genuinely stretched, and given how much Bilardo had altered his squad, nobody knew whether they were firing on all cylinders or idling along, primed to click up by a gear or two.

The home comforts of Querétaro, where West Germany had been drawn to play all three of their group fixtures, was of no help when it came to facing Denmark. Beckenbauer rang the changes for the final group match and out dropped Briegel, Augenthaler, Magath and Littbarski. Back came Brehme, along with Jakobs, who had appeared from the bench against Scotland, plus the first sightings of Herget and Rolff.

With Briegel nursing a minor injury and Magath ill, both would return for the last 16, but this was the end of the World Cup for Augenthaler. He would play every match for Beckenbauer at the 1990 World Cup, but in Mexico he succumbed to an injury that prematurely ended his tournament. He was badly missed against Denmark, and Herget was handed the role of sweeper. He failed the audition. It would be his only appearance in Mexico. Jakobs would take on the position from the beginning of the knockout stages. With Augenthaler injured and Herget having fumbled his opportunity, Beckenbauer's indecision over the position was taken out of his hands, as Jakobs was essentially the last man standing.

Perhaps hardest done by was Littbarski, who had the biggest cause for complaint. Key to both of West Germany's goals against Scotland, he returned to the bench against Denmark and remained there for the rest of the tournament. Ironically, Rummenigge, the man who might well have been expected to replace Littbarski, also remained on the bench, despite being passed as fully fit.

When it comes to lessons learned, the one handed to them by Denmark was arguably the most sobering and pertinent of all absorbed by Beckenbauer during his first two years in the job. Two years and one day beyond West Germany being outplayed in Querétaro by Denmark, Beckenbauer returned the compliment by the very same scoreline in Gelsenkirchen at the 1988 European Championship. West Germany on the upcycle, Denmark on the downward arc.

Back in 1986, the most startling thing about West Germany's loss to Denmark was the simplicity with which they were taken apart. This despite Sepp Piontek making four changes of his own, inclusive of being bold enough to rest his first-choice goalkeeper.

While West Germany would now have to travel the 438 miles north to Monterrey and have one day fewer than Denmark to recover for their next match, their opponents weren't as daunting as the one they had gifted to Denmark. West Germany were to face the surprise winners of Group F, Morocco. Meanwhile, back in Puebla, Argentina were faced with an evocative fixture in the last 16. Uruguay were awaiting Bilardo and Maradona.

Two age-old rivals separated geographically by the Río de la Plata, they had contested the very first World Cup Final in Montevideo in 1930. Stories have been told of how Argentina supporters had sailed across the river to be in attendance. The depth of their rivalry can be gauged by the fact that by the time they fought it out at the Estadio Centenario for the Jules Rimet trophy in July 1930, the two great neighbours had already played each other over 100 times. In Puebla, at the Estadio Cuauhtémoc, it was the 165th playing of the fixture. It was, however, the first time that Argentina and Uruguay had gone head to head in the World Cup finals since that iconic 1930 final in Montevideo.

Uruguay had been fined £8,000 for their part in the ugliness of their clash with Scotland, while their coach, Omar Borrás, was banned from the touchline for the last-

16 match. As comic book villains go, Argentina were mere amateurs in comparison to Uruguay. Spiritedly, they put in an immediate appeal to have their sanctions overturned, only to see this rejected out of hand just as swiftly.

Bilardo made just one change to his line-up, Pasculli returning in preference to Borghi. The switch paid off and the Lecce striker scored the only goal, but the 1-0 scoreline did a roundly entertaining match no justice. Argentina were outstanding, Maradona was majestic, Pasculli was both the hero and the villain. Uruguay behaved themselves, despite still picking up four yellow cards, and they defied gravity to almost take the match into extra time, having had their on-pitch orders barked to them down a walkie-talkie attached to Borrás's hand, way up in the stands of the Estadio Cuauhtémoc.

This was the version of Uruguay who played during the first half against West Germany; this was the likeable version of Uruguay, a version that might well have beaten Scotland in style, had Borrás set his stall out in a similar manner.

If any doubts about Maradona's capabilities to own his World Cup surroundings remained at kick-off, they had been completely blown away by full time. On an individual basis, he created an early, credible yet wasted goalscoring opportunity for Valdano, he hit the crossbar with a free kick from immense distance, he had a second-half goal harshly disallowed, he skipped past Uruguay defenders as if they weren't there, almost teasing them, before cueing up for Pasculli to miss another clear-cut chance.

Childlike enthusiasm flowed through Maradona's movements. He pleaded for clemency to the referee when his goal was disallowed. Further chances that Argentina created collectively were missed: a Ruggeri header drifted over the crossbar, when vast quantities of time and space were generously permitted by the Uruguayan defence; Valdano had a far-post header deflected wide, when it initially looked like he'd wasted the opportunity; and another chance fell for Burruchaga, which was cleared off the line when it appeared easier to score. Álvez also pulled off a fine save from Maradona, when the Argentina captain wriggled free in the penalty area once more.

A win garnered without a hint of egotism, Bilardo and Maradona surely knew that only hard work, vision, unity, power, skill and desire would see Argentina past Uruguay. The true Uruguay had only minimally been on show up to this point. They still simmered below the surface, and while confident in their own abilities, Argentina showed the perfect amount of respect to deal with and dispose of their neighbours from across the Río de la Plata.

The one goal Argentina did score was a fitting one to grace and decide such a match, a wonderful 12-pass move that was instigated by Pumpido and concluded by Pasculli when it had opened up the Uruguay defence for the latter to score. From Pumpido to Pasculli, from one end of the pitch to the other, the ball travelled with a skill and measure that was both illuminating and hypnotic. The ball passed through Maradona along the way, but rather than him being the puppet master in this one, he was merely one of the collective, facilitating just one of the 12 passes, yet the one on which the whole move pivoted. In a tournament blessed by an abundance of artistic individual goals, this one was arguably the best team goal of the 1986 World Cup.

Given how one-sided so much of this match was, Uruguay had Argentina hanging on at the end of it. Uruguay's early attempts were in short supply, rushed and clumsy when they did materialise. The great Enzo Francescoli and his teammate Wilmar Cabrera contrived to get in each other's way when one rare opportunity fell in their combined direction. On another occasion, an innocuous Francescoli free kick from distance, which Pumpido fumbled, created a more dangerous situation than necessary. It all worked to focus Argentina upon the threat that Uruguay posed. In a sense, Uruguay were the sleeping dog that Argentina feared disturbing.

At 1-0 it was always finely poised. Uruguay had spent the near entirety of it weathering the Argentinian storm, then hitting on the break. Jorge da Silva, a half-time replacement for Cabrera, pounced on a slip in the Argentina defence, Pumpido pushed the ball to his left, then collided with Francescoli, who had every right to challenge for the ball. A scuffle broke out. It was one of only a small number of truly contentious flashpoints in an atmosphere that crackled.

As Uruguay pushed for a late equaliser, Argentina were now the team hitting on the break. Maradona, always looking to carry the ball, sent Pasculli running free into a sparsely populated Uruguay half, where he wasted a one-on-one situation, taking the ball too close to the goalkeeper. Pasculli left his foot in, much to Álzev's displeasure, the Uruguayan goalkeeper then appearing to catch the Argentine striker with his studs when stepping over him. The matter escalated, as he then got to his feet and punched Álvez in the face, when the shot-stopper went to help him up. It would have been a certain red card had it been spotted. As it was, these were the final few seconds of Pasculli's World Cup. He wouldn't appear again beyond facing Uruguay.

Uruguay were undeniably second best throughout this match, but they fought to the final whistle. They were more than an added extra, however; they were a compelling support actor. In his commentary for BBC Television, John Motson showed admiration for the approach Uruguay took, when he declared, 'Uruguay making a fight of it, in the best sense of the word.' It still didn't stop the delivery of one more hack at Maradona's shins, deep into stoppage time.

These were the final few acts of a match that isn't given the credit it deserves. One that's masked by the low scoreline, one that's shielded because of the attention history affords the ones that followed this for Argentina. An ebullient and underrated game of football that goes largely forgotten, thanks to the fact that it was more of a parochial, neighbourhood dispute. With the Uruguay of the 1986 World Cup being one of the most unloved football teams in the tournament's history, it takes a strong stomach to elect to seek out their matches retrospectively from that summer, but it's worth doing, because their performances touch upon virtually every facet of human nature, from the good, to the bad, and then back again.

For Argentina, they would be heading back to Mexico City from Puebla. This time the Estadio Azteca would be their destination and there they would stay. This meant that the three stadiums Argentina would grace at the 1986 World Cup all resided within a circumference of under 90 miles.

At the Estadio Universitario in Monterrey 24 hours later, it was West Germany's turn to embrace the knockout stages. With no return to fitness for Augenthaler and the torrid time Herget had been given by Denmark, Jakobs inherited the sweeper role, in a West German defence that was also boosted by the return of Briegel. Brehme dropped down to the bench, as Beckenbauer altered his formation slightly to accommodate Rummenigge. The form of both Allofs and Völler had been one of the few definitive positives about the World Cup so far for West Germany. It would have left Beckenbauer with an impossible choice of which of the two should be removed to make way for Rummenigge, had the coach stuck to the same formation.

Within this, allowing the Rummenigge, Allofs, Völler conundrum to dictate the framework of his team was one of a cluster of almost un-Germanic decisions by Beckenbauer that could have cost West Germany their place in the quarter-finals. You could almost suggest there was a lack of discipline with Beckenbauer and his squad at the 1986 World Cup, be that the pre-tournament arguments he had with Schumacher, his denouncement of West Germany's chances of winning a third World Cup, or their insistence in conceding the first goal in all three of their group matches.

Possibly underestimating the capabilities of Morocco, not only did Beckenbauer opt for a three-man forward line, but he also brought Magath back into the team after illness had kept him out of the Denmark match. Contrary to what his future pragmatic coaching approach might say to you about Magath, as a player he was an attacking midfielder with a keen eye for a killer pass and an appetite for goals of his own. Factor in Matthäus, and against Morocco this made for a very attacking line-up.

The main problem was that it was built upon a disjointed foundation. While Jakobs, Briegel and Förster would be the answer to Beckenbauer's central-defensive problems, the addition of Rummenigge as an extra attacking element left too much responsibility on Berthold and Eder to position themselves higher up the pitch, in support of the midfield, from their traditionally deeper roles.

West Germany vs Morocco was an awful game of football, but it was one that reconciled Beckenbauer with the reality that he would have to bring Brehme back into his line-up and opt for two from the three of Rummenigge, Allofs and Völler. Beckenbauer might well have been the bright young mind that the DFB needed, but he would need to work those new ideas into the existing template. This was a pattern written in stone by Herberger and reworked by Schön and Derwall during their respective eras. For Beckenbauer to dare to deviate from the pattern was arguably brave, yet potentially foolhardy. Either way, he didn't do it again. He went back to the blueprint and, like Schön and Derwall before him, Beckenbauer reinvented West Germany's successful wheel.

Taking Morocco lightly had been a risk. As a player, Beckenbauer had faced them at the 1970 World Cup in León, where West Germany had been on the receiving end of a sizeable scare. Their 2-1 victory was earned from a half-time deficit, and Gerd Müller's winning goal had come late, with a reasonable slice of luck. Sixteen years on, West Germany were made to sweat for their success once again. Brehme, on the bench, had been in the West Germany Olympic team that faced Morocco in 1984, at the Stanford Stadium in California. It was ironic that he might have brought not only a better balance to Beckenbauer's team in Monterrey, but also an on-pitch insight into how stubborn Morocco could be.

Perhaps inspired by Steaua Bucharest's approach to that year's European Cup Final, Morocco barely ventured forward. They were instead happy to see whether the baking conditions could take a toll on West Germany for them, before pouncing late in the match. Similar tactics had accounted for the draws they had gained during the group stages against Poland and England, before showing a much more expansive version of themselves against Portugal. In fact, it was one of the biggest disappointments of the tournament that Morocco didn't face West Germany in the same frame of mind that they had faced Portugal.

A belated change in shape was made by Beckenbauer, when he replaced Völler with Littbarski for the last 17 minutes. It made no aesthetic difference, however, and the match looked set to drift into extra time until Matthäus hit his beautifully low-struck free kick, just two minutes from the end, arcing it wide of a badly formed Morocco defensive wall and just beyond the despairing reach of Badou Zaki, Morocco's goalkeeper and captain.

Boos and jeers rained down from the stands of the Estadio Universitario upon the final whistle. It had been an unsatisfactory match to the naked eye, and in the BBC studio Emlyn Hughes stated his relief that they had all been spared a further 30 minutes.

Unlike his critical analysis of his team's performance after their only other win of the tournament, against Scotland, Beckenbauer was guarded in his appraisal this time, focusing on Morocco's reluctance to play an open game and pointing to José Faria's approach to Morocco's encounters against Poland and England. In reply, Faria downplayed West Germany's chances of going further into the tournament, proclaiming mischievously that England had been Morocco's hardest opponents throughout their adventures in Mexico.

Both West Germany and Argentina had progressed to the quarter-finals by virtue of 1-0 victories, but the stories behind the scorelines were vastly different. For Argentinian skill, verve and endeavour against Uruguay, West Germany had been frustrated and had struggled to find the answers to Morocco's stubborn questions. Argentina had been inspiring, West Germany uninspiring.

Leapfrogging Argentina in the order of play, West Germany would remain in Monterrey, where they would welcome the host nation, Mexico, four days beyond progressing against Morocco. It made for a peculiar situation, where the hosts were almost the visitors, having played their previous four matches at the Estadio Azteca. There might have been a partisan and vocal support for Mexico at the Estadio Universitario, but they were facing opponents who had the advantage of playing on turf and within surroundings where they had very recently won.

Faced with further, and even literal, sleepless nights, in the build-up to the quarter-final, Beckenbauer had to deal with the breaking of the squad curfew by four of his players, who returned to the team hotel at 2am on the Thursday morning prior to the Mexico match on the Saturday afternoon.

Citing 'technical reasons' for their lateness, Jakobs, Augenthaler, Stein and Hoeneß succeeded in bringing another un-Germanic plot twist to Beckenbauer's campaign. The West German coach wasn't short of headaches already, which were added to when Völler picked up an injury that would mean he'd play no part against Mexico. While the loss of Völler meant that Beckenbauer was spared having to make the difficult decision between Rummenigge, Völler and Allofs for the two striking positions available against Mexico, it simply blunted any potential plan B he might have wished to have up his sleeve in the event of a stalemate at the Estadio Universitario.

In the absence of Augenthaler, Jakobs was the only one of those set to start the quarter-final who broke Beckenbauer's curfew, but the injury to Völler brought Hoeneß into play too, among the substitutes. With Rummenigge, the only survivor from the two teams that faced each other in Argentina eight years earlier, still searching for peak match-fitness, the captain would last just short of the hour mark, when he would be replaced by Hoeneß. In fact, as the match limped into extra time and on to a penalty shoot-out, it meant that Hoeneß played a longer active role than Rummenigge.

As Völler dropped out, it was Brehme that returned, as did West Germany's more familiar formation. It might not have seemed like it at the Estadio Universitario, but Völler's absence from the quarter-final had an unexpected positive side-effect to the balance of Beckenbauer's team. Völler would return beyond the match against Mexico, yet only in cameo appearances from the bench, in the same manner Rummenigge began the tournament. They essentially switched roles, to spectacular effect.

An intriguing, if awful game of football, it was certainly the worst of the quarter-final fixtures, and West German proficiency from the penalty spot was the difference. There was also the stubbornness of Beckenbauer's team when playing with one player fewer, and their ingenuity in provoking Mexico to join them in a match of ten players apiece for the last 20 minutes of extra time.

Earlier in the day, France had overcome Brazil in their iconic quarter-final at the Estadio Jalisco in Guadalajara, and as sad as it was to see the hosts eliminated, the anticipation of another West Germany vs France semi-final was massive. West Germany's progress to the semi-finals meant that there was strong sense of foreboding and almost pre-match acceptance that they would once again get the better of a French team that would be carrying a lot of 1982-themed baggage into the meeting, and so it proved to be.

With Argentina having navigated their way past England to now face Belgium in the last four, despite media fears of another major international final between West Germany and Belgium, you could see an Argentina vs West Germany final looming on the horizon from the moment Fernando Quirarte missed Mexico's second penalty in their quarter-final shoot-out.

Semi-finals day came three days later, this still being the era when the two games took place on the same day. The only other occasion since 1986 when both of the last four days took place within a couple of hours of one another was in the USA, in 1994. There was something special about the era which the two semi-finals were played out within a close procession of each other. A definitive answer of who would contest the final was attained within a six-hour timespan, and there would be no rumbling discontent from one of those finalists about how their opponents were benefiting from an extra 24 hours' rest before the trophy-deciding match was to be played.

This double-header felt more even-handed, like a greater occasion than the future splintering of the two matches into consecutive days. In an era when live football was still a rarity, World Cup semi-finals day was the cherry on a very sweet cake. Starved of live football, here was this oasis of pleasure, with a double helping of intense drama on one day.

Up first were West Germany and France in Guadalajara at the Estadio Jalisco, where Henri Michel's team went dry of mouth and fumbled the lines that most observers had hoped they would be able to utter to avenge the events of 1982. It wasn't to be, and having shown a surprising amount of dysfunctionality along their path, West Germany were in yet another World Cup Final, their fifth from the last nine, having reached the semi-final of two of the years when the final eluded them.

A few hours later, at the Estadio Azteca, Maradona's sorcery was all too much for Belgium, although they did manage to hold them at bay until the 51st minute, before two moments of genius won Argentina their place in the World Cup Final, goals separated by 12 minutes.

The only question that was to be asked as the second semi-final approached wasn't how Belgium could win, but how on earth could they stop Maradona. Given that nobody could stop Maradona, nobody really considered how Belgium might set about winning the match. Thys did try to stop him, deploying two players to mark him, in the hope that Argentina were as much of a one-man band as most observers suggested. By the time the match had ended, still nobody was sure of the answer to this question, but at least everyone was clear that Maradona was unstoppable.

His two goals against Belgium were magical. The run he makes, the ball stabbed to him by Burruchaga, and the flick of his left foot, chipping the ball over the advancing Jean-Marie Pfaff. Maradona is off and away to celebrate towards the corner flag, before evading one team-mate to find Burruchaga and thank him for the pass, which was a work of art in itself. A glorious first goal.

As good as his first goal was, it's Maradona's second goal of the semi-final that refuses to dislodge itself from the mind's eye, however. Laid the ball by Cuciuffo, Maradona is midway inside the Belgium half, central to goal, and while Cuciuffo continues his run forward he never receives a return pass. Argentina's No. 10 slaloms past four Belgian shirts before slashing the ball across Pfaff and into the net. Magnificent goal, it's the celebration that stays with you for the longest, as Maradona staggers away, doing well to keep his feet, while the biggest smile in the Estadio Aztetca is beamed into millions of homes around the world. A punch of the air, and Olarticoechea is the first to embrace him. There were 27 minutes remaining, but the match could have ended there and then as far as Belgium were concerned.

Four days later came the final. Expansion up against pragmatism. Argentina facing down West Germany. Even if the South Americans didn't have the best player in the world within their ranks, they would have still had history in their corner. No European nation had won the World Cup away from European soil, a quirk that would remain in place for another 24 years. The task for West Germany to prevail was a very big one indeed. Stop Maradona, and once you've done that, confound footballing history.

Argentina in their traditional stripes, West Germany in green shirts, the Estadio Azteca awash with a vibrancy of sight and sound. It would be the last great World Cup Final of purpose for decades.

Pre-match, West Germany's perceived lack of exceptional talent was projected to be their expected undoing. Yes, they no longer had a Beckenbauer on the pitch, nor did they boast a Paul Breitner, a Günter Netzer or a Gerd Müller, but what they did have was a lot of knowledge at their disposal, the type of knowledge that had been good enough to see off France in the semi-final.

There's nothing quite as dangerous in football as underestimating a German team, and Argentina kind of did that for a while in the final. Unlike Thys, Beckenbauer opted for one marker on Maradona, and there was only one man for the job, Matthäus, fresh from his missions of antagonism against Denmark, Mexico and France.

When the 1986 World Cup Final is debated, Maradona's selflessness often comes to the fore. Having been the master individual of the tournament all the way up to the final, he operated as the textbook team man when the trophy was on the line. There's a lot of truth in this theory, but given the chance, Maradona would undoubtedly have loved to throw off the shackles and have been as omnipresent against West Germany as he was against Uruguay, England and Belgium. It was the attention of Matthäus that stopped him from doing so.

So effective was Matthäus in his task that Maradona was relegated to support act in the final, albeit the most valuable one imaginable, as he indirectly influenced all three Argentina goals, although he went through all manner of frustration before getting there. Before the breakthrough was made, Maradona had already earned himself a yellow card for arguing with the referee over the positioning of an Argentinian defensive wall for a free kick he felt should never have been given.

Luckily enough, Matthäus then picked a yellow card up himself four minutes later, having hacked Maradona down after being caught out with a cute back-heel. It meant that Matthäus had cheaply sold the advantage of being able to subtly wind Maradona up, safe in the knowledge that he could save a yellow-card offence until deeper into the match.

Two minutes beyond Matthäus's yellow card, Argentina had the lead, edging ahead midway through the first half. José Luis Brown headed in from a Burruchaga free kick from the right, Schumacher having been coaxed into the gap when keeping an eye on the location of Maradona.

For West Germany this completely went against their proposed script of first-half containment, and a second period of counter-attacks. Argentina's goal drew Beckenbauer's team from their shell, and it would be something that they would forget to retract back into later to such dramatic match-losing effect.

Ten minutes into the second half Argentina had their second goal, and seemingly the World Cup tied up in their favour. Facilitated by a pass from Maradona, Héctor Enrique released Valdano into acres of space, within which he closed in on the West German penalty area and the now exposed Schumacher. Opening his body up, Valdano left Schumacher guessing on his intentions, before intelligently placing the ball to the right of him, low into the net to double Argentina's lead. It was a fantastic breakaway goal, with Beckenbauer's team committing to attack. It also made up for a few opportunities that Valdano had failed to take against Belgium, goals that would have given a truer reflection of the balance of play in the semi-final.

With Völler already having been introduced for the start of the second half as a direct replacement for Allofs, Beckenbauer had no option but to throw caution to the wind. He introduced Hoeneß just beyond the hour in place of

Magath, going three up front and potentially surrendering the midfield to Maradona, given that Matthäus's remit would now be a much wider one. As alterations go, it was one that could have resulted in Argentina matching the four goals that Brazil had scored in the 1970 World Cup Final, but instead Bilardo's players struggled to get to grips with the change of pattern.

Within 12 minutes of the introduction of Hoeneß, West Germany had clawed a goal back, Rummenigge reacting fastest when Völler flicked on a Brehme corner. It was a goal that came within a pivotal few minutes, as Burruchaga hadn't long been denied a certain goal by a last-gasp back-post clearance at a time when a third Argentina goal had seemed inevitable.

Seven minutes later the final was level. Another Brehme corner from the left, more defensive indecision, a header won, and there was Völler to guide the ball in. Argentina were suddenly paralysed by an unknown aerial weakness, and West Germany's propensity to get the job done was now in danger of completing a comeback that would have mirrored the one they achieved in the 1954 World Cup Final against Hungary.

With nine minutes to go, this was now a match that could go either way, while neutrals everywhere were baying for extra time. Possibly carried away by their success in fighting back from 2-0 down, however, and with potential notions of winning within 90 minutes, West Germany ignored the basics of defending what they had reclaimed. Also fatigue will have played its part. As much as their comeback had been so shocking, so too was the way they threw it all away just three minutes after levelling the scores.

Maradona, just inside his own half, saw the pass was on and that Burruchaga had begun his run. West Germany's defence was holding a high line, apart from Hans-Peter

Briegel, who was deeper and isolated. It was an open invitation for Argentina to pounce. A burst of pace into the West German penalty area, and Schumacher was drawn forward. Burruchaga held his nerve and rolled the ball past him. It was a swift, simple and effective move. It just so happened to be the World Cup-winning goal, and it totally drained the spirit of the West German players who, despite having another six minutes to save themselves, couldn't lift themselves again.

A pitch swamped by photographers and well-wishers, a trophy cradled like a baby, then proudly lifted for the crowd to see. It was an utterly iconic moment, and one that was a worthy sibling to the greatness of Brazil's celebrations in 1970.

Afterword

WHETHER IT was ultimately by hook or by crook, for a nation that was handed a World Cup with only three years' notice to plan for it, and despite all the glaring imperfections that undoubtedly marred so much of it, the tournament was an unmitigated success in terms of its legacy. All this, despite the breakdowns in broadcasting links, the often-substandard nature of the local organisation committees, which even prompted FIFA to lose their cool, the poor standard of refereeing at times, the noon and 4pm kick-off times that put frankly dangerous demands on players and, of course, the concept of four third-placed nations being able to progress to the knockout stages.

Even at the time, watching on television, some five and a half thousand miles away from the action, somewhere in the north-west of England, the 1986 World Cup finals left a deep imprint. They imparted an eternal love so strong for the Danish national team that, when Hummel reissued replicas of Preben Elkjær's No. 10 shirt in 2021, a man in his late 40s, who was 12 in the summer of 1986 and should be knowing better three and a half decades later, was straight online to order one.

Is it wrong that I tracked the order's delivery on an almost hourly basis until it finally arrived? Regardless, I'm still waiting impatiently for Adidas to do likewise with the Soviet Union shirts, Topper to rerelease the Brazil shirt, and Le Coq Sportif to launch reproductions of Argentina's shirt.

Some 36 years later, everything about the 1986 World Cup still catches the eye. The kits, the ball, the shimmer of the television images and the scratchy sound of the commentators. The flight of the ball through the thin air, the obvious heat on display. It's all beautiful.

Feeling cold on a winter's day, but concerned about rising heating bills? No problem, simply Google for footage of the France vs Brazil quarter-final and you'll soon feel hot under the collar.

Then there are the injustices. The early exits of Denmark and the Soviet Union in the last 16, the loss of Brazil in the quarter-finals, Spain's defeat at the same hurdle, also on penalties, France being thwarted by West Germany once again.

Every nation offered a positive, even the perceived bad guys. Strip away the 'Hand of God' and there is so much more to Argentina's success, while West Germany's kits were magnificent. To be honest, there wasn't really a bad kit among the 24 competitors, although some were better than others.

The main thing I tried to do with this book, aside from the shameless rose-tinted time travel and unabashed homage given, was to make sure every nation that qualified was heard, that their stories were told, along with a few of those who failed to qualify too. For many of the big nations, it was about looking at the fine detail of their campaigns and charting the forks in the road they took towards glory, or failure as the case regularly was. For the smaller nations it was about how they came to be in Mexico in the first place and the noble fights they put up when they got there. A team might well have played three and lost three, but there's always a hero that needs to be known about.

In constructing the shape of this book, I agonised long over how to set it out. In the end, as always winds up being the case, I followed my instinct. Beyond chapters about the 'Hand of God' and Paco's Panini Album, the teams that receive star billing throughout each chapter are generally the ones that topple out of the tournament as it rolls along, the teams that vanquish them being merely an incidental extra until it's their time to bid farewell to Mexico.

An incredible World Cup that was an utter privilege to write about and a joy to watch as it unfolded at the time, while the 1986 tournament wasn't perfect, it did take place at the optimum moment for me. Utterly impressionable and with a thirst for as much football as possible, June 1986 made for a glorious month, when the sun seemed to shine every day and the most beautiful football unfolded.

Denmark still should have won it though.